Howard MacQueary

The Evolution of Man and Christianity

Howard MacQueary

The Evolution of Man and Christianity

ISBN/EAN: 9783337167301

Printed in Europe, USA, Canada, Australia, Japan

Cover: Foto ©ninafisch / pixelio.de

More available books at **www.hansebooks.com**

THE

EVOLUTION OF MAN

AND

CHRISTIANITY

BY THE
REV. HOWARD MACQUEARY

NEW YORK
D. APPLETON AND COMPANY
1890

TO PROF. JOSEPH LE CONTE, LL. D.,
BERKELEY, CAL.

My Dear Sir:

This book, the first-fruits of my pen, I dedicate to you, not simply because I would associate my name with that of one so eminent for piety and learning as yourself, nor because I would hold you responsible for any opinion it contains, but rather because I would fain express my heart-felt appreciation of the unfailing sympathy and invaluable assistance I received from you during the long, dark period of mental and spiritual struggle which resulted in my emancipation from the thralldom of a crude and irrational Traditionalism.

Earnestly trusting that this humble effort may be the means of promoting the great cause we have at heart—the cause of truth—I am, with deep respect,

Very Cordially Yours,
HOWARD MAC QUEARY.

CANTON, OHIO, *Oct. 1889.*

PREFATORY.

"THERE can be little doubt in the mind of the thoughtful observer that we are now on the eve of the greatest change in traditional views that has taken place since the birth of Christianity. This change means not a readjustment of details only, but a *reconstruction of Christian theology.*" *

It is because I am firmly convinced of the truth of these profound words that I have written this book.

Three great forces, among others, will effect the theological and ecclesiastical revolution predicted—viz., Physical Science, Biblical Criticism, and the Social Movement. Our young men and women who enjoy the privileges of the higher education are becoming thoroughly imbued with the teachings of Physical Science, which, backed by Biblical Criticism, is aiming deadly blows at the *miraculous* features of popular Christianity, and, as will appear from the following pages, it is destined to profoundly modify our idea of miracles, and this means a complete reconstruction of traditional and popular theology. Evolution is "in the air," and its fundamental tenets are being accepted (perhaps unconsciously) by all classes of minds—from a Huxley to a hod-carrier. It behooves us,

---

* Prof. Joseph Le Conte, "Evolution and Religious Thought," p. 277.

then, as religious teachers to recognize this fact, and adjust our theology accordingly. The Social or Labor movement is assuming (has assumed) an anti-church attitude. The laborer imagines that the Church is not his friend, and that its doctrines—its "fish-stories," etc.—have been exploded by Darwin, Spencer, Huxley, and others. I speak from personal knowledge as well as from the testimony of others.* The Church (i. e., primarily the Clergy and secondarily the Laity) must arouse itself to an exact recognition of the facts of the case and prepare to meet the issues before it. This book is written in the hope of drawing attention more generally to the salient points of the work before us. No one is more conscious of its defects than its author, but he asks his readers to give him credit for at least honesty and loftiness of purpose.

He has not hesitated to reject the teachings of the most venerable and the most eminent when they seemed to him to conflict with fact and reason. He has done this, however, not from presumption and conceit, but simply because his conscience and intellect would not allow him to accept such teachings. He is conscious of having used strong language in some places, but he begs his readers to remember that he did not mean to stoop to personal abuse, but only spoke strongly because he felt strongly, and because strong language alone can impress certain minds. Every person, whose views I oppose in this book, has my profound respect, and indeed it is because I respect them that I oppose their theories; and, could we be thrown together, they would find in me a warm-hearted friend.

Of course, I anticipate great opposition from various quarters, and any courteous criticism of my position will be thankfully received and duly considered, but the prime

---

* See Prof. R. T. Ely's "Labor Movement in America," pp. 244, 245.

object of the book is not to stir up bitter controversy, but to help those, of all classes, who are troubled by the difficulties of traditional and popular theology, to a plane of thought from which they may espy the Celestial City and escape the miasmas of time-worn Traditionalism. It is needless to say that I have drunk deeply of the quiet waters of popular " Orthodoxy," and hence can sympathize with those who still find in it a haven of rest for their souls. It is also needless to say that in putting forth from that haven I have experienced the usual storms of mental and spiritual disturbance which beat upon one in his voyage over the ocean of free thought. "It is an awful moment," says Frederick Robertson, "when the soul begins to find that the props on which it has blindly rested so long are many of them rotten, and begins to suspect them all; when it begins to feel the nothingness of many of the traditionary opinions which have been received with implicit confidence, and in that horrible insecurity begins also to doubt whether there be anything to believe at all. It is an awful hour—let him who has passed through it say how awful—when this life has lost its meaning, and seems shriveled into a span; when the grave appears to be the end of all, human goodness nothing but a name, and the sky above this universe a dead expanse, black with the void from which God himself has disappeared. In that fearful loneliness of spirit, when those who should have been his friends and counselors only frown upon his misgivings, and profanely bid him stifle doubts, which for aught he knows may arise from the fountain of truth itself, to extinguish as a glare from hell that which for aught he knows may be light from heaven, and everything seems wrapped in hideous uncertainty, I know but one way in which a man may come forth from his agony scathless: it is by holding fast to those things which are certain still, the grand, simple landmarks of *morality.* In the darkest hour through which a human soul can pass, whatever else is doubtful, this at least is certain.

"If there be no God and no future state, yet, even then, it is better to be generous than selfish, better to be chaste than licentious, better be true than false, better to be brave than to be a coward. Blessed beyond all earthly blessedness is the man who, in the tempestuous darkness of the soul, has dared to hold fast to these venerable landmarks. Thrice blessed because his night shall pass into clear, bright day. At last he will stand upon the rock, the surges stilled below him, the last cloud drifted from the sky above, with a faith, and hope, and trust which neither earth nor hell shall shake thenceforth forever."* Whoever launches out on the river of thought involved in the word "Evolution" will experience the tempest thus eloquently described; he will be carried out into a sea which has its dangers, its quicksands, its deceitful currents; and it will require wary sailing and good pilots in order to make a safe voyage: but it ought to be a subject of earnest thought whether it is better to be sailing there, on to something better in the Infinite, or riding at anchor in the tranquil, landlocked bay of Traditionalism.

During the preparation of this book I have been asked more than once, how could I hold such views consistently with my ordination vows? And as this question may be asked by the different readers of the book, I shall here answer it. As a clergyman in the Protestant Episcopal Church I was asked at my ordination this question: "Are you persuaded that the Holy Scriptures contain all Doctrine required as necessary to eternal salvation through faith in Jesus Christ? And are you determined out of

---

* Robertson's "Life and Letters," by Brooke. "Second Address to Workingmen."

the said Scriptures to instruct the people committed to your charge, and to teach nothing, as necessary to eternal salvation, but that which you shall be persuaded may be concluded and proved by the Scripture?" To which I answered, "I am so persuaded, and have so determined, by God's grace," and I am of the same opinion still. Let us compare with this ordination vow the Sixth of the Thirty-nine Articles of Religion. It reads, " Holy Scripture containeth all things necessary to salvation, so that whatsoever is not read therein, nor may be proved thereby, is not to be required of any man, that it should be believed as an article of the Faith, or be thought requisite or necessary to salvation." It then gives a list of the generally accepted "canonical books" which we understand to be Holy Scripture.

Now observe, first, that the ordination vow and the article both assert plainly the *Right of Private Judgment*: each man is to study the Bible and ascertain for himself what things in it are necessary articles of faith.

The creeds and articles, therefore, are mere summaries of what their originators considered the essential truths of the Bible, but every one must test them by the Bible, and this I claim to have done in the following pages. For instance, in refusing to accept the literal meaning of the story of the Virgin-Birth of the Saviour, I claim to be following Isaiah. I attach to the word "virgin" the meaning he gave it—namely, that of "*young woman.*"

And, again, in rejecting the doctrine of a gross material resurrection I claim to be following II Peter, iii, 10, which teaches, with modern physical science, that "*matter*" *is not to be eternal.*

Secondly. Neither the ordination vow nor the article asserts any *theory of Inspiration:* they merely say, " Holy Scripture *containeth* all things necessary to salvation," and this I heartily believe.

Thirdly. Nowhere does our Church lay down any formula concerning the *authorship* of the books of the Bible. The Sixth Article merely enumerates these, but says not a word as to when or by whom they were written, and hence every Episcopalian is at liberty to freely investigate this subject for himself.

Fourthly. Theories of the Godhead, the Atonement, etc., find no place in our formulas, and an evolutionist holding the views expressed in the following pages can conscientiously use our Liturgy; at least, I for one experience no pangs of conscience in using it.

Fifthly. On the vexed question of Future Punishment our Church has not a single line save in the Litany, where we pray to be delivered from "everlasting damnation." But, as Archdeacon Farrar long ago pointed out, this is no *formula*, and, even if it were, the words "everlasting damnation" could only mean what they mean in Holy Scripture, and what that meaning is I have explained in the chapter on "Evolution: Heaven and Hell."

Finally. On the question of man's *origin* our Church has not a single word, and the Ninth Article (on "Original Sin") may be dealt with in one of two ways: we may either appeal from it to Holy Scripture, as I do in this work, or we may claim that the state of *original innocence* which it speaks of is, in the evolutionist's opinion, merely the period during which man existed as an irresponsible animal—i. e., the period between his origination and the birth of his moral sense or "Conscience." I think, however, that the Ninth Article is a crude, Calvinistic statement of the Biblical idea of *Sin*. The Bible emphasizes, not the supposed fall of Adam, but the universal *fact of Sin*. Theologians, mistaking an allegory for literal history, have supposed that whenever the Bible speaks of sin it means that in Adam all mankind fell from a state of perfect righteousness into a state of utter moral depravity.

This, I attempt to show, is false. It seems never to have occurred to my interrogators that their questions had presented themselves to my mind at an early stage of my inquiries, and, by earnest thought and the help of bishops, doctors, and professors, I had been enabled to avoid taking the course of a "Robert Elsmere." The truth is, Episcopalians—and more especially non-Episcopalians—do not fully realize the real *catholicity* of our Church. They think that the "Church of Henry VIII" (falsely so called) is as narrow as any sect in Christendom, and it is mainly because I wish to show that it is at least *as broad as the Bible itself* that I write this preface. A Channing or a Beecher might have found a comfortable home within our fold, *so far as the Prayer-Book's teaching is concerned*, and if "the powers that be" will only act in the spirit of the Prayer-Book, the American Episcopal Church may yet become the rallying-point of many broad-minded men and women, who else would drift away into vague *un*belief or absolute *dis*belief; and this is not my opinion merely, for, in a letter to me, Prof. Alexander Winchell, a Methodist, said, "It has been my good fortune to find several church rectors with views as broad and liberal as the truth itself." Then, mentioning those "rectors" by name, he added, "It looks as if Episcopal rectors were destined to become leaders in liberal Christian thought." One can not help being reminded by these words of our Kingsleys, Maurices, Stanleys, Robertsons, Farrars, Arnolds, Fremantles, etc.—all of whom, however much they may have differed on minor points, were and are distinguished as "leaders in liberal Christian thought," and they believe that they are loyal to the real spirit and meaning of the Prayer-Book.

"These are the men," to apply Dean Stanley's words to his own class—"these are the men, wherever they are, and whosoever they may be, and howsoever they may be neglected, or assailed, or despised—these are the silent healers, who must bind up the wounds of their age in spite of itself; they are the good physicians who must knit together the dislocated bones of a disjointed time; they are the reconcilers who must turn the hearts of the children to the fathers, or of the fathers to the children. They will have but little praise or reward from the partisans, who will be loud in indiscriminate censure and applause.

"They will be attacked from both sides; they will be charged with not going far enough or with going too far; they will be charged with saying too much or with saying too little; they will be regarded from either partial point of view and not from one which takes in the whole. But, like Samuel of old, they will have a far higher reward in the Davids who are silently strengthened and nurtured by them in Naioth of Ramah—in the glories of a new age, which shall be ushered in peacefully and happily after they have been laid in the grave."*

This school has been more than once accused of teaching "negative theology," † and I have reason to anticipate such a charge against this book. Let me say, then, once for all, that my aim has been to *substitute new truths in the place of the old;* and while I have been compelled to tear down certain theories, in NO case have I failed to offer what I consider more rational, credible, and Scriptural views in their place. I claim, therefore, a decidedly *positive* character for my theology. But let it ever be remembered that Christianity consists, not in *theories* of any sort, but in a Personal Life—the life of Jesus. He is its center and circumference, and my aim in this book—nay, the effort of my whole life—is, and shall be, to lead

---

* Stanley's "Jewish Church," lecture xviii.
† Robertson's "Life and Letters," introduction, p. vii.

men's minds away from all theories, whether of my own making or of somebody else's, to Him—to the humble, self-renouncing, noble, Godlike Son of Man.

If this is "negative theology" I rejoice to "plead guilty," and cry for more such negation. Where is the man that can say aught against Him? Who is ashamed to take his stand by His side? Where is the father who would not have his son follow His example—be His disciple? When even an R. G. Ingersoll can say, "For the man Christ I have infinite respect; to that great and serene Man I gladly pay—GLADLY PAY—the tribute of my admiration and my tears," surely there is no need of insisting on his transcendent character. We do not realize what a treasure we have in that Character; we do not realize how we dishonor that Character by our irrational or imperfect theories about it; we do not know what infinite harm we do to religion by giving men the stones of dogmatic theology instead of the bread of that grand Life. If this book hammers down any of the stone walls that have been built round that inviolable shrine and makes men cling more closely to the Rock of Ages—if it leads any one to think less of Theology and more of Christ —the charge of preaching "negations" can not be justly brought against its author. I long to hear the Master's summons re-echo through his church, "*Follow me.*" I long to see his test of religious character applied once more, and if I can help in its application, I can bear even the charge of "negative theology," which is often another name for positive Christianity.

I conclude this too extended "preface" by making one request, which I earnestly hope all readers of this book will grant: If they should feel inclined to criticise it, they will greatly oblige the author by *reading, before they make such criticism, all the books referred to which they may not have read, if there be any.*

A bit of experience which I had during the preparation of this work leads me to make this request. I was corresponding with a bishop on some of the questions discussed, and I asked him what he thought of Dr. Keim's views of the birth and resurrection of Jesus. He did not, in his reply, answer directly this question, and I remarked to a friend to whom I read his letter that I did not believe the bishop had read Keim. He laughed at the idea of a *bishop's* not having read this work; but in a correspondence with another (an English) bishop, a very learned and liberal man, I found that *he* had not read Keim, but judged him from quotations which others made from his writings. This bishop was good enough, however, to buy Keim's great work and to read it. At first he thought that Keim agreed essentially with Renan, Baur, and their followers; but he discovered his mistake. This experience proved to me two things:

First, that many learned people are not as widely read as they are supposed to be; and,

Secondly, it is a great mistake to judge one from hearsay. Dr. Keim's work, it will be noted in the sequel, is one of the most important works cited, and I specially insist on my readers studying his views and those of other Biblical critics quoted, if they have not studied them, for, as a learned friend who has seen the manuscript of this book tells me, "the chapter on New Testament Scriptures (Introduction to Part II) will be unsatisfactory to some, because it is necessarily so brief; such (he adds) will, or ought to, consult the originals from which you quote." It is not presumption, then, nor a reflection on any one's intelligence to make such a request as this.

The book is intended to be *popular and suggestive—* to suggest lines of thought which every one may follow out for himself, and hence he should consult all the works referred to, if he have not, and others which they refer to

—provided, of course, he be not satisfied with the views herein expressed.

If he should imagine, for instance, that, because he is familiar with Renan, Strauss, and Baur, he can judge of Keim's position and conclusions (as the good bishop did), he may greatly err. Keim may advance an argument or state a fact on some particular point which others have ignored or merely glanced at, and this argument or fact might absolutely change one's opinion. So with other writers.

But there are many, even now, who "would not be persuaded though one rose from the dead." As a friend, already quoted, says: "Most people won't receive a great new truth, not because of want of evidence, but because it requires a complete readjustment of their mental furniture; and most people's furniture is *screwed down* to the flooring of the mind in such wise that it requires a ripping up of the whole mental structure."

But while I can not hope to influence this class of minds, yet there are others who are not so stereotyped in prejudice as to be absolutely unimpressible by facts and reasons, and there are some, even in the Church, who may gladly receive old truths in new forms.

THE AUTHOR.

CANTON, OHIO, *October, 1889.*

CONTENTS.

PART I.

THE EVOLUTION OF MAN.

CHAPTER	PAGE
I.—God and Nature	21
II.—Man's Origin according to Science	37
III.—Man's Origin according to Theology	72
IV.—The Age of the Human Race	84
V.—Man's Primitive Home and Condition	113

PART II.

THE EVOLUTION OF CHRISTIANITY.

	PAGE
Introduction—The Documents	138
I.—Evolution and Miracles	191
II.—Evolution and Inspiration	231
III.—Evolution and the Trinity	256
IV.—Evolution and the Divinity of Christ	277
V.—Evolution and the Atonement	295
VI.—Evolution: Heaven and Hell	312
VII.—Evolution and the Problem of Evil	337
VIII.—Evolution and Bodily Resurrection	363
IX.—Evolution and Immortality	376
X.—The Church of the Future	394

THE EVOLUTION OF MAN
AND CHRISTIANITY.

CHAPTER I.

GOD AND NATURE.

None but the fool can say, "There is no God," and, as a matter of fact, the deepest thinkers even among the agnostics acknowledge the existence of God, although they prefer another name for Him. Thus Mr. Herbert Spencer, the Corypheus of agnosticism, says: "One truth must grow ever clearer—the truth that there is an Inscrutable Existence everywhere manifested, to which man can neither find nor conceive either beginning or end. Amid the mysteries which become the more mysterious the more they are thought about, there will remain the one absolute certainty that he is ever in the presence of an Infinite and Eternal Energy from which all things proceed."* And when he adds, elsewhere, that it is this same Power which "in ourselves wells up under the form of consciousness," we find it quite unnecessary to dispute with him on this subject. Call Him what you will, God is; and the only remaining question is, What is His character?

---

* Spencer's "Ecclesiastical Institutions," p. 843; cf. p. 839.

Mr. Spencer thinks that this is "utterly inscrutable," but many, even among the members of his own school of thought, disagree with him on this point. Thus Prof. John Fiske, one of Spencer's most ardent admirers and brilliant disciples, says: "Though we may not by searching find out God; though we may not compass infinitude or attain to absolute knowledge, we may at least know all that it concerns us to know, as intelligent and responsible beings. Deity is unknowable just in so far as it is not manifested to consciousness through the phenomenal world—knowable just in so far as it is thus manifested; unknowable in so far as infinite and absolute—knowable in the order of its phenomenal manifestations—knowable, in a symbolic way, as the Power which is disclosed in every throb of the mighty rhythmic life of the universe— knowable as the Eternal Source of a moral law which is implicated with each action of our lives and in the obedience to which lies our only guarantee of the happiness which is incorruptible, and which neither inevitable misfortune nor unmerited obloquy can take away. There is a "reasonableness," he adds, "in the universe such as to indicate that the Infinite Power, of which it is the multiform manifestation, is *psychical*, though it is impossible to ascribe to Him any of the limited psychical attributes which we know or to argue from the ways of man to the ways of God." No wonder, then, that our author should say: "How far my view agrees with his" (Mr. Spencer's) "I do not undertake to say. On such an abstruse matter it is best that one should simply speak for one's self."* I do not see

---

* Fiske's "Idea of God," preface, pp. xxiv, xxviii, xxix, etc.

what more a Christian could desire from science than this. Indeed, Dr. Martensen, whose learning and piety will not be questioned, expresses essentially the same view when he says: "We may have a *true*, though not an adequate knowledge of the nature of God. We can not have an adequate knowledge of God—that is, a *knowledge coextensive in every feature with its subject.* We can, however, have a true knowledge; that is, a knowledge true in principle, true in its tendency, and true in the goal at which it aims—true, because it goes out from and leads to God." He further assures us that "even the profoundest speculative knowledge must be supplemented by a believing ignorance; and the deepest attempts to fathom the mystery of God reveal to us unfathomable abysses which no eye can reach." *

Theologians and Scientists being thus agreed as to the knowledge of God attainable by man, it seems unnecessary to consider this subject at length. We may have a true though not a perfect or complete knowledge of God, and that knowledge is obtained in two ways: viz., by the contemplation of man, and by the study of the external world.

It is not, however, my purpose to undertake to prove the existence of God, since all that it is necessary to say on this point will be said incidentally in the following pages. But I may remark, in passing, that while the doctrine of Evolution has exploded the *forms* in which the old arguments for God's existence were cast, the essence of those arguments is not destroyed but rather cleared and strengthened by Evolution. Thus, we may not, in Paley-fashion, argue, "The hu-

---

* Martensen, "Christian Dogmatics," pp. 90, 91.

man eye shows as much *intelligent design* in its construction as an eye-glass does, and, therefore, its Designer must be a being like unto the optician."

Evolution reveals an important difference between the formation of the eye and of the eye-glass: the one grows from a little speck, and the other is made all of a piece. Hence we must go back to the *germ* and urge that the Power which originated a germ *capable of developing* into Man, with his wonderful powers of mind and body, must be infinitely superior in wisdom and might to a finite being, like Man. In other words, we can no longer confine our attention to some special feature of the process of Evolution or Creation, but we must take a larger view; we must consider it as a whole, and if we do this, we shall understand the profound truth of Prof. Huxley's words on this subject.

"The teleology," he says, "which supposes that the eye, such as we see it in Man or one of the higher vertebrates, was made with the precise structure it exhibits, for the purpose of enabling the animal which possesses it to see, has undoubtedly received its death-blow" (from Mr. Darwin). "Nevertheless, it is necessary to remember that there is a *wider teleology which is not touched by the doctrine of Evolution, but is actually based upon the fundamental proposition of Evolution.*" *

Evolution affords the very strongest evidences of the existence of an Infinite Intelligence and Will back of and in Nature. God is the Alpha and the Omega of all Evolution. Without Him it could not begin or continue its mighty work, but the God of Evolution is not

---

* "Critiques and Addresses," p. 305, cited in "Popular Science Monthly," June, 1888, p. 212.

the God of traditional or popular theology; and since it is absolutely necessary to have as clear a notion on this subject as possible—since much that will follow can not otherwise be understood—since, in a word, it seems to the writer that a more or less vague and erroneous view of God vitiates and obscures much that is said and written by even learned theologians on Evolution, I have determined to state as clearly as I can the theory of Divinity which will be applied in this book.

God and Nature are the opposite poles of all thought, and so we can not discuss the one apart from the other. What, then, shall we think of Nature? What *is* it? Three answers are given to this important question:

First, one school of thought—the Materialistic—says, "Matter and Force" constitute the sum and substance of Nature. Matter is that which occupies space —as, for instance, this pen with which I write, which is composed of infinitely small particles called "atoms," that are held together and in certain positions by "forces" residing within them. But Prof. Huxley most effectually disposes of this view in the following masterful manner: "When I was a mere boy," he says, "with a perverse tendency to think when I ought to have been playing, my mind was greatly exercised by this formidable problem, What would become of *things* if they lost their *qualities?* As the qualities had no *objective* existence, and the thing *without qualities* was nothing, the solid world seemed whittled away —to my great horror. As I grew older, and learned to use the terms 'matter' and 'force,' the boyish problem was revived—*mutato nomine*. On the one hand, the notion of matter without force seemed to resolve the world into a set of geometrical ghosts too dead even to jabber. On the other, Boscovich's hypothesis, by which matter was resolved into centers of force, was very attractive. But when one tried to think it out, what in the world became of force considered as an objective entity? Force, even the most materialistic philosophers will agree with the most idealistic, is nothing but a name for the cause of motion. And if, with Boscovich, I resolved things into centers of force, then matter vanished altogether, and left immaterial entities in its place. One might as well frankly accept idealism and have done with it. I must make a confession," he adds, "even if it be humiliating. I have never been able to form the slightest conception of those 'forces' which the materialists talk about, as if they had samples of them many years in bottle. They tell me that matter consists of atoms, which are separated by mere space, devoid of contents; and that, through this void, radiate attractive and repulsive forces whereby the atoms affect one another. If anybody can clearly conceive the nature of these things which not only exist in nothingness, but pull and push there with great vigor, I envy him for the possession of an intellect of larger grasp, not only than mine, but than that of Leibnitz or of Newton.

"Let it not be supposed," he concludes, "that I am casting a doubt upon the propriety of the employment of the terms 'atom' and 'force' as they stand among the working hypotheses of physical science. As formulæ which can be applied with perfect precision and great convenience in the interpretation of Nature, their value is incalculable; but, as real entities, having objective existence, an *indivisible* particle, which, nevertheless, occupies space, is surely inconceivable; and with respect to the operation of that atom, where *it is* *not* by the aid of a 'force' *resident in nothingness*, I am as little able to imagine it as I fancy any one else is." *

With such arguments, and backed by such authority, we may set the materialistic view of Nature on one side, and pass to the second—the Idealistic—view, of which that great Irishman, George Berkeley, Bishop of Cloyne, who lived two hundred years ago, was one of the most eminent advocates. "Idealism," says Dr. Krauth, in his admirable edition of Berkeley's "Principles of Human Knowledge," (page 66) "is on the whole, with reference to the part it has played in the history of human thought, the greatest of systems. Like England, its drum-beat follows the sunrise till it circles the world." "The essence of idealism," says Frederick Schlegel (ibid., page 67), "consists in holding the *Spiritual* alone as actual and truly real, in entirely denying to bodies and matter existence and reality, in explaining them as mere appearance and illusion, or at least *transmuting and resolving them into Spirit.*"

Accordingly, Berkeley remarks: "It is an opinion strangely prevailing among men that houses, mountains, rivers, and, in a word, all sensible objects, have an existence, natural or real, *distinct from their being perceived by the understanding.*" But he maintains that "there is not any other substance than Spirit, or that which perceives. . . . It is said," he adds, "that extension is a mode of matter, and that matter is the substratum that supports it. Now, I desire that you would explain to me what is meant by matter as supporting extension. It is evident 'support' can not here be taken in its usual or literal sense, as when we say that pillars support a

---

* "Popular Science Monthly," February, 1887, pp. 499, 500.

building; in what sense, therefore, must it be taken? For my part, I am unable to discover any sense at all that can be applicable to it."

Thus, Berkeley denies that matter is the "substratum" of things, and asserts that "Spirit is the only substance"; and hence he inverts the popular thought on this subject, putting Mind in place of Matter, and allowing only a relative existence to the latter. He does not deny utterly all reality to Matter, but only its independent, absolute existence. He believes it exists *in relation to Mind*, somewhat as the shadow is related to the body which reflects it. The shadow has an existence, but not apart from the body; and so Berkeley says: "The table I write on exists—that is, I see and feel it; and if I were out of my study I should say it existed, meaning that if I were in my study I might perceive it, or *that some other spirit actually does perceive it.*" *

Hence, Dr. Krauth well observes that "the absolute existence of sensible objects—i. e., in themselves or without a mind—is the principle Berkeley argues against as either meaningless or contradictory." And it is because so many fail to clearly grasp this fundamental proposition of Berkeleyism that they misunderstand and misrepresent it. When our philosopher says that the table in his study exists either in relation to his mind or to "some other Spirit" that "actually does perceive it," he sounds the key-note to his whole system. He teaches that all sensible objects exist only in relation to the Divine or Human Mind. Nature is mere "visible Spir-

---

* Berkeley's "Principles of Human Knowledge," Krauth's edition, pp. 195-205.

it"; is the Living Garment, in which the All-Beautiful has robed His mysterious loveliness—is simply and only "an outward and visible sign of an inward and Spiritual" Being—an *externalized, objectified mode of the Divine Mind.*

Now, while Prof. Huxley thinks that any hypothesis which may be held on the subject in hand is only a speculation incapable of demonstration,* yet it is interesting to read these words from his pen: "The good Bishop Berkeley, if he were alive, would find such facts" (as those revealed by physical science) "fit into his system without the least difficulty."† And many others, even among those who are not Idealists, say the same; and hence, in these days, when theology and physical science are at swords'-points, a large number of thinkers is found turning to Berkeley for relief. For my own part, I think that something like Berkeleyism is the only philosophy which can meet the demands of the case. Science has forever exploded the low view of God, which regarded (and regards) Him as a sort of Man, and has taught us that a close and vital union exists between Him and Nature; and yet we are apt to be lost in the whirlpool of Pantheism—to think of the Deity as One "whose body Nature is," if we give up the old view of God which holds that He exists apart from and above the world.

What is needed above all things is a philosophy which will reconcile the old and the new views; which, while it teaches God's immanence in Nature, also as-

---

* "Science and Culture," pages 268-270. D. Appleton & Co., 1882.
† "Popular Science Monthly," February, 1887, p. 503.

serts His transcendental character; and the Berkeleyan system seems to me to afford at least the *basis* for such a philosophy.

Canon Fremantle says: "God may be conceived of as transcendental—that is, as transcending all the visible cognizable universe, as existing apart from it and working upon it from without; or, as immanent, dwelling within it as its moral and spiritual center, its guiding force. The two ideas are by no means incompatible; they are both of them expressed in Scripture, and it would probably be a great spiritual loss so to dwell upon one of them as to exclude the other. But it is certain that the thought of a transcendental God dealing with the world *ab extra* has been dwelt upon in the past in such a way as to exclude the thought of an immanent God working upon the world from within. It is certain, also, that this idea of a transcendental God is one which by seeming to imply continual interference with the regular course of the world is peculiarly difficult to grasp in a scientific age."* It is certain that not only has the idea of a transcendental God been dwelt upon to the exclusion of the idea of a God immanent in Nature, but even a lower view prevails among many otherwise well-informed people, especially among the laity. What Prof. Fiske says about his idea of God when he was five years of age is true of many more matured notions. "I imagined a narrow office," he says, "just over the zenith, with a tall standing desk running lengthwise, upon which lay several ledgers bound in coarse leather. There was no roof over this

---

* Fremantle's Bampton Lectures, 1883, "The World as the Subject of Redemption," p. 17.

office, and the walls rose scarcely five feet from the floor, so that a person standing at the desk could look out upon the whole world. There were two persons at the desk, and one of them a tall, slender man, of aquiline features, wearing spectacles, with a pen in his hand and another behind his ear, was God. The other was an attendant angel. Both were diligently watching the deeds of men and recording them in the ledgers."* Most men doubtless entertain some such notion of God as this at some period of their lives, and in my own case it clung to me for quite a while after I began the study of theology. When I realized that " God is without body, parts, or passions "—pure, invisible, intangible Spirit—I experienced a painful shock which lasted for several days, and which others of my acquaintance have experienced when they have been made to realize the same deep truth. But, of course, it would be said just here, "Only half-educated people hold the low view of God just stated"; and there is truth in this assertion, yet I am thoroughly convinced that men's early notions of God, in many cases, cling to them with a more or less firm grip through life, and unconsciously influence their philosophizing on this subject. While, therefore, they do not hold the anthropomorphic conception in all its crudeness, as stated by Prof. Fiske, yet their notion of a *Personal* God is so inextricably blended with the idea of a Man-God—a *Bodily-God*—that it vitiates much of their reasoning on this ubject.

The doctrine of God's personality undoubtedly contains a great and indispensable truth ; it emphasizes the

---

* "Idea of God," p. 116.

fact that He is Intelligent Power; but it seems to me that we should express His personality as Christ did when he said, "God is Spirit." At any rate, throughout this work I shall use the word "God" to denote the Infinite Spirit who resides *in* and presides *over* the material world; and if I be asked to illustrate my idea more clearly, I can not do it better than by citing Charles Kingsley's remark that "souls secrete their bodies as snails do their shells." God secretes physical Nature as the snail secretes its shell; and, although this illustration not only fails to illustrate perfectly, but also savors of Pantheism, I know of no more perfect illustration (for what *can* illustrate the Infinite?), and I can simply assert that it is not intended to teach Pantheism.

But if Canon Fremantle's assertion that the notion of a transcendental God is not incompatible with that of an immanent God be true (and I think it is true), I can scarcely formulate this idea of God otherwise than as I have attempted to do.

The physical universe, according to my view, floats, so to speak, in an ocean of Spirit; this infinite Spirit permeates somewhat as the ether is supposed to permeate all things, sustains all things, transcends all things, and is essential intelligence.

But, before saying anything more on this subject, I must glance at the third and last view of Being which it is possible to hold, viz., the Agnostic theory. If I understand Agnosticism, it teaches that *mind and matter are neither of them real substances, but only passing manifestations of an unknown and unknowable reality;* are mere bubbles on the great ocean of Being, which appear for a little while and then vanish away.

"The Unknowable," says Mr. Herbert Spencer, the

acknowledged authority on this subject, "as manifested to us within the limits of Consciousness in the shape of Feeling, being no less inscrutable than the Unknowable as manifested beyond the limits of Consciousness in other shapes we approach no nearer to understanding the last by rendering it into the first," and hence he concludes that "our only course is to recognize our symbols ('Mind' and 'Matter') as *symbols only of some form of Power absolutely and forever unknown to us.*" *

In the first quotation Mr. Spencer rejects Idealism; in the second he defines and accepts Agnosticism.

We have already seen that Prof. Fiske—a Spencerian, when not a Fiskean—thinks that the Infinite Power of which the universe is the multiform manifestation is by no means so unknowable as Mr. Spencer considers it. On the contrary, he says not only that "Deity is knowable just in so far as it is manifested to consciousness through the phenomenal world," but, further, that "there is a *reasonableness* in the universe such as to indicate that the Deity is psychical." This is precisely my own view. "If there were not intelligence at the root of things, it could not be turned up as the crown of the development of life"; and since this Intelligence, as far as we can ascertain, is coextensive with the universe; since it manifests itself *to us* and *in us*, we must believe that *so far* we have a true knowledge of Deity, although this knowledge is not complete—that is, it is not "a knowledge coextensive in every feature with its subject." However, if any Agnostic object to this view, then I would take an entirely different position. "You admit," I would say, "that

---

* Spencer's "Principles of Psychology," vol. i, pp. 159, 162.

any theory—Materialistic, Idealistic, or Agnostic—which may be formulated on the subject in hand must be only a speculation, a working hypothesis,* and hence you must admit that one has a right to—nay, *must*—adopt whatever hypothesis seems to him to satisfy all the demands of the case. The Idealistic view seems the most rational to my mind—it alone, I think, satisfactorily explains the reasonableness everywhere manifested in Nature, and so I adopt it, granting you the same privilege of choice."

Two facts recognized by the best physical science of the day seem to lend confirmation to the Idealistic view:

First, as Prof. Huxley so ably and clearly shows, the material "atom" can not stand a close and searching analysis, but must be regarded as a hypothetical entity.

Second, while "material *force*" shares the same fate, yet we *ourselves are powers*, as consciousness demonstrates, and hence we have a right to argue from the nature of the Self-Power as revealed in consciousness to the Non-Self-Power manifested around us. This argument need not be complicated by any consideration of the freedom of the human will. Whether the will be absolutely free or not (no one believes this †), all must admit the *fact* that it is a force—a power—and from it alone can we form any notion of force. While, therefore, we are landed in hopeless difficulties if, with the Materialist, we look *outside* ourselves and analyze Nature as though it were an absolutely independent, self-existent machine, yet if we turn the eye *inward* and contemplate Self we may get, first, an idea of *Being;*

---

* Huxley's "Science and Culture," p. 270.
† Canon Row, "Present Day Tracts," No. 30.

secondly, an idea of *Power;* and, thirdly, an idea of *Intelligence;* and with these we may proceed to formulate a view of the world which none can destroy and few will attack. Such a view would be somewhat as follows:

Spirit—i. e., Intelligent Power—is the only Eternal Absolute Substance. Nature is an outward and visible sign of this inward-underlying-Energy or Being. Its phenomena are naught else than *objectified modes* of the Eternal I Am; the forces of Nature are naught else than *different manifestations* of one Divine Will; the laws of Nature, naught else than the regular *modes of operation* of that will, unchangeable because He is unchangeable.*

The great doctrine of the "Correlation of Forces," so triumphantly established by modern Science, confirms this view. It means simply *that what we call "forces of Nature" are different forms of one and the same thing.* Thus the "force" which causes a stone to fall to the Earth ("gravity"), the "force" by which two gases unite to produce the dew-drop ("chemical affinity"), the "force" which causes the grass to grow ("Life"), and Man to think ("Mind"), are all streams issuing from one fountain-head; and that fountain-head is believed to be Spiritual or psychical in its nature, since otherwise the reasonableness everywhere displayed in the universe is inexplicable.

The Evolution of the idea of God thus imperfectly sketched will be further considered in the chapter on

---

* Prof. Joseph Le Conte. "Evolution and its Relation to Religious Thought," p. 283. Cf. Prof. Winchell's admirable paper on "Speculative Consequences of Evolution," in University of Michigan Philosophical Papers, Second Series, No. 2.

"Evolution and the Trinity," and so I need only say that Prof. Fiske,* Mr. Herbert Spencer,† Sir John Lubbock,‡ Dr. E. B. Tylor, and others, have laid at least the foundation of a true theory of the development of ideas of Deity. I say "at least the foundation," for we may not accept either or all of their theories *in toto*.

---

* "Idea of God." ‡ "Origin of Civilization," chaps. v-vii.
† "Sociology," I, chaps. xx-xxvi.

CHAPTER II.

MAN'S ORIGIN ACCORDING TO SCIENCE.

"EVERYBODY nowadays," says a brilliant writer, "talks about Evolution. Like Electricity, the Cholera-germ, Woman's rights, the great mining boom, and the Eastern question, it is 'in the air.' It pervades society everywhere with its subtile essence; it infects small talk with its peculiar catchwords and slang phrases; it even permeates that last stronghold of rampant Philistinism, the third leader in the penny papers. Everybody believes he knows all about it and discusses it as glibly as he discusses the points of race-horses he has never seen, the charms of peeresses he has never spoken to, and the demerits of authors he has never read. Everybody is aware, in a dim and nebulous semi-conscious fashion, that it was all invented by the late Mr. Darwin, and reduced to a system by Mr. Herbert Spencer, don't you know, and a lot more of those scientific fellows. It is generally understood in the best-informed circles that Evolutionism consists for the most part in a belief about Nature at large essentially similar to that applied by Topsy to her own origin and early history.

"It is conceived, in short, that most things 'growed.' Especially is it known that, in the opinion of the Evolutionists as a body, we are all of us ultimately descended from men with tails, who were the final offspring and improved edition of the common gorilla.

"It is scarcely necessary," our author adds, "to inform the intelligent reader, who, of course, differs fundamentally from that inferior class of human beings known to all of us in our own minds as 'other people,' that almost every point in the catalogue thus briefly enumerated is a popular fallacy of the wildest description.

"Mr. Darwin did not invent Evolution any more than George Stephenson invented the steam-engine, or Mr. Edison the electric telegraph. We are not descended from men with tails any more than we are descended from Indian elephants. There is no evidence that we have anything in particular more than the remotest fiftieth cousinship with our poor relation—the West African gorilla.

"Science is not in search of 'a missing link'; few links are anywhere missing, and those are for the most part wholly unimportant ones. If we found the imaginary link in question, he would not be a monkey, nor yet in any way a tailed man." *

As an illustration of this profound ignorance of the nature, scope, and truth of Evolution, even among those who are supposed to be very learned people, I may mention the fact that an eminent Doctor of Divinity in a city in which I once lived, said in a public lecture, "When a crab develops into a monkey and a monkey into a man, I will accept Evolution"! And this absurd ignorance passes for learning! Hence it is necessary to briefly state the nature and scope of Evolution.

---

* "Popular Science Monthly," March, 1888, pp. 636, 637.

Prof. Joseph Le Conte, of the University of California, thus defines Evolution: "Evolution is (1) continuous *progressive* change, (2) according to certain *laws*, (3) and by means of *resident forces.*"

The first part of the definition is well illustrated in the development of the individual. Each one of us is an evolution. We begin our existence as a minute germ, which adds cell to cell, tissue to tissue, organ to organ, and function to function, until we are finally evolved as infants; and then we continue to develop into men and women. Here we see "progressive change"; and this happens according to certain laws which are, generally speaking, three, viz., the Law of Differentiation, the Law of Progress of the Whole, and the Law of Cyclical Movement.

The Law of Differentiation simply means the law of *divergence*, and is illustrated by the development of the acorn into the oak. The tree begins as a little seed, and by successive branching and rebranching, each branch taking a different direction and all growing wider and wider apart (differentiating), it finally stands forth as monarch of the forest. So, too, with the plant and animal kingdoms. Birds and reptiles, or fishes and reptiles, for instance, started from a common stock or root, and by successive branching and rebranching, each branch taking a different direction, and all growing wider and wider apart (differentiating) the movement has at last resulted in the present bird, reptile, and fish classes. Of course, in this process, during the long time of development, many intermediate forms—"connecting links"—would die out, just as the buds and branches of a tree die and disappear; and so the connecting links between bird and reptile, fish and reptile, man and the lower animal, may be forever lost; yet this fact is quite unimportant: evolution rests on a different and more solid basis.

Each branch of the bird and reptile classes has been traced back to the point where they shade into each other, so that it is impossible to say whether we should call the first known bird *a reptilian-bird or a bird-like reptile*, and the significance of this fact can not be misunderstood by the thoughtful mind. But the half hath not been spoken.

There are myriads of little creatures which may be called *plant-animals* or *animal-plants;* for there are just as many reasons for naming them plants as there are for calling them animals; and, on the other hand, there are just as many reasons for classing them among animals as there are for considering them plants.

The conclusion, therefore, is irresistible that "the difference between animal and plant is one of *degree* rather than of *kind;* and the problem whether, in a given case, an organism is an animal or a plant, may be essentially insoluble." *

Suppose, then, that in the beginning of the history of life on earth, there existed creatures with plant-animal (or animal-plant) natures, which began to develop the one or the other side of such nature; by successive branching and rebranching, each branch taking a different direction and all growing wider and wider apart (differentiating), we would in due time be presented with the plant and animal kingdoms as we now have them. This is what is meant by the Law of Differentiation in the sphere of living organisms.

---

* Huxley, "Science and Culture," p. 186.

But can we go further? Can it be shown that *Life itself* has been developed from some lower form of force? There are two radically different views, as is well known, on this subject: one holding that Life was an essentially *new* force infused into Nature at a certain point in the process of evolution; the other claiming that Life is *only another manifestation of that Energy* which on a lower plane is called " gravity " or " chemical affinity."

In support of the first view it is urged that Life can not *now* be produced by any combination of physical and chemical forces; it must come from a living germ. But, in answer to this, Evolution urges that, in the beginning, the earth was in a different condition from what it now is, and hence combinations of lower forces or manifestations of the one eternal Energy may have occurred then which never can occur again in the history of terrestrial life. Evolution must, of course, insist on this view, and I for one think it highly rational and probable, and see no more Materialism or Atheism in it than in that which holds that Life was specially created—i. e., was a new force infused into Nature at a given time; for, even if we grant that Life was produced by a combination of lower forces, under peculiar conditions, the question inevitably arises, *Whence came those forces and peculiar conditions?* This takes us to the root of this whole matter—to the time when " the earth was without form and void," when only a mighty cloud of atoms filled the realms of universal space. Further back than this Science can not take us; here the mighty evolution of things commences. Beginning with this original *nebula* or cloud of atoms, with its inherent forces, evolutionists argue that by branching and rebranching, each branch taking a different direction and all growing wider and wider apart (differentiating) the universe in all its magnificence and complexity has been produced. And this is what is meant by the Law of Differentiation as applied in evolutionary philosophy.

The second Law is that of Progress of the Whole. "Many imagine," says Prof. Le Conte, "that *progress* is the one law of evolution; in fact, that evolution and progress are coextensive and convertible terms. They imagine that in evolution the movement must be upward and onward in *all* parts; that degeneration is the opposite of evolution. This is far from the truth. There is, doubtless, in evolution, progress to higher and highes planes, but not along *every* line nor in *every* part; for this would be contrary to the law of differentiation. It is only progress of *the whole organic kingdom in its entirety*." An illustration will make this clear: "A growing tree branches and again branches in *all directions,* some branches going upward, some sidewise, and some downward—anywhere, everywhere, for light and air; but the whole tree grows, ever taller in its higher branches, larger in the circumference of its outstretching arms, and more diversified in structure. Even so the tree of life, by the law of differentiation, branches and rebranches continually in all directions, some branches going upward to higher planes (progress), some pushing horizontally, neither rising nor sinking, but only going farther from the generalized origin (specialization); some going downward (degeneration), anywhere, everywhere, for an unoccupied place in the economy of Nature, but the *whole tree* grows ever higher in its highest parts, grander in its proportions, and more complexly diversified in its structure."

The third Law of Evolution is that called the Law of Cyclical Movement. In other words, although the evolutionary movement has ever been onward and upward, yet it has not traveled at a *uniform rate* in the whole, much less in the parts, but it has moved in successive *cycles*. "The tide of evolution rose ever higher and higher, without ebb, but it nevertheless came in successive *waves*, each higher than the preceding and overborne by the succeeding." This successive culmination of higher and higher classes of beings has also been aptly compared to a growing tree—to the flowering and fruiting of successive higher and higher branches.

"Each uppermost branch, under the genial heat and light of direct sunshine, received in abundance, by reason of position, grew rapidly; but quickly dwindled when overshadowed by still higher branches, which, in their turn, monopolized for a time the precious sunshine." But when each ruling class declined in importance, it did not perish altogether, but continued in a subordinate position—a degenerated state—a sort of stepping-stone to higher things—an Ichabod of Evolution.

Thus, the first two sections of our definition of Evolution, namely, that it is a progressive change according to the laws of differentiation, cyclical movement, and progress of the whole, have been explained. The last section, which teaches that *these changes are produced by forces residing in the organisms themselves*, is perhaps the most important. But I dispose of this part of the subject in the judicious and philosophic words of Prof. Le Conte. "When the Evolutionist," he says, "speaks of the forces that determine progressive changes in organic forms as *resident* or *inherent*, all that he means, or ought to mean, is that they are resident in the same sense as all natural forces are resident; in the same sense that the *vital forces of the embryo* are resident in the embryo—in other words, they are natural, not supernatural. This does not, of course, touch that deeper, that deepest of all questions, viz., the *essential nature and origin of natural forces;* how far they are independent and self-existent, and how far they are only modes of Divine Energy. This is a question of philosophy, not of science." * And I have given my views on this subject in the first chapter of this work.

Having now given an idea of the laws and scope of evolution, I pass to its *factors or causes*. But I shall mention only the five chief factors so far ascertained. First, there is *Environment* or surrounding conditions, climate, food, light, water, etc. When an oyster, for instance, is transferred from the shores of England into the Mediterranean Sea, its shell undergoes certain changes which are due to a change of external conditions. When Ohio sheep are transferred to Texas, in a few years their wool loses the distinctive quality it formerly had, and takes on a new character belonging to the breeds of Texas. Indeed, the common fact that one has to become "acclimated" to a new region illustrates this, as some believe, "the primordial factor of organic Evolution"—e. g., Spencer, Riley.†

A second cause of Evolution is *use and disuse* of organs. The athlete develops his muscles by exercise, while he reduces them when he deserts the gymnasium

---

* "Evolution and its Relation to Religious Thought," pp. 8–31.
† "Popular Science Monthly," February, 1889, p. 489.

or the field for the study. The giraffe has, probably, acquired its long neck by constant reaching up to the boughs of trees; the monkey has acquired its opposable thumb by constant grasping at the neighboring branches; and the serpent has acquired its sinuous shape by constant wriggling through the grass of the meadows. At least, this was the view of the great French naturalist, Lamarck, who flourished during the first half of this century, and the two factors in question are now generally recognized by scientists. To these Mr. Charles Darwin added two other factors, namely, "Natural Selection" and "Sexual Selection." The first simply means that, among the manifold varieties of plants and animals which are constantly originated in Nature, some are better adapted to surrounding conditions than are others, and by virtue of this constitutional advantage they survive in "the struggle for existence" which rages everywhere in the animal and vegetable world, while their weaker fellows are killed off, and thus better varieties, species, genera, races, etc., are produced. Illustrations of this law will occur to every mind. The little pig ("runt"), for instance, which is beaten away from the trough by his more vigorous relations until he dies of abuse and starvation, affords a very common instance of the operation of "Natural Selection."

"Sexual Selection" means that choice of the strongest and most attractive males which the females generally exercise in selecting family partners. "Among all animals," says Mr. Darwin, "there is a struggle for the possession of the female. Hence the females have the opportunity of selecting one out of several males, on the supposition that their mental capacity suffices for such a choice." This being generally true, the females select the strongest and most attractive, and thus improve and diversify their species. Perhaps our "society belles," who select the "dudes," instead of men of superior intellectual and moral character, might learn a lesson from their humbler relations. To these four factors—modification by environment, modification by use and disuse of organs, Natural Selection, and Sexual Selection—must be added that formulated by Dr. Romanes, called "Physiological Selection." This eminent scientist observed and emphasized the fact that the *reproductive organ* is, of all other organs, the most subject to *variation in its degrees and kinds of fertility*, and this, he thinks, explains the origin of many so-called "species."

Owing to the extreme variability of the reproductive organ, radical variations from the parental type would occur, by which the offspring would be rendered infertile with the parent stock, and yet they would be perfectly fertile among themselves. Here, then, we would have the beginning of a (so-called) species. To illustrate: the common dog was made by a mixture of several species of wolf. Suppose that, in the beginning, there occurred some variation in the wolf type due to a change in the reproductive organ by which a "doggish" offspring was produced which was infertile with the parental stock, but fertile with animals which varied in the same direction. A cross between these, which would naturally and necessarily happen, would, of course, produce a more "doggish" creature, which, in turn, would produce another, and so on, until the common dog would be the result. It thus appears that "Physiological Selection" throws much light upon the origin of species, and especially upon the knotty question of hybridism. The common objection, based upon the fact that a cross between certain animals (an ass and a horse, for instance) produces a hybrid (a mule), which is incapable of breeding, has received not a little attention from scientists, and Physiological Selection answers, to a very great extent, this objection. By virtue of the operation of this law, infertility is produced between certain branches of the animal kingdom, and these continue to *grow farther and farther apart* until the possibility of interbreeding them becomes as hopeless as the attempt to unite the ends of a tree's boughs; we must go down the trunk, begin at the bottom, and work upward. But the thoughtful reader is, of course, asking: "*What makes the reproductive organ, or, indeed, any other organ, vary from its original type?* What is the *prime* factor in this process?" To which I reply: It is *just here* that those differences of opinion arise which half-informed people — but only these — fancy are fatal to the whole theory of evolution, or rather to the fact of evolution; for it should be carefully borne in mind that the *theory* of evolution and the *fact* of evolution are two entirely different things. All, or nearly all, scientists accept the latter; but there are many and different schools (Lamarckian, Darwinian, Spencerian, etc.) of evolutionists, and these are characterized by the advocacy of the different theories concerning the causes of evolution which Lamarck, Darwin, or Spencer has formulated. I am an evolutionist. I believe that man has been evolved, *body and soul*, from a lower animal form; but without accepting any of the aforementioned theories, I aim to separate the chaff of error from the grain of truth. I believe, with Mr. Spencer and others, that "it is as yet far too soon to close the inquiry concerning the causes of organic evolution." * Mr. Spencer's discussions on this subject, together with what Darwin wrote in his various works, and what Semper wrote in his " Animal Life," express the most satisfactory view of the subject; while Prof. Riley's admirable address before the (1888) meeting of the American Association for the Advancement of Science is an excellent popular exposition of the causes of variation.† A careful perusal of these authors will—or ought to—convince the most skeptical that the day is not distant when a satisfactory theory of evolution will be formulated. But, however this may be, let it be remembered that the fact of evolution is fully established and almost universally accepted by those who are authorities in science. Thus, Prof. Le Conte says: "We are confident that evolution is *absolutely certain;* not, indeed, evolution as a special theory—Lamarckian, Darwinian, Spencerian—for these are all more or less successful modes of explaining evolution; nor evolution as a school of thought, with its following disciples—for in this sense it is still in the field of discussion—but evolution as a law of derivation of forms from previous forms; evolution as a law of continuity, as *a universal law of becoming.* . . . The words *evolutionism* and *evolutionist* ought not any longer to be used, any more than gravitationism and gravitationist." ‡

Hence it would be well for those who fancy that an explosion of Mr. Darwin's or Mr. Spencer's theories is

---

* " Popular Science Monthly," June, 1886, p. 205. Cf. Principles of Biology I, Plate III, Chapter viii-xi.

† " Popular Science Monthly," February and April, 1889.

* " Evolution and its Relation to Religious Thought," pp. 65, 66.

the destruction of evolution, to look more carefully into the subject.

The evidences of man's development from a lower animal form are derived chiefly from *four* sources, viz., Paleontology, Morphology, Variability, and Embryology.

I. It is a most significant fact *that the farther back in time we go, the simpler the forms of animal and plant life become, and those forms occur, in the order of their origination, just as if they were developed one from another.* The lowest and oldest form of animal life so far found in the bowels of the Earth is the *Eozoön,** or "Dawn Animal," discovered and named by Prof. J. W. Dawson, of McGill University, Canada. *Eozoön* "seems to have been a sessile creature resting on the bottom of the sea, and covering its gelatinous body with a thin crust of carbonate of lime, or limestone, adding to this, as it grew in size, crust after crust attached to each other by numerous partitions, and perforated with pores for the emission of gelatinous filaments. . . . In the modern seas, among the multitude of low forms of life with which they swarm, occur some in which the animal matter is a mere jelly, almost without distinct parts or organs, yet unquestionably endowed with life of an animal character." These small and often microscopic animals are not so large as *Eozoön,* which somewhat resembles them. *Eozoön* is not the oldest organism, but only the oldest yet discovered. "The existence of such creatures," says Prof. Dawson, "supposes that of other organisms, probably microscopic

---

* "There is much doubt *now* as to the nature of *Eozoön,* whether organic or mineral in origin."—LE CONTE.

plants, on which they could feed. No traces of these have been observed, though the great quantity of carbon in the beds probably implies the existence of larger sea-weeds. No other form of animal has yet been distinctly recognized in the Laurentian limestones, but there are fragments of calcareous matter which may have belonged to organisms distinct from *Eozoön*." * It is not necessary to my purpose to discuss either the question of organisms lower than the *Eozoön*, though, of course, on evolution principles, such must have existed, or the question whether such organisms were developed from non-living matter (I have already given my opinion on this subject); but I may take *Eozoön* as the starting-point of animal life, and coming up the scale (see diagram), we notice that higher and more complex organisms arise until the progress ends in man, " the lord of creation."

Beginning with the " Protozoa " (*Eozoön*, etc.), we find Crustaceans, Corals, and Mollusks; then Fishes and Amphibians; then Reptiles and Mammals; and, finally, Man. Of course, there are many missing pages in this geological history; for instance, " between the time when *Eozoön Canadense* flourished in the Laurentian period and the Cambrian age a great gap (Huronian period, see diagram) evidently exists in our knowledge of the succession of life " (Dawson), and this imperfection of the geological record has, of course, been cited by anti-evolutionists as a complete refutation of the doctrine of descent. But there is just about as much reason in this procedure as there would be in citing " the gap " in a book, some of whose leaves had been torn out,

---

* Dawson's "Story of the Earth and Man," pp. 23-25.

Diagram of the Earth's History.

PERIODS.		ANIMALS.	PLANTS.
Neozoic.	Modern. Post-pliocene. Pliocene. Miocene. Eocene.	Age of Man and Mammals.	Age of Angiosperms and Palms.
Mesozoic.	Cretaceous. Jurassic. Triassic.	Age of Reptiles.	Age of Cycads and Pines.
Palæozoic.	Permian. Carboniferous. Devonian. Silurian. Cambrian. Huronian.	Age of Amphibians and Fishes.	Age of Acrogens and Gymnosperms.
		Age of Mollusks, Corals, and Crustaceans.	Age of Algæ.
Eozoic.	Laurentian.	Age of Protozoa, Eozoon, etc.	Plants not determinable.

which yet had an *index* to show that such leaves must have once existed. We shall see that Embryology furnishes an index to the book of life which *necessitates* the existence of the missing leaves in the geological record. None are more fully aware of the imperfection of the geological record than evolutionists themselves, and they have successfully met all the objections of their opponents. Thus, Prof. Le Conte, while generously acknowledging that there is much force in the objection under consideration, disposes of it in a most satisfactory manner. He gives several solutions of the difficulty, the most conclusive of which is the following: "The steps of evolution *are not uniform*. Nearly all evolutionists have assumed and even insisted on uniformity, as the opposite of catastrophism and of supernaturalism, and therefore as essential to the idea of evolution. They say that the constancy of the action of the forces of change necessitates the uniformity of the rate of change.

"But, in fact, this is not always nor even usually true. *Causes or forces* are constant, but *phenomena* everywhere and in every department of Nature are *paroxysmal.*" To illustrate: "Water running with great resistance in small pipes is checked, but soon accumulates additional force, which overcomes the resistance, only to be again checked, and so on, and therefore runs in pulses. Now, the course of evolution of the whole earth may be likened to such a current: there are forces of movement and forces of resistance—progressive forces and conservative forces. The progressive force is accumulative, the resisting force is constant. Thus, in all evolution or history, whether of the earth or of society, there are periods of comparative quiet during which the forces of change are gathering strength and periods of revolution or rapid change, during which these forces show themselves in conspicuous effects.

" The consequence is, that there is an apparent break (oftentimes) in the continuity of life-forms; but undoubtedly this is only apparent, and if we could recover the record, as indeed we sometimes do, we should find in all cases that there is no break, but only more rapid rate of change at these times."*

When "the gaps" in the geological record may be thus easily explained, it is surely folly to insist that they present insuperable difficulties. Prof. Alexander Winchell, of Ann Arbor, summarizes the *paleontological* evidence of evolution thus:

"In spite of all this (imperfection), paleontology has been able to establish the following principles:

"1. There has been *gradual improvement* in the structural rank of the leading type of animals as the history advanced from age to age.

"2. The earlier condition of each animal type was a *comprehensive* one, in which certain characteristics of two or more families or orders were united in one species.

"3. The tendency of change has been toward the *resolution of comprehensive types*, so that the characteristics of each separate family or order should finally be embodied in separate species.

"4. While this process of resolution of comprehensive types has been in progress, still further differentiations and specializations, both in the comprehensive and the resolved forms, have taken place.

---

* " Evolution and its Relation to Religious Thought," pp. 232-247.

"5. The progress of discovery has gone so far that we have established not only a steady progression upward in the animal series at large, but also in several ramifications of the series."

Prof. Winchell traces the line of development in the Bird, the Camel, and the Rhinoceros series; but to avoid, as much as possible, the use of technical terms, I shall trace the evolution of the Horse only, which instance will sufficiently illustrate the evolution of other animals. "The horse," says Prof. Le Conte, "came from a five-toed, *plantigrade* ancestor, but we are not able to trace the direct line of genesis quite so far. The earliest stage we can trace with certainty, in this line of descent, is found in the *Eohippus* of Marsh. This was a small animal, no bigger than a fox, with three toes behind and four serviceable toes in front, with an additional fifth palm-bone (splint) and perhaps a rudimentary fifth toe like a dew-claw. This was in early Eocene times" (see diagram). "Then, in later Eocene, came the (higher form) *Orohippus*, which differs from the last chiefly in the disappearance (absorption) of the rudimentary fifth toe and splint. Next, in the Miocene (diagram) came the *Mesohippus* and *Miohippus*. These were larger animals (about the size of a sheep), and had three serviceable toes all around; but in the former the rudiment of a fourth splint in the fore-limb yet remained. Then in the Lower Pliocene (diagram) came the *Protohippus* and *Pliohippus*. These were still larger animals, being about the size of an ass. In the former the two side-toes were shortening up and the middle toes becoming larger. In the latter the two side-toes had become splints. Lastly, only in the *Quaternary* (latest formation) comes the genus *Equus*, or true horse. The size of the animal is become greater, the middle toe stronger, the side splints smaller; but in the side splints of the modern horse we have still remaining the evidence of its three-toed ancestor. Similar gradual changes may be traced in the two bones, which have consolidated into one; in the teeth, which have become progressively longer and more complex in structure, and therefore better grinders; in the position of the heel and wrist, which have become higher above-ground; in the general form, which has become more graceful and agile; and, lastly, in the brain, which has become progressively larger and more complex in its convolutions—to give greater battery power—to work the improved skeletal machine." *

This beautiful instance of evolution illustrates Prof. Winchell's remark that there has been "not only a steady progression upward in the animal series at large, but also in several separate ramifications of the series." The first known bird (as we have seen) may be considered either a reptilian-bird or a bird-like reptile, so nearly does it approach the bird and reptile series; in short, it is "the connecting link" between these, and they have both been differentiated and developed from this common source, as Prof. Winchell shows. Lastly, he says: "The tendency of fresh discovery is continually to fill up pre-existing gaps. Serial successions are being completed from year to year; connecting links are coming to light; terms thought misplaced are found, through new discoveries, to be in proper successional order. . . . We anticipate, accordingly, that in the course of time it will be shown that our earth has been

---

* "Evolution and its Relation to Religious Thought," pp. 108–110.

the abode of complete successions of animal types leading backward from each of our modern generic or family groups by ever-converging lines, toward ancestral centers, and from these centers other lines pointing toward some common center in the remoter past. We expect to see the consecutive terms in these various series graduating structurally into each other; and every characteristic conformed and arranged *as if* there had been a gradual descent of all our modern mammals along a set of diverging lines from some primitive, plantigrade, five-toed ancestor.

"This is the generalization which the known facts and the known tenor of the facts authorize us to draw." *

If, now, the radical skeptic, deaf alike to the voice of reason and fact, still insist that, although the forms of animal life do occur in the history of the earth *just as if* they were developed out of one another, yet we can not *demonstrate* such development, we reply by citing the facts of embryology which Prof. Winchell truly says *do* " demonstrate that the derivative relation of such terms as paleontology presents is an ever-repeated reality."

II. Next, we consider the Morphological evidence of evolution—that is, the evidence afforded by a study of the *structure* of various animal types; and here again I follow Prof. Winchell, partly because his summary of evidence is brief and masterly, but especially because I hope the words of a Christian and a practical scientist may have more weight in certain quarters than either my own opinion or those of agnostic and skeptical natu-

---

* Winchell's "Sparks from a Geologist's Hammer," pp. 339–341.

ralists. "Every one," says Prof. Winchell, "understands what is meant by saying one person bears a family resemblance to another. It implies that there is a blood connection between them. In some generation more or less remote their lineage converges, and the same parents stand as common ancestors to both persons. Precisely the same thing is involved in the statement that the dog, the wolf, and the jackal have a family resemblance—or the cat, the lynx, the ounce, and the panther. The resemblances in these families are not so close as in the human family; but they are of the same kind, and they impress themselves on us in the same way and with the same effect. The children of John Smith are quite certain to resemble their parents, and may reproduce predominantly traits of their grandparents or remoter progenitors."

This happens, of course, according to the well-recognized law of heredity. "It is certainly safe," continues Prof. Winchell, "on grounds of natural evidence, to admit that family resemblances among animals, as among mankind, imply community of descent.

"This principle achieved, very much is found involved in it. Resemblances of the same nature as those called family resemblances exist between groups of animals and plants quite widely differentiated from each other. We do not say the mouse and the rhinoceros possess a family resemblance, but it is demonstrable that they do possess profound resemblances aggregating vastly more than all their differences. Their differences relate to size, covering, habits, and other trivial circumstances; while their resemblances include skeletal framework, circulatory, digestive, respiratory, and reproductive organization, as well as the general plan, arrangements, juxtaposition, connection, and coaction of these systems, and all the minuter plan, substance, structure, development, and action of bone, nerve, skin, fibers, membranes, etc. Finally, both have warm blood, respire air, and nourish their young with milk.

"How can we escape the conviction that these animals, also, owe their amazing similarity of constitution to their common descent from some remote ancestor?" *

If this conclusion seems startling to any of my readers, it will appear less so the more they study Morphology.

Thus, Prof. Le Conte shows, by a comparison of the fore-limbs of mammals, birds, reptiles, and fishes, that they are all constructed on the same fundamental plan. He traces the gradual changes in the collar-bone, in the position of the elbow, in the bones of the forearm, in the position of the wrist, in the tread, number of toes, modifications for flight, etc. He concludes by saying that, in an early period of the earth's history, "fishes were the only representatives of the vertebrate (back-bone) type of structure. The vertebrate machine was then *a swimming-machine.* In the course of time, when all was ready and conditions were favorable, reptiles were introduced. Here, then, is a new function—that of locomotion on land. We want a *walking-machine.* Shall we have a new organ for this function? No; the old swimming-organ is modified so as to adapt it for walking. Time went on, and birds were introduced. Here is a new and wonderful function, that of flying in the air. We want a *flying-machine.* Nature (unlike

---

* "Sparks from a Geologist's Hammer," pp. 333-335.

man) modifies the fore-limbs for this new purpose. If we must have wings, we must sacrifice fore-legs. We can not have both without violating the laws of Morphology.

"Finally, ages again passed, and, when time was fully ripe, man was introduced. Now we want some part to perform a new and still more wonderful function. We want a *hand*, the willing and efficient servant of a rational mind. But, if we want hands, we must sacrifice feet. Again, therefore, the fore-limbs are modified for this new and exquisite function. Thus, in the fin of the fish, the fore-paw of a reptile or mammal, the wing of a bird, and the arm and hand of a man, *we have the same part variously modified for many purposes.*" Prof. Le Conte, in the chapter immediately following the one just referred to, discusses the structures of the *Articulates*, or *jointed animals*, such as worms, crayfishes, lobsters, etc., and shows that, whether they originated by derivation one from another or not, "it is certain that the structure of the articulate animals is exactly such as *would* be the case if all these animals were genetically connected and came originally from a primal form something like one of the lower Crustaceans, or perhaps a marine worm." *

Hence it is incumbent upon the anti-evolutionists to formulate a more rational theory of creation, which, we feel sure, can not be done.

Such, then, is what Morphology has to say about the origination of the manifold forms of plant and animal life; and what an inspiring study it is! What infinite wisdom is displayed in the marvelous modifications of

---

* "Evolution and its Relation to Religious Thought," pp. 92–130.

the original forms! How much nobler is this view than that which presents us with a "workshop" of the Almighty Maker, thus reducing Him to a sort of tinker!*

III. The *third* source of evidence proving man's evolution from a lower form is found in the facts of *Variability*. What is meant by this will appear from the following anecdote told me by a friend, a pigeon-fancier: He once made a bet with a friend that within a year from that time he could get a pair of perfectly white pigeons out of his flock, although he had no bird with a single white feather in his plumage to begin with. Of course, the bet was accepted, and my friend eagerly awaited the advent of some pigeon with a white feather in his coat. In due time one came from a neighbor's yard, and he caught and cooped him up with one of his own birds. The result was the production of an offspring with some white feathers in its plumage, and my friend continued to *select* and match together the birds which varied in the white feather direction until, sure enough, he got his white pair of pigeons within a year, and won his bet. And it is well known to pigeon-fanciers that all pigeons—the pouters, tumblers, carriers, fantails, etc.—are descendants from one kind—the Rock Pigeon. Having in mind the doctrine of evolution, I asked my friend if he thought it possible by artificial selection to entirely change the type of the pigeon, to make another bird out of him. "Oh, no," he replied, "it will always be essentially a pigeon." Now, this has been the universal opinion until a com-

---

* See Dawson's "Story of the Earth and Man," p. 27, where this phrase is actually used.

paratively recent period. Species were (and are still in some quarters, chiefly theological) considered groups of plants or animals staked off from certain others by insurmountable barriers. But it was the glory of the late Mr. Charles Darwin to show, in his great work, "The Origin of Species," that some such process as that adopted by my friend takes place among wild animals, and he earnestly and ably contended that there is no such thing as an absolutely unchangeable Species. The terrible storm which his book created in the scientific and theological world has scarcely died away even now; but its thunders are only heard in the distance, and his views are pretty generally accepted among scientists, while they are growing in favor with theologians. "Some cases of transmutation of species," says Prof. Winchell, "have actually been traced, and evidence has been gained that the gradational series connecting species of animals and plants long regarded as distinct, are, in truth, only transitional states of one of the species in its passage over to the other."

In the case of birds, for instance, "certain forms have long been known from widely separated regions and universally regarded as distinct species—as distinct as any. But by minute examinations of intermediate regions, a complete series of intermediate forms has been picked up. This has occurred not only in one case, but in many cases, and not only in birds, but in many other classes; examples increase with our increasing knowledge. The only answer to such evidence is, that *these are not true species.* Now, see the fallacy lurking here. Anti-Evolutionists define species as forms distinct and without intermediate links, and require us to find such intermediate links; and, finally, when with infinite pains, some such links are found, they say: "Oh, I see we were mistaken; they are only varieties." "But there are some cases in which this subterfuge will not do. There are cases in which the transitions are between forms so extreme that they can not, by any stretch of the term, be called varieties. In Würtemberg (Germany), near the little village of Steinheim, are found certain fresh-water deposits which are extremely rich in fossil shells, especially of the genus called *Planorbis*. As the deposits seem to have been continuous for ages, and the fossil shells very abundant, this seemed to be an excellent opportunity to test the theory of derivation." Accordingly, Prof. Alpheus Hyatt, of Boston, made a most thorough examination of these shells in 1880. "In passing from the lowest to the highest strata the species change greatly, and many times, the extreme forms being so different, that, were it not for the intermediate forms, they would be called not only different species, but different genera. And *yet the gradations* are so insensible that the whole series is nothing less than a *demonstration*, in this case, at least, of origin of species by derivation with modifications. The case is striking, partly because it is a very favorable one, but mainly because it has been so carefully studied. There can be no doubt that equally careful study would reveal the same transitions in many other cases. Nor are such transitions confined to the lower forms of life, though they are probably more abundant there. According to Prof. Cope, the nicest gradations may be traced between some of the extinct mammalian species so abundant in the Tertiary deposits of the West," and Prof. Le Conte thinks that "the same is probably true of many extinct species of the horse family." *

Thus, at last, this common but superficial objection to evolution has been exploded. "The sum total of the variational evidence shows us that the derivative origin of types in paleontological history is a natural possibility."

IV. But, in the fourth place, we have the *Embryological evidence*—that is, proofs afforded by the development of each individual from a minute speck called the *embryo*. "This seems to us to bring all the other evidence to a focus and complete the conviction that the derivative origin of species is a fact. It affords not only a picture of the succession of extinct forms, but it is a picture in which the successive terms are *known* to be derivatively related to each other." (Winchell.)

"It is a curious and most significant fact," says Prof. Le Conte, "that the individual animal in embryonic development passes through temporary stages which are similar in many respects to permanent conditions in some of the lower forms in the same group. To give one example for the sake of clearness: the frog, in its early stages of embryonic development, is essentially a fish, and if it stopped at this stage would be so called and classed. But it does not stop; it passes through the fish stage and several other stages. In its tadpole (or first) state it is a gill-breather. It has, therefore, its gill-arches, three on each side, like a fish, and for the same reason viz., the aëration of the blood. But when its gills dry up and lung-respiration is established, its now

---

* "Evolution and its Relation to Religious Thought," pp. 61, 236–239.

useless gill-arches still remain as aortic arches to attest their previous condition." Take another example, the lizard. "If one examines the large vessels *going out* from the heart of a lizard, he will find *six arches* (called aortic arches), i. e., three on a side. These all unite below the heart to form one descending abdominal artery. Now, there is no conceivable use in having so many of these arches, as we know from the fact that birds and mammals have only one aortic arch, and the circulation of the blood is as effective as, nay, much more effective in these than in reptiles. The explanation of this anomaly," Prof. Le Conte adds, " is revealed at once as soon as we examine the circulation of a fish. The multiplication of aortic arches is here, of course, necessary, for they are the gill-arches. If, now, a lizard were ever a fish and afterward turned into a lizard, changing its gill-respiration for lung-respiration, then, of course, the useless gill-arches will remain to tell the story.

"Now, although a lizard never was a fish in its *individual* history, yet it was a fish in its *family* history, and therefore it yet retains, by heredity, this curious and useless structure as evidence of its ancestry." We thus see that "the embryo of a higher animal of any group passes *now* through stages represented by lower forms, *because in its evolution its ancestors did actually have these forms.* From this point of view, then, the history of each individual (its development) is a brief repetition as it were, from memory, of the main points of family history. . . . It is a most curious and significant fact that, in the early embryonic condition of birds and mammals, including man, we find on each side of the neck several gill-slits, each with its gill-arch, and there are several aortic arches on each side precisely as we have already described."

These arches are subsequently, some of them, obliterated; some modified to form the one aortic arch, and some of them still more modified to form the other great arteries coming from the heart to supply the head and fore-limbs. This is a beautiful and convincing example of evolution. "See, then, the gradual process of change through the whole vertebrate (backboned) department. In the lowest of all vertebrates, if vertebrate it may be called (for what corresponds to its backbone is an *unjointed* fibrous cord)—i. e., in the lancelet—there are about forty gill-arches on each side. As we rise in the scale of fishes, these are reduced in number. In the lamprey there are seven; in the sharks usually five; in ordinary fishes there are four, sometimes only three on each side, the others being aborted. Thus far the change is only by diminution of numbers, but the further change is one of *adaptive modification*. In some reptiles (the lizard for instance) the three gill-arches on each side all retain the form of aortic arches; in some reptiles only two retain this form. In birds and mammals only one arch is retained, in the form of aortic arch, the others being modified to form the great outgoing vessels of the heart, or else aborted."

Having thus made it clear, I hope, that "the individual higher animal in embryonic development passes now through temporary stages which are similar in many respects to permanent or mature conditions in some of the lower forms in the same group," and this "because in its evolution its ancestors did actually have these forms," I now quote Prof. Le Conte's masterly sketch of the evolution of man's brain, which shows that he is a descendant of fishes, reptiles, birds, and mammals:

"The very early condition of the human brain" (in embryo), says our author, "is nothing more than the intercranial continuation of the spinal cord enlarged a little into three swellings (ganglia). . . . This stage may be regarded as lower than that of the ordinary fish. I have, therefore, called it the *sub-fish stage*. The cerebellum is a subsequent growth from the medulla, as is the cerebrum and olfactive lobes from the thalamus. This next stage, therefore, may be said to represent fairly the *fish-stage*. Henceforward the principal growth is in the cerebrum and cerebellum, both of which are subsequent outgrowths of the original simple ganglia, the medulla, and the thalamus.

"The cerebrum especially increases steadily in relative size, first becoming larger than but not covering the optic lobes. This represents the *reptilian stage*. Next, by further growth it covers partly the optic lobes. This may be called the *bird stage*. Then it covers wholly the optic lobes, and encroaches on the cerebellum behind and olfactive lobes in front. This is the *mammalian stage*. Finally, it covers and overhangs all, and thus assumes the *human stage*."

Prof. Le Conte, in the chapter from which I have thus quoted at length,* gives woodcuts of all these stages of development of man's brain; and any one who will read the chapter carefully and understand it must, I think, be convinced that the human brain passes through such stages of development because and only because

---

* "Evolution and its Relation to Religious Thought," Part II, chap. vi.

man is a descendant of animals which possessed brains corresponding to these temporary stages of embryonic evolution. "Fishes," says Prof. Le Conte, "were the only vertebrates living in the Devonian times (see diagram).

"The first form of brain, therefore, was that characteristic of that class. Then reptiles were introduced; then birds and marsupials; then true mammals; and, lastly, man. The different styles of brains characteristic of these classes were, therefore, successively made by evolution from early and simpler forms." Man's development, therefore, in embryo, "is a brief repetition from memory, so to speak, of his family history."

To prevent misunderstanding, it seems necessary to quote and emphasize Mr. Spencer's remarks on the popular misapprehension of this argument made by popular treatises on evolution. "An impression," he says, "has been given by those who have popularized the statements of embryologists, that, during its development, each organism passes through stages in which it resembles the *adult* forms of lower organisms; that the embryo of a man is at one time like a fish, and at another time like a man. This is *not* a fact. The fact established is, that *up to a certain point the embryos of a man and a fish continue similar, and that then differences begin to appear and increase—the one embryo approaching more and more toward the form of a fish, the other diverging from it more and more.*

"And so with resemblances to the more advanced types. Supposing the germs of all kinds of organisms to be simultaneously developing, we may say that all members of the vast multitude take their first steps in the same direction; that at the second step one half of this vast multitude diverges from the other half, and thereafter follows a different course of development; that the immense assemblage contained in either of these divisions very soon again shows a tendency to take two or more routes of development; that each of the two or more minor assemblages thus resulting shows for a time but small divergences among its members, but presently again divides into groups which separate ever more widely as they progress; and so on, until each organism, when nearly complete, is accompanied in its further modifications only by organisms of the same species; and, last of all, assumes the peculiarities which distinguish it as an individual—diverges to a slight extent to the organisms it is most like. The reader must also be cautioned against accepting this generalization as exact. The likenesses thus successively displayed are not precise, but approximate."

But the important question is, *Why these approximate likenesses?* Why should there be any such striking embryonic resemblances, if all animals be not *genetically* related—do not belong to one great genealogical tree? Mr. Spencer replies, with all other evolutionists, that this question is unanswerable except on the evolution-hypothesis. He believes, as firmly as any other evolutionist, that the embryonic resemblances are due to community of origin.*

And so, to quote Prof. Winchell's forcible summary of the evidences of man's development from lower forms: "*Palæontological* history exhibits a series in which the continued interpolation of newly discovered terms pro-

---

* "Principles of Biology," I, p. 143; cf. Part III, chap. v.

duces the suspicion of a perfectly graduated and genetic line. It suggests material continuity as a *possibility and a promise*. *Morphological* relations present such continuity as something which within the range of observation is a *probability*. The phenomena of *Variability* reveal a disposition and an aptitude on the part of Nature to fulfill the 'promise,' and make the 'probability' completely a fact. The data of *Embryology* (note well) *demonstrate* that the derivative relation of such terms as paleontology presents is and ever—repeated actuality. Now, with the work completed in the ontogenetic epitome, and with this proof of Nature's *method* and the variational proof of Nature's *method* and *means*, it is little stretch of belief to grant that Nature pursued the method of derivative originations during the whole period of paleontological history." *

Under the pressure of these and similar facts and arguments, some scientists and theologians have been compelled to grant that man's *physical* organism has been developed from a lower animal form, but they draw a line at his *spiritual* nature ; assert that his spirit could not have been evolved from the *anima* of animals But the ground is being rapidly cut from under their feet by Mr. Herbert Spencer, Prof. Romanes, and others.† For my own part, I see no possibility of drawing so imaginary a line, and therefore I accept the

---

* "Sparks from a Geologist's Hammer," p. 348. Compare Mr. Spencer's "Biology," I, chapters iv–vii, on the Evidences of Evolution, and Dr. Romanes's pamphlet on "The Scientific Evidences of Organic Evolution," Humbolt Library, No. 40.

† Spencer's "Psychology," Romanes's "Animal Intelligence," "Mental Evolution in Animals," "Mental Evolution in Man," etc.

evolution of man, *body and soul*, from the lower animals. We have been compelled to grant evolution in Astronomy, Geology, and Biology, and it is folly to ask the evolutionists to stop short at Psychology and Sociology. We should gratefully accept their deliveries on these subjects and readjust our theology accordingly. In saying this, however, I would not be understood as indorsing or adopting any particular theory of Evolution (Lamarckian, Darwinian, Spencerian, or other); but I mean to say we should accept the *fact* of evolution in all its length and breadth and depth and height, and give due weight to all the *factors* or causes of evolution which the different scientists discover, waiting patiently till all the laws and causes of evolution be discovered before we formulate an evolutionary creed. In view of the statements just made concerning the evolution of man's mind, it may be thought that I should give the facts and reasons upon which such statements are based. This I shall not do, for two cogent reasons: First, space will not permit it; and, secondly, if one accept the evolution of man's physical nature, he will not hesitate very long to accept mental evolution—especially if he will read Mr. Spencer's "Psychology" and Prof. Romanes's works referred to above. These able treatises seem to me quite satisfactory, and therefore I content myself with referring the reader to them. Let me add that no one is more conscious than I am of the imperfection of the sketch of Man's evolution thus given; but it was impossible to make it more perfect in the space allotted to me, and my simple object has been to give the reader the right point of view, to break down popular superficial objections to the doctrine of evolution, and to show that it is on chimera, but a fact. If I have succeeded in doing this, I am satisfied to refer my reader for full information to the works of Mr. Darwin,* of Mr. Spencer,† of Prof. Huxley,‡ of Prof. Dawson (an anti-evolutionist),# of Prof. Le Conte, ‖ of Prof. Winchell,△ and other leading scientists.

---

* "Origin of Species," "Descent of Man," etc.
† "Synthetic Philosophy."
‡ "Man's Place in Nature," "Science and Culture," "Lay Sermons," etc.
\# "Story of the Earth and Man," "Origin of the World," etc.
‖ "Evolution and its Relation to Religious Thought," etc.
△ "Sparks from a Geologist's Hammer," etc.

CHAPTER III.

MAN'S ORIGIN ACCORDING TO THEOLOGY.

WE rejoice in the enlightenment and tolerance of our age, but the historian of the future will have the painful duty to perform of recording instances of intolerance and bigotry which find their prototypes in the history of the sixteenth century. Not only were Mr. Darwin and his co-evolutionists denounced and anathematized by the pulpit and religious press, but even so late as the year 1888 an ecclesiastical assembly (Presbyterian) deprived a theological professor of his chair because he inclined to accept a modified form of evolution—believed that Adam was formed not of inorganic but of organic dust. If the rack and thumb-screw are abolished, the *odium theologicum* still exists and produces essentially the same effects, albeit by more refined and excruciating methods. "Persecution," said the late Rev. Frederick Robertson—and he spoke from bitter experience—" persecution is that which affixes penalties upon *views held*, instead of upon *life led*. Is persecution *only* fire and sword? But suppose a man of sensitive feeling says, The sword is less sharp to me than the slander; fire is less intolerable than the refusal of sympathy!" The man who adopts certain "views" need never expect ecclesiastical preferment. Protestantism is quite as intolerant as Romanism. Although no Protestant church has a specific dogma on the subject of man's origin, yet the general consensus of Protestant theologians is so decidedly anti-evolution in spirit that a clergyman who aspires to be a "doctor," "professor," or "bishop," would better beware of "science falsely so called." True, the fundamental tenet of Protestantism is the "Right of Private Judgment" in religious matters, and hence no one has a moral (and no one ought to have an ecclesiastical) right to debar one the honors of the Church on account of *views*, but nevertheless "the powers that be" have and exercise such authority.

Not only has Protestantism no dogma concerning man's origin, but theological writers who claim that "Man is a special creation"—a being "created in the image of God"—"out of the dust of the ground"— seem utterly unable to tell us exactly what they mean by these phrases. Thus, Dr. Van Oosterzee asks, "Whence, then, is man? . . . It is not enough," he answers, "to say that he, as everything else, has his origin from God. The question is whether any more accurate definition concerning the proper origin of the human race can be attained. Without reason this question is put on one side, as not belonging to the domain of Theology but to that of Physical Science."* When I read these words my heart leaped for joy, for having looked in vain through the works of other theologians and scientific advocates of "special creations" for an "accurate definition" of man's origination, I thought that at last I had found it. Imagine my disappointment when I read the following definition: "Man, the

---

* Van Oosterzee, "Christian Dogmatics," vol. i, p. 360.

most excellent being upon earth, owes his origin to a definite creative act of God, in consequence of which he may in no sense be called the merely natural product of a lower order of creatures, but rather a link in the chain of animated beings." Let us analyze this definition: First, who doubts that man is "the most excellent being on earth"? Nobody. Secondly, who doubts that "a definite creative act of God" takes place in the production of *every* creature? None but the atheist. Mr. Spencer recognizes "An Eternal Energy" from which all things proceed, and this by most "definite" acts. Thirdly, Dr. Van Oosterzee, like so many other theologians, uses the word "Natural" in an *undefined sense*, and he would do well to ponder the words of Prof. Huxley on the meaning of the terms "Natural Order," "Laws of Nature," etc.* These are mere names applied to certain phenomena, but they by no means explain those phenomena. Finally, we are told that man is "a separate link in the chain of animate beings," but not one word is said about how this link was forged. In short, this "accurate definition" is meaningless.

Another definition of man's origin is given by the Rev. Dr. Charles Hodge, in the second volume of his large work on "Systematic Theology" (p. 3), where he quotes the account of man's creation in Genesis (i, 22, 27, and ii, 7), and adds: "Two things are included in this account. First, that man's body was formed by the immediate intervention of God. It did not grow; nor was it produced by a process of development. Secondly, the soul was derived from God. He breathed into man the 'breath of life.'"

---

* "Popular Science Monthly," January, 1888, p. 355.

One question explodes this "definition," viz., *What is meant by "the immediate intervention of God"?* This is precisely what we desire to have defined, but our author is so haunted by "anti-Scriptural theories" of creation that he has no time to formulate a Scriptural theory. There is plenty of denunciation of "Naturalism," etc., in the writings of both these eminent divines, but I have looked in vain for an "accurate definition" of what they consider the Biblical idea of man's origination. Surely they do not mean that God came down (or up) to some spot, say in the plains of Mesopotamia, and took up dust and made a mud man, and breathed into his nostrils the breath of life. Nor can they mean that the Energy (God) which constantly operates in Nature, causing the stone to form, the plant to grow, and the animal to think, on one occasion, by a peculiar exertion of itself (Himself), made the particles of dust collect themselves into a human form, into which the same Energy infused the power of motion, life, and thought. If they mean this, let it be said in plain words, but let us not be expected to accept vague, general terms as "definitions."

The question, therefore, returns with redoubled force: If man's body (and soul) were not derived, according to the well-recognized laws of Morphology, Embryology, and Psychology, from a lower animal form; if the human frame is not genetically related to lower organisms, how was it produced? It is interesting to note that Dr. Hodge, in his little book on "What is Darwinism?"—a most unsatisfactory production in every respect—virtually contradicts his opinion just quoted. He says: "Man is, according to the Scripture, as concerns his body, of the earth. So far he belongs to the animal kingdom."* But if man's body were formed by "the immediate intervention of God," how can it belong to the animal kingdom? The doctor evidently grew—became more of an evolutionist—between the time of the publication of his "Theology" and this later work; he inclines to accept the physical evolution of man; but this, as already remarked, involves his mental evolution. Other advocates of the special creation of man, be they scientists or theologians, fail as absolutely as the two just quoted to tell us exactly what they mean by such a creation.

Dr. Cunningham Geikie, in his "Hours with the Bible" (Vol. I, Chaps. X and XI), discusses man's origin quite fully, and attempts to refute the evolutionary theory, but formulates no other theory. Dr. Martensen, in his "Christian Dogmatics" (page 136 *et seq.*, T. and T. Clark's Library), talks most mystically about man's creation in the image of God, but gives us no definite idea concerning the mode of his origination. Dr. Arnold Guyot is equally unsatisfactory,† and Principal Dawson does not help his theological friends out of their dilemma, although he has written one work specially for this purpose.‡ But while the advocates of "special creation" can not tell us exactly what they mean by this phrase, they, nevertheless, insist that man *was* a new creation—a new link in the chain of life, radically different in soul, and probably also in body, from all lower animal forms. On what do they base this claim? On the facts of Morphology, Embryology, Paleontology, etc.? No; for we have seen that all

---

* "What is Darwinism?" p. 5.
† "Essay on Creation." p. 122 *et seq.*
‡ "Origin of the World."

such facts point to man's derivation from the lower animals. What, then, constitutes the foundation of the theological view? *A document whose meaning and authorship are so hopelessly uncertain that the most learned and devout minds can not agree on either the one or the other.* It is now generally acknowledged, among even "conservative" commentators, that the Book of Genesis consists of traditions, oral or written, which were handed down from patriarchal times. Thus, to quote only one "conservative" writer, Bishop Harold Browne says: "It is not necessary to deny that Moses had certain documents or traditions referring to the patriarchal ages, which he incorporated into his history. Indeed, it is most likely that such traditions should have come down through Shem and Abraham to Joseph and the Israelites in Egypt; and there can be no reason why an inspired historian should not have worked up such trustworthy materials into the history of the ancestors of his people."* The idea of "an inspired historian" working up another's documents into a production of his own seems utterly absurd, for why could not and did not the Inspirer originate an entirely new account? Surely it would have been quite as easy as it was to inspire Moses to use traditions which had existed for hundreds of years, perhaps in oral form, and may have been corrupted.

Surely the Inspirer had no reason for economizing his sources of wisdom. If so, the documentary theory does not prove it. That theory really gives up the Mosaic authorship of those parts of Genesis which consist of the said traditions. And when the reader re-

---

* "Speaker's Commentary," vol. i, Introduction, p. 2.

members, or is informed, that the late George Smith, among others, discovered "A Chaldean Genesis"—i. e., accounts of creation, the deluge, etc.—written on clay tablets, brought from that section of the country where Abraham was reared—Ur of the Chaldees (Genesis xi, 28-31)—he will not be long in concluding that our Genesis is only one of several accounts of creation which originated among the religious poets and sages of that age and country; and although it is superior to any of those accounts, and most valuable as a monument of ancient philosophy, the student will not accept it as absolutely and literally infallible *until it is proved to be so.*

It is utter folly to ask us to accept a document as Divinely inspired without giving a single reason for so wonderful a conclusion—without even telling us who wrote that document. "But hold!" cries the advocate of traditionalism; "Christ and His Apostles indorsed Genesis as an inspired work—the work of Moses."

"If we consult the Bible" (says Dr. Van Oosterzee), "we learn from the Lord Jesus that it is God who has made them male and female (Matthew xix, 4). St. Paul speaks in a like sense (I Corinthians xi, 8-12, and I Timothy ii, 3), and his words are only the echo of the Old Testament. All these voices refer us to the records of Moses (Genesis i, 26, and ii, 7)." Upon this it may be observed:

First. The genuineness and authenticity of a document can hardly be established by citing statements from still more questionable documents. For all well-informed people know (and the uninformed reader will subsequently learn) that the authorship of the *Gospels* is no more certain than that of Genesis. It would be well for those who are ever trying to press our Lord into the service of Biblical Criticism and Dogmatic Theology to remember that He never wrote out His views on such subjects, and it *is much more probable that we have in the books of the New Testament the opinions of pious Jews than it is that we have our Lord's views.*

We may be sure at any rate that He, if He were on earth to-day, would be the last one to fly in the face of fact and reason in order to preserve the letter of the first and second chapters of Genesis. *He* regarded Nature and the Human Spirit as no less revelations of God than the Bible. But—

Secondly. Even granting that Christ and St. Paul did utter the words (the latter certainly wrote First Corinthians) which are attributed to them, those words neither prove the authorship and inspiration of Genesis nor disprove man's derivation from the lower animals. Nobody doubts that "God created them male and female," but the question is, *How* did He so create them? Neither Christ nor St. Paul answers this question, because they were teachers of religion, not of physical science, and it was sufficient for their purpose to say, "God did it." They therefore merely refer to or "echo" the account in Genesis, but do not explain the precise meaning of that account, which is exactly what we now desire to have done. We are therefore forced to interpret Genesis as best we can, and the following seems to be the only view which modern discovery permits us to hold: The accounts of creation, the deluge, etc., in Genesis were written probably about fifteen hundred or two thousand years before Christ, in Chaldea, by some of the religious sages who there pondered the great problems of Being. When Abraham left "Ur of the Chaldees," he gathered together these accounts, took them with him, and handed them on to his children; they passed them on to their children, and finally they were embodied (by Moses or some one else) in the Pentateuch, and so became the heritage of the Jewish Nation. These narratives can not be interpreted literally, and, as a matter of fact, no one attempts to so interpret them.

They were not written to give a scientific account of the origin of the world, but for a strictly *religious* purpose. The author's (or authors'—for there may have been several) contemporaries were Nature-worshipers, and so he (they) aimed a deadly blow at such worship by proclaiming "that the heavens and the earth" were "created," and hence men should worship a higher Being; and the lesson which he (they) aimed to teach has to be learned by many of this materialistic generation; but it is simply folly to cite these narratives as refutations of a scientific theory so well established as the theory of Evolution.

Two facts, however, stated in Genesis (ii, 7) concerning man's origin modern science confirms, viz.: first, that man's body consists of dust; and, secondly, that the soul of man is not identical with his body. While the commonly observed fact of decomposition at death may have suggested the first truth to the ancient sage, yet his apprehension of the second is surely wonderful. Our modern *savants* can tell us something of the process of the formation of man's body and also something of the Divine inspiration (breathing into man) of the soul; their elder brother did not concern himself with "processes," as he was teaching religion and not science. He merely proclaimed that God created all things, and, although man's body should molder into its original dust, yet his soul was a reflection, an "image," a spark flashed forth from the Eternal Light, and hence partook of its nature and (it was necessarily implied) man should live worthy of his Divine parentage. The strange account of Woman's creation (Genesis, ii, 21, 22) was doubtless suggested by the fact of her *dependence* on the man, and was designed to impress the beautiful truth involved in this fact: "And Adam (the Man) said, This is now bone of my bone, and flesh of my flesh; she shall be called woman because *she was taken out of* man. Therefore shall a man leave his father and mother and shall cleave unto his wife; and they shall be one flesh."

How profoundly significant to the divorce-lovers and wife-abusers of our day; but how much more significant to the adulterous generations of antiquity!

Interpreted in this, or a similar, manner Genesis will teach us profound moral truths; but the moment we attempt to make it teach science, we are landed in hopeless difficulties. From the birth of physical science to the present day attempts have been made to stop the onward march of Science by citing texts of Scripture and issuing conciliar decrees, but all such attempts have resulted in disaster to the Church. It is, therefore, high time that theologians should surrender the whole domain of cosmology to the scientists and interpret those passages of Scripture which refer to natural phenomena by the light of Science and History. As a moral and religious guide the Bible will never be surpassed—will ever remain indispensable—but it will henceforth be treated not as a verbally and infallibly inspired account of all things in heaven and earth, but as "the *record* of a progressive (religious) revelation, divinely adapted to the hard heart, the dull understanding, and the slow development of mankind." *

The account of creation given in Genesis, considering the time when and the circumstances under which it was produced, is a marvelous product of religious genius; and this, notwithstanding the possible relic of polytheism involved in the plural form (Elohim) of the name of the Creator. But it is chiefly valuable as a gem of ancient thought. It shows us that the men of those far-off ages meditated profoundly on the great problems of Being which exercise the philosophic minds of our own generation. It brings those old seers and sages near to our hearts; and while we are able, by the light of science, to penetrate further into the dark corners of Nature's Temple than they could, yet over its portal we must inscribe their immortal words, "IN THE BEGINNING GOD CREATED THE HEAVENS AND THE EARTH." Let not, then, an arrogant Theology destroy the poet's strain or mar the seer's vision by inflating it with a tone or meaning it never could have had.

From what has been said we conclude that Theology has no explanation of man's origin to offer, while its attempted refutation of the evolutionist's explanation rests on no sure warranty of Scripture, and is contradicted by all the facts so far discovered. The evolutionary theory has its difficulties; all the "gaps" are not yet filled up; but all the facts point in this direction, and, as it is the only explanation worthy of the name of the great problem in hand, it should be accepted —at least, until a better one is established.

---

* Archdeacon Farrar, "History of Interpretation," Bampton Lectures for 1885, Preface, p. x.

Science and Theology have been arrayed against each other long enough. They are wasting precious energies fighting each other which might be used to better purpose. They are divinely ordained twin-sisters: "What God hath joined together, let not man put asunder."

CHAPTER IV.

THE AGE OF THE HUMAN RACE.

UNTIL recently it was generally believed that the age of Man did not exceed six thousand years, and this is still considered, in some quarters, "the orthodox view," but whether it is "orthodox" we shall now see. On what grounds does this opinion rest? On the authority of an archbishop in the Church—Dr. Usher, who lived about three hundred years ago. On what did he base his estimate? On the facts of archæology? This science was not then born. "His leading data," therefore, to quote the Rev. Dr. William Smith, editor of "Dictionary of the Bible," etc., "were, first, the adoption of the numbers of the Hebrew text for the patriarchal genealogies.

"Secondly, the reckoning of the four hundred and thirty years from the call of Abraham to the Exodus; and, lastly, the adhering to the four hundred and eighty years for the period from the Exodus to the building of the Temple of Solomon." *

How utterly unreliable are such data will appear when we consider two facts: First, numbers of all things are even now most liable to change, but before

---
* Smith's "Old Testament History" (Student's Series), p. 39.

the days of the printing-press, when metals, brick tablets, animal-skins, papyrus ("the paper reed" of Egypt), and vellum were used instead of paper, and the stylus took the place of the sharp pen, or the well-defined "type" of the printer, how much more liable were figures to be mistaken and numbers changed! * But, secondly, when it is remembered that, in the original language of the Old Testament (the Hebrew), *letters* were used to signify numbers, and some of these letters have only the slightest variations from one another, it will at once be understood how easily an ancient scribe or copyist might unintentionally mistake these letters, and so introduce endless confusion and irreconcilable discrepancies into his estimate. Thus the letter ו (pronounced *Vâv*) equals six (6), while ר (*Resh*) equals two hundred (200); and the reader may imagine how readily a copyist, in reading an old papyrus manuscript, might mistake Resh for Vav, and thus make a difference of one hundred and ninety-four (194) in the original estimate. In this way, among others, serious errors have arisen in the Bible numbers. To cite only one of many striking instances of such errors, we are told in II Chronicles (xxi, 20) that Jehoram, King of Judah, "was thirty-and-two years old when he began to reign, and he reigned in Jerusalem eight years, and departed."

Hence he died when he was forty years old. In the next chapter (xxii, 1, 2) we are informed that "the inhabitants of Jerusalem made Ahaziah his youngest son king in his stead; forty-and-two years old was Ahaziah when he began to reign." Therefore the youngest son of King Jehoram must have been two years older than

---

* "Encyclopædia Britannica," article on "Palæography."

his father! A friend, who first called my attention to this mistake, said that his good mother (*Requiescat in pace!*), when he, as a boy, discovered this error and insisted that it was an error, told him that "the Bible was God's word, and he must not question any of its statements. Such passages were doubtless inserted to try one's faith!" Let no one smile at this good woman's "faith," for it is of a piece with the "faith" of many profound theologians—at least of "sixty years since."

The correct age of Ahaziah is probably given in II Kings (viii, 26), where it is said he was only "two-and-twenty years old" when he began to reign; he was, therefore, something less than eighteen years younger than his father; but this passage contradicts that of II Chronicles, and hence we see how hopeless is the attempt to maintain the inspiration of Biblical figures.

Dr. Smith, who is a decidedly "conservative" writer, makes some wise remarks on this subject in the note already referred to. "The generations of the patriarchs which form our only guide" for the period between the Creation and the Flood, he says, "are given differently in different copies of the Scriptures; the sum being in the LXX six hundred and six years longer, and in the Samaritan Pentateuch three hundred and forty-nine years shorter than in the received Hebrew text. The ancient Chronologers give further variations." "The LXX" thus referred to is the Septuagent (seventy) or Greek Version of the Old Testament, supposed to have been made by "seventy" (or rather seventy-two) scholars at Alexandria in Egypt about 280 years before Christ. It is of special importance as the version of the Scriptures which the early disciples used, while its variation in the age of the world from that of the Hebrew original is more especially worthy of note, as we shall presently see.

The tribe of the Samaritans originated about 675 years before Christ by an Assyrian king's colonizing Samaria, which he had conquered, with the population of other conquered cities and districts. From that day to the time when our Lord talked to the Samaritan woman by Jacob's well (John iv, 9) the Samaritans and Jews had no dealings with each other, but rather set up opposing systems of worship, the former on Mount Gerizim—where they are found to-day—and the latter at Jerusalem. But they had one thing in common, viz., the Pentateuch, or Five Books ascribed to Moses.

The origin of the Samaritan Pentateuch has given rise to much controversy. The two most usual opinions are: 1. That it came into the hands of the Samaritans as an inheritance from the Ten Tribes of Israel, whom they succeeded. 2. That it was introduced by King Manasseh, at the time of the foundation of the Samaritan sanctuary on Mount Gerizim. As Dr. Smith says, "the ancient chronologers give further variations" in the dates found in the numerous versions of the Old Testament. Indeed, one chronologer tells us that "he collected upward of two hundred different calculations, the shortest of which reckons only thirty-four hundred and eighty-three years between the creation of the world and the commencement of the vulgar era, and the longest sixty-nine hundred and eighty-four."

The difference amounts to thirty-five centuries; surely we must, therefore, agree with him that " the so-called era of the creation of the world is a purely conventional and arbitrary epoch"; * or with another, that Revelation, whatever its authenticity, has not revealed the age of the world." †

The first fact, then, to be clearly grasped and borne in mind is that "the Bible has no chronology." The dates we find in it, especially the genealogies of the patriarchs, are the most uncertain of all uncertain quantities, and hence the accepted chronology—i. e., Archbishop Usher's estimate—is only one of two hundred worthless estimates. It is amazing, therefore, that so much anxiety should exist to preserve Usher's estimate, and that so much opposition to the scientists' demand for a lengthened chronology should be manifested. Even Dr. Geikie and Canon Rawlinson, while acknowledging the unreliability of the data upon which Usher founded his system, and confessing that the age of man is somewhat greater than is commonly supposed, yet strive most earnestly to press human history within a period of six thousand years. ‡

Having thus disposed of the popular view of the antiquity of man—having seen that this view rests on so unreliable data that we can not put any confidence in estimates based on such a foundation—we are now free to hear what Science has to say on this interesting subject. I arrange the evidence it affords under the following somewhat arbitrary but convenient heads:

First, that furnished by the general principles of evolution. If man is the last link in the chain of animal life—that is to say, if, as we have ample reason to

---

* "Encyclopædia Britannica," article on "Chronology."
† Winchell, "Preadamites," p. 105.
‡ Geikie's "Hours with the Bible," I, chapters ix, x; Rawlinson, "Origin of Nations."

believe, man was developed from a lower organism and did not come into existence miraculously endowed with knowledge and civilization—then it certainly must have taken many thousands of years for him to learn, in the School of Experience, language, arts, religion, etc. "The starting-point is the hard point," says the wise proverb, and so we can not estimate the early progress of the human race by the rate of its modern progress. The movement of mankind resembles that of a large rolling stone, which, starting very slowly, gathers momentum and so increases its speed the further it rolls. These truths may be accepted by even the anti-evolutionist. Whether one believes that man has been developed from a lower organism or not, he must admit that civilization is a *slow growth;* that man has gradually and painfully toiled upward either from a state of original simplicity or from a state of savagery. On either hypothesis, it must have taken many centuries for him to attain to the lofty pinnacle of modern civilization; and we shall see that the period of such development commonly assigned is far too short.

In the second place, we have the evidence of man's extreme antiquity afforded by *Geology.* "One of the most remarkable phenomena affecting the conditions of life in Europe in recent geological epochs is the existence of a period of long duration throughout the northern hemisphere of a temperature resembling that of the Arctic regions at the present time. The mountainous regions of Scotland and Wales—then probably of a much higher elevation—resembled Greenland at the present time; and this Arctic temperature gradually extended southward to the Alps and the Pyrenees. The glaciers (gigantic ice-mountains), formed under the influence of perpetual frost and snow, descended from those and other mountains into the valleys and plains over the greater portion of central Europe and northern Asia; and this condition of things, pertaining to what is known as the *Glacial Period,* was one of prolonged duration." Subsequently, "a gradual but persistent rise of temperature carried the lines of ice and perpetual snow farther and farther northward, excepting in regions of great elevations, as in the Swiss Alps," where to this day, as is well known, are found immense relics of this Ice Period—the delight of modern travelers. This rise of temperature was necessarily accompanied by the melting of the vast glaciers accumulated in the mountain valleys throughout the protracted period of cold. The broken rocks and soil of the highlands were swept into the valleys by torrents of melted ice and snow; the lower valleys were hollowed out and reformed under this novel agent; and the landscape received its present outlines of valley, estuary, and river-beds from the changes wrought in this "Diluvian Epoch," as it has been well called.

Within this late *Tertiary or Quaternary* Period are found the remains of animal life contemporary with primeval man and his earliest art. "Here are the remains of now wholly extinct species of mammoth, elephant, bear, hyena, reindeer, elk, etc., buried with flint instruments, and other ingenious traces of primitive art." *

In those days, a brilliant writer assures us, "From a country now known as Picardy (in France) the ancient inhabitants of Abbeville or Amiens could pass into

---

* "Encyclopædia Britannica," article "Archæology."

Great Britain without crossing the English Channel. The British Isles were united to Gaul (France) by an isthmus which has since been submerged. The level of the Baltic and of the North Sea was four hundred feet higher than it is at the present day. The valley of the river Somme was not hollowed out to the depth it has now attained"; it was in places more than two hundred feet above its present level. "Sicily was joined to Africa, Barbary to Spain. . . . Hence," he adds, "we know with certainty that European man was contemporaneous with the extinct species of the quaternary period (already mentioned), that he witnessed the upheaval of the Alps,* and the extension of the glaciers; in a word, that he lived thousands of years before the dawn of the remotest historical traditions." †
Next, we have the abundant and conclusive evidence of man's extreme antiquity afforded by *Archæology*. "Classical antiquity," says M. Joly, "tells us of four successive ages—the ages of gold, silver, bronze, and iron. Under the reign of (the god) Saturn—that is, during the golden age—men enjoyed a long life, which they spent in the midst of happiness, peace, and plenty. But the horrors of war were soon let loose among them; iron took the place of gold; a rapid decadence began, and man retains at the present day only faint traces of his primitive perfection and happiness."

"Another myth of later date, and more in harmony with the facts observed, tells us that the earth was originally inhabited by a race of giants, and, by a sub-

---

* "The Alps was upheaved at end of *Eocene*. There may have been continental but not mountain upheaval in the Glacial period."—LE CONTE.

† Joly's "Man before Metals," pp. 183, 184.

sequent creation, of a race of dwarfs. The giants dwelt among the rocks, and built their walls of Cyclopean masonry; they carried stone clubs, and were ignorant of the use of metals. The dwarfs, far weaker but at the same time far more industrious than the giants, inaugurated the age of bronze. They sought this metal in the bowels of the earth, and, with the help of fire, forged precious ornaments and shining arms, which they gave to men. Finally, giants and dwarfs gave place to the men of the iron age, and were forced to abandon the land. It is curious to see poetry thus forestall history, and mention distinctly the series of epochs which are generally admitted by modern science.

"Archæology combines with Geology to show that human civilization has passed through three more or less distinct stages, in Europe at least, for which the names of stone, bronze, and iron ages have been retained, although they may be, perhaps, too suggestive of the myth."* "The Stone Period, as the name implies, is that in which the rude aboriginal arts, which the commonest necessities of man call into operation, are assumed to have been employed on such available materials as stone, horn, bone, etc. The Bronze Period may admit of subdivision, though the term is constantly employed in the most comprehensive sense for that era of progress in which the metallic arts appear to have been introduced and slowly developed; first, by the simple use of native copper, followed by the application of fire, the construction of molds, and the discovery of such chemical processes as the alloying of copper and tin, and the consequent production of bronze.

---

* "Man before Metals," pp. 19, 20.

"The Iron Period marks the era of matured metallurgic arts, and the accompanying progress consequent on the degree of civilization, which is the inevitable consequent of such a state of things."* It may be well to refute, just here, an objection to this division of prehistoric ages which some writers allege. "The theory," says Dr. C. Geikie, "of widely separate ages for old and new stone tools, and for bronze and iron, is one of those scientific fancies which further investigation overthrows." He then quotes the Duke of Argyll's remark that "there is no proof whatever that such ages ever existed in the world."† Both of these authors think that, because all nations have at certain times used stone tools, and because the ages shade into one another, and are often simultaneous, we have no right to talk of stone, bronze, and iron periods. But it is difficult to see the force of such reasoning. Archæologists recognize all this, and yet feel justified in using such terms. Thus, M. Joly says: "It is sometimes rather difficult to draw the line sharply between the various ages we have just enumerated; the work of one is often carried on into another." And again: "The three ages of Stone, Bronze, and Iron have not been in all places and at all times successive, but very often simultaneous. Though they mark three stages in the civilization of nations, it does not follow that all have passed through them at the *same period*. The chronological value of these ages is not always, therefore, absolute and general, but sometimes purely local and rela-

---

* "Encyclopædia Britannica," article, "Archæology."
† "Hours with the Bible," i, p. 134; Argyll's "Primeval Man," p. 181; compare Lubbock's "Origin of Civilization," Appendix, pp. 496, *et seq.*, a reply to the Duke of Argyll.

tive."* This is precisely what might have been expected. It would be unreasonable, contrary to the fundamental proposition of evolution, to expect that in every case tribes and nations would suddenly leap from the stone to the bronze, or from the bronze to the iron age; these periods ought to shade into each other like light and darkness. It would be equally irrational to suppose that all nations have passed through these stages of development at the same period. Assuming, then, that the ages in question really existed, I proceed to discuss the phenomena of each.

The Stone Age, as already intimated, is divided into the Old or Palæolithic and the New or Neolithic Periods. The cave-dwellers of the Old Stone Age were, to all appearances, contemporaneous with the extinct animals aforementioned—the mammoth, the woolly-haired rhinoceros, the great cave-bear, etc. In the first chapter of his admirable little book, already quoted more than once, M. Joly gives a history of the discoveries of that great naturalist, Boucher de Perthes, who, "among the ancient tombs, the caves, the peat-mosses, the diluvian of the valleys, and of the bone-caves," sought and collected the various remains of prehistoric times, which finally established the extreme antiquity of man. . . . On March 23, 1863" (we are careful to give this memorable date), "M. Boucher de Perthes was gratified by the discovery, at Moulin-Quignon, of the famous jaw-bone, or rather the part of a human jaw-bone, which became the subject of so much controversy. It lay imbedded about five yards deep in the dark, sandy gravel. The same bed contained carved

---

* " Man before Metals," pp. 20–30.

flint axes and teeth of the mammoth." The excitement produced by this discovery was so great that a congress of the most eminent French and English scientists was assembled, and, after a thorough "trial of the jaw-bone," " the immense majority of geologists, both French and foreign, declared that the man of Moulin-Quignon had witnessed the geological phenomenon which had deposited the beds of diluvian gravel." The discovery of other bones (skulls) confirmed this opinion.*

In the third chapter of his work (Part I) M. Joly discusses "the bone-caves," of which Kent's Cavern in Devonshire, England, is one of the most famous. Its "lowest deposit is a breccia of water-worn rock and red clay, interspersed with numerous bones of the great cave-bear. Over this a stalagmitic flooring had been formed, in some places to a depth of several feet, by the long-protracted deposition of carbonate of lime, held in solution by the drippings from the roof above this ancient flooring, itself a work of centuries; later floods had superimposed a thick layer of cave-earth, in some cases even entirely filling up extensive galleries with a deposit of drift-mud and stones, within which are imbedded the evidences of contemporaneous life—bones and teeth of the fossil elephant, rhinoceros, horse, cave-bear, hyena, reindeer, Irish elk; and along with these numerous weapons and implements of chipped flint, horn, and bone—the unmistakable proof of the presence of man. These, again, have been sealed down, in another prolonged period of rest, by a new flooring of stalagmite; and thus the peculiar circumstances of those

---

* " Man before Metals," pp. 42–47.

cave-deposits render them specially favorable for the preservation of a coherent record of the period."*

"It is incontestable that Kent's Cavern long served as a dwelling to the primeval inhabitants of the country, that they had their meals in it, and worked in flint and bone there, etc., until the day when the thick layer of stalagmite which covers the ossiferous sediment was formed."† "But, besides the actual deposits in the caves, the *river gravels* of the same period have their distinct disclosures. The spear-heads, disks, scrapers, and other large implements of chipped flint are of rare occurrence in the cave breccia. Their size was sufficient to prevent their being readily dropped and buried beyond reach of recovery in the muddy flooring of the old cave dwellings; and the same cause preserved them from destruction when exposed to the violence involved in the accumulation of the old river drifts. In the north of France, and England from Bedfordshire southward to the English Channel, in beds of ancient gravel, sand, and clay of the river valleys, numerous discoveries of such large flint implements have been made.... The twenty centuries of French and English history form but a fraction of the time which has elapsed since the stone implements of prehistoric tribes were first buried under beds of gravel and sand by the rivers now represented by the Thames and the Somme. Still vaster, however, is the idea of antiquity suggested by the geographical conformation of such valleys as those in which these rivers flow. These drift-beds lie on their sides often one to two hundred feet, and even

---

* "Encyclopædia Britannica," article "Archæology."
† "Man before Metals," p. 62.

more, above the present flood-levels. As such highest deposits seem to mark the time when the rivers flowed at heights so far above the present channels, it follows that the drift-beds, and the men whose works they inclose, must have existed during a great part of the time occupied by the rivers in excavating their valleys down to their present beds."* "But," replies Dr. C. Geikie, "all this is unsatisfactory. It is indeed quite impossible to fix the age of such drift-deposits. Local floods work great changes and the shifting of river-beds also works great changes, and all rivers are much larger in a state of nature than when human settlement has drained off the surface water." † "Granting it as possible," answers Dr. E. B. Tylor, "that the rivers by which this enormous operation (the deposition of drifts) was performed were of greater volume and proportionately still greater power in flood-time than the present streams, which seem so utterly inadequate to their valleys, and granting, also, that under different conditions of climate the causing *débâcles* by ground-ice may have been a powerful excavating agent, nevertheless, with all such allowances the reckoning of ages seems vastly out of proportion to historical chronology." ‡ "The great alluvial valley of the river Forth (Scotland) has yielded relics of the fossil elephant connecting it with man. In at least one case its tusks were found in such perfect condition as to be available for the ivory-turner, though lying imbedded at a depth of twenty feet in the bowlder clay. But in the neighboring valley the fossil whale has not only

---

* "Encyclopædia Britannica," articles on "Archæology" and "Anthropology."
† "Hours with the Bible," i, p. 134.
‡ "Encyclopædia Britannica," article "Anthropology."

been repeatedly found far inland, buried in the alluvial soil, at levels varying from twenty to twenty-five feet above high-water mark, but in at least two instances the rude lance or harpoon of deer's horn lay alongside of the skeletons; and near another of them were found pieces of stag-horn, artificially cut, and one of them perforated with a hole about an inch in diameter. Flint implements, an oaken quern, and other ingenious traces of primitive art recovered from the same alluvial soil, all tell of a time when the British savage hunted the whale in the shallows of a tide at the base of hills now between twenty and thirty feet above the highest tides and seven miles distant from the sea." * Every one in the least familiar with archæology will also remember that "borings made in the alluvium of the Nile Valley to a depth of sixty feet" revealed "fragments of burned brick and pottery, showing that people advanced enough in the arts to bake brick and pottery have inhabited the valley during the long period required for the Nile inundations to deposit sixty feet of mud at a rate probably not averaging more than a few inches in a century." These, of course, are only a few instances of the cave-deposits and river drifts, but they serve as examples of the evidence of man's extreme antiquity, and I think any one who will fairly consider such facts will, notwithstanding certain superficial objections which may be raised, acknowledge that six thousand years is far too short a period to assign to the human race.

The Old Stone (Palæolithic) Period, thus briefly glanced at, with its characteristic implements of chipped flint, was followed by the second or New Stone (Neo-

---

* "Encyclopædia Britannica," article "Archæology."

lithic) Period, characterized by weapons of *polished* stone. "The discovery and exploration of the ancient lake dwellings of Switzerland and other countries, including the Crannoges of Ireland and Scotland, and the refuse-heaps of Denmark, Scotland, and elsewhere, have greatly extended the illustrations of this period, and given definiteness to the evidences of its antiquity." An eminent Danish naturalist (Steenstrup), who paid special attention to the peat-mosses of his country, thinks that "ten to twelve thousand years went to the accumulation and transformation of the remains of the vegetation" which constitutes these peat-bogs; the vegetation has partly or wholly disappeared from the district. "The Stone Age terminates with these forests." * The Bronze Period begins apparently with "the recognition of the native copper as a malleable metal, and then as a material capable of being melted and molded into form by the application of heat, which was followed up by the art of smelting the crude ores so as to extract the metal."

"It was long assumed, alike by historians and antiquarians, that the beautiful bronze swords, spear-heads, shields, torques, etc., so frequently discovered, were mere relics of foreign conquest or barter, and they were variously assigned to Egyptian, Phœnician, Roman, or Danish origin. But this gratuitous assumption has been disproved by the repeated discovery of the molds for molding them, as well as of the refuse castings, and even beds of charcoal, scoriæ, and other indications of metallurgy, on the sites where they have been formed."

---

* See Joly's masterly discussion of this point, "Man before Metals," chapters v-vii, inclusive.

The abrupt transition from the Stone to the Bronze Period in Europe the author just quoted explains by the supposition that "the metallurgic arts of the north of Europe are derived from a foreign source, either by conquest or traffic. The direct intercourse between the countries on the Mediterranean Sea and the Tin Islands —as the only known parts of the British Islands are called in the earliest allusions which are made to them by the ancient historians—Herodotus, Aristotle, and Polybius—abundantly accounts for the introduction of such knowledge to the native Britons at a very remote period."

The Iron Age is that in which iron superseded bronze for arms, sword-blades, spear-heads, axes, daggers, knives, etc., and from this period we reach the era of authentic history during which man has struggled upward through the savage, hunter state and the pastoral state to his present agricultural and civilized stage.

A word now on prehistoric man in America, and I pass to the documentary evidence of man's extreme antiquity. "The Indian red-skin," says M. Joly, "living in a state of barbarism at the time of the conquest can not be called the primitive American, nor were the luxuriant forests where he hunted his prey truly primeval, for they were preceded by other forests, which themselves did not deserve the name of virgin since they had already been trodden by the foot of man, whose remains lie buried beneath their own. At New Orleans, on the banks of the Mississippi, an entire human skeleton was found buried beneath four ancient forests. Dr. Dowler attributes an age of fifty-seven thousand years to these remains. We can not guarantee the accuracy of these figures, but, if this single fact were established beyond dispute, it would be in itself a proof of the great antiquity of the human race in America. Other discoveries of no less weight corroborate our opinion." Human bones have been found near Natchez deeply buried with long-extinct species of animals. From a coral reef in Florida, which Prof. Agassiz considers to be "more than ten thousand years old," human bones were extracted. In the caves of Brazil human remains were found entombed with the bones of fossil animals; while the burial-places of Peru, the celebrated "Mounds" in Wisconsin, Illinois, Ohio, and elsewhere have yielded to the researches of the archæologists treasures as valuable as they were unexpected. Their age is unknown; but many of them date, it would seem, from a period anterior to the Neolithic Age of the New World." * Dr. Charles C. Abbott, the eminent anthropologist of Trenton, N. J., in an able paper read before the American Association for the Advancement of Science (Cleveland, Ohio, August, 1888), said: "There was a time when to all appearances American archæology would have to be squeezed into the cramped quarters of ten thousand years; but we are pretty sure of twenty or even thirty thousand now." And he gave facts and reasons to prove this conclusion. He closes his paper with these eloquent and significant words: "As I wander along the pleasant shores of the Delaware River, seeing it but a meager stream between high banks, in midsummer; or in winter, swollen and choked with ice, until these are almost hidden, I recall what time this same stream was the mighty channel of gla-

---

* "Man before Metals," Part I, chap. vii.

cial floods pouring seaward from the mountains beyond, and picture the primitive hunter of that ancient time, armed with but a sharpened stone, in quest of unwary game. And later, when the floods had abated and the waters filled but the channel of to-day, I recall that more skillful folk, who with spear and knife captured whatsoever creature their needs demanded—the earlier and later Chippers of Argillite. These passed, and the Indian, with his jasper, quartz, copper, and polished stone, looms up, as others fade away. His history, reaching forward almost to the present, I leave in the hands of others to record."

The fourth and last source of the evidence proving man's extreme antiquity which we shall glance at is the documentary evidence.

Here it is important to remember at once the fact that, according to the traditional and popular view, the human race has had *two beginnings*—one in Adam, the other in Noah. All the Adamic race, except Noah's family, was destroyed by the Flood, and hence all the nations on the globe to-day are, according to this view, descendants from those eight persons in the Ark. Noah's Deluge, according to Usher's chronology, occurred 2348 B. C., and therefore we are to believe that the mighty civilizations of Egypt, Babylonia, China, India, etc., originated within that period. Abraham went down into Egypt about 1921 B. C., and he there found a great monarchy in existence—nay, more, he left behind him large empires, with magnificent cities, arts, sciences, religion, over which ruled such kings as Sargon I. And we are to believe that such civilization—such immense nations—grew up within the short period of four hundred and twenty-seven years—this too, from three families. Impossible! except, of course, upon the supposition of repeated *miracles;* but when Miracle comes in, Science steps aside and doffs her cap. But this is not all. The conservative Canon Rawlinson assures us that "the establishment of a settled monarchy in Egypt occurred between B. C. 2450 and B. C. 2250." That is to say, the Egyptian monarchy existed in a "settled" form *one hundred and two years before its founder—Ham—left the Ark!* "Oh, no," our author replies, "according to the Septuagint (Greek) version of the Bible, the date of the deluge was certainly anterior to B. C. 3000."* But we have seen that the Septuagint Version is contradicted by the Hebrew original, and, since this is accepted by all theologians as the most authentic record —the foundation of all other versions—we set aside Dr. Rawlinson's appeal to the dates of the Septuagint as simply the result of a preconceived theory which landed him in a dilemma from which there was no other way of escape. But even if we grant the Canon the use of the Septuagint date, yet we might forcibly urge that a "settled" monarchy like that of Egypt at the time referred to could not have grown up in those days of slow progress during the short period of five hundred and fifty years from one man's family or even from Shem, Ham, and Japheth combined, unless they were civilized *nations* which no Ark ever built by man could hold. The civilizations, therefore, of the great Eastern monarchies—Egypt, Chaldea, Assyria, Babylonia, India, etc.—could not possibly have grown up during the short period which the popular chronology

---

* "Origin of Nations," p. 32.

assigns. The history of Egypt alone explodes the traditional view. We must also give up the popular notion that Ham was the founder of this nation. These facts, added to what has been said on Biblical dates and the geological and archæological evidence of man's extreme antiquity, ought to prepare us to accept Dr. Tylor's opinion that "the first appearance of man, though comparatively recent, is positively so remote that an estimate between twenty and a hundred thousand years may fairly be taken as a minimum." * At any rate, two facts ought to be clear:

First. The age of the human race is not settled by the Bible, since equally devout and learned chronologers from the same data draw utterly contradictory estimates. This, by the way, should silence those who accept Usher's view, and object to the scientific estimate because anthropologists differ in their opinions.

Secondly. Whatever objections may be raised to the geological, archæological, and historical evidences of man's extreme antiquity, yet his history can not be compressed within a period of four to six thousand years; but if we give up this the popular view, then we may safely let the anthropologists settle the question among themselves.

Closely connected with what has been said on the age of man is the question of "Preadamitism." The first question which meets us in considering this subject is that of the unity of the human race. Did it originate from a single pair, male and female, or from many individuals and centers? It must suffice to quote in answer the eminent scientists, Prof. Huxley and Dr.

---

* "Encyclopædia Britannica," article "Anthropology."

E. B. Tylor. Says the former: "I am one of those who believe that at present there is no evidence whatever for saying that mankind sprang originally from any more than a single pair. I must say that I can not see any good ground whatever, or even any tenable sort of evidence, for believing that there is more than one species of man. Nevertheless, as you know, just as there are numbers of varieties in animals, so there are remarkable varieties of men."* "The opinion," says Dr. Tylor, "of modern zoölogists, whose study of the species and breeds of animals makes them the best judges, is against the view of several origins of man, for two principal reasons:

"First. That all tribes of man, from the blackest to the whitest, the most savage to the most cultured, have such general likeness in the structure of their bodies and the working of their minds, as is easiest and best accounted for by their being descended from a common ancestry, however distant.

"Second. That all human races, notwithstanding their form and color, appear capable of freely intermarrying and forming crossed races of every combination, such as the millions of mulattoes and mestizoes sprung in the New World from a mixture of Europeans, Africans, and native Americans. This again points to a common ancestry of all races of man. We may accept the theory of the unity of mankind as best agreeing with ordinary experience and scientific research." †

An apparent objection to a consideration of "Pre-adamitism" may be urged just here. "Why," it may

---

* Huxley's "Origin of Species," p. 113.
† Tylor's "Anthropology" (International Scientific Series), pp.

be asked, "should we consider the question whether there were Preadamites when we do not know when Adam lived?" In answer, Prof. Alexander Winchell, one of the most eminent advocates of "Preadamitism," would say, "Though we may not know the exact year of 'Adam's' birth, we may *approximately* ascertain it, and this is sufficient for our purpose." In a letter to the author on this subject he said: "The Biblical Adam lived, say, six to ten thousand years ago; men who lived before Adam, however remote they were, I denominate Preadamites." In his able work on "Preadamites," Prof. Winchell maintains that the Biblical Adam was not the first man, but the first *white man*, and I can not do better than give a brief synopsis of his views on this subject, and then pass judgment upon the general question. "There are two alternative positions," says our author, "which may be assumed in reference to Adam: 1. Adam was absolutely the first human being, and was in every respect such as to fill the requirements of that position. 2. Adam was the immediate progenitor of the nations which figure in Biblical history, and hence must not be expected to answer to the requirements of the primitive ancestry of all mankind."* In attempting to refute the first and to establish the second proposition, Prof. Winchell adduces "Biblical, linguistic, ethnological, archæological, and other evidence," which certainly deserves most respectful and careful consideration; for, if it do not conclusively prove his theory, it at least destroys many of the popular notions as to the origin of nations. He claims, and gives strong arguments in support of his claim, that the scope of Biblical

---

* "Preadamitism," p. 5.

Ethnography was limited.* "We fix our attention," he says, "upon the land of Canaan, and observe that its position is nearly central between the limits of the Genesiacal dispersion. From this center the vision of the sacred ethnologist went forth and discovered the distribution of the nations of his day. . . . The whole geographical extent of the Noachidæ (descendants of Noah) does not embrace more than one fifteenth of the territory which we now find populated by man.

"Was this an attempt to explain the origin of all the nations of the world?

"Does this genealogical map (Genesis x) imply that the regions beyond its limits were then occupied by human beings? Does it mean that the various tribes and nations which are now spread over the earth have arisen from the wider dispersion of the Sons of Noah? Have the black tribes of Africa and Australia and Melanesia, and the brown nations of Asia and America and Polynesia, been produced from the posterity of Noah during the interval which separates us from the flood? To all these questions I reply in the negative; and I shall show not only that science sustains the negative, but that the Record itself both implies and demands it.†
. . . In the purview of Genesis," he adds further on, "all the world is the region over which the Semitic people were dispersed" (which he considers in Chapter IV), "or, in the widest sense, it stretched no farther than the tribes of Gomer on the north, Madai on the east, Seba on the south, and the posterity of Mizraim on the west. With such a purpose, and the silence which such a purpose imposed, the later Jews undoubtedly

---

* "Preadamitism," chapter vii.   † Ibid., pp. 89, 90.

came to believe literally that all the races of men had descended from Noah." * He then shows "the invalidity of this belief." In showing that the Bible itself favors " Preadamitism," he considers the well-known passages about Cain's banishment and the "sons of God" intermarrying with "the daughters of men." "When Cain" (he says), "according to the Biblical account, was convicted before Jehovah of the murder of his brother, he was banished as a fugitive from the land of his parents. The culprit, reflecting on the condition to which he had been doomed, exclaimed : ' My punishment is greater than I can bear. *Every one that findeth me* shall slay me.' And Jehovah said unto him, ' Therefore, *whosoever slayeth Cain*, vengeance shall be taken on him sevenfold.' "

And Jehovah set a mark upon Cain, lest *any one finding him* should kill him. And Cain departed and dwelt in the land of Nod, on the east of Eden (Gen. iv, 13–24). It is next mentioned, in the continuation of the narrative, that Cain had *married a wife*, and a son had been born, whose name was Khanok (Enoch). Cain is next reported to have *built a city*, which he named after his son. From Enoch descended generations represented by Irad, Mehujael, Methusael, and Lamech, who *married two wives*. Jabal, the son of one wife, " was the father of all *such as dwell* in tents and of such as have cattle. Jubal, his brother, was the father of such as *handle the harp and organ*. The other wife bore Tubal-Cain, an instructor of every artificer in brass and iron."

Following out, in another place (Gen. vi, 1–4), the

---

* " Preadamitism," p. 132.

line of the Adamites and their contemporary annals, the sacred account informs us that, "When men began to multiply on the face of the earth and daughters were born unto them, the sons of God saw the daughters of men that they were fair and took them wives of all which they chose," and the children of such union became mighty men, which were of old men of renown.

"Now, I think," continues our author, "that a natural and unsophisticated interpretation of the foregoing Biblical statements demonstrates that they imply the existence of Preadamites:

"1. Cain recognizes the existence of some people in the regions remote from Eden, from whom he might apprehend bodily danger. He does not anticipate this because they would recognize him as an offender, but because he would be a foreigner and a stranger.

"2. Jehovah recognizes the existence of a foreign people and the danger to which Cain would be exposed, and provides some means by which he would be protected from the effects of intertribal or inter-racial antagonism.

"3. Cain went toward the east—and found a wife in the region to which he removed. On the current pseudo-orthodox intepretation Cain must have married his sister or his niece, and the married woman must have followed him into banishment for some unnamed offense. I say 'followed him,' for at the date of his banishment Adam's daughters are not stated to have been born. . . . His wife (it is concluded) was a woman of the country to which he fled. She was a daughter of the Preadamite race.

"4. Cain built a city. How did Cain build a city with only a wife and baby? Or did the population of the city await a natural increase of a family? How many citizens is it probable that Cain himself furnished during his lifetime? It will be suggested that Enoch probably assisted him; but where did Enoch obtain a wife? Did he marry one of his aunts, or one of his possible sisters? Is it probable that an eligible aunt would give her hand to the son of her brother's murderer? I would reply that Enoch intermarried with the people among whom his father had settled.

5. "'And Irad begat Mehujael.' Who was Mehujael's mother? Was she his aunt, a sister of Irad? Or was she his great-aunt, a sister of Enoch? The popular and traditional interpretation supplies another muddle at this point."

Prof. Winchell, also, considers "the sons of God" who intermarried with "the daughters of men"—i. e., the daughters of Adam—Preadamites.* Of course, by supposing that *miracles* were constantly wrought—that men produced offspring by the thousands in those days where they now produce tens—that moral obligations were not the same then as now—that is to say, by *making a great number of gratuitous assumptions*—we can "explain" away all the difficulties which Prof. Winchell brings forward; but, if we are asked to give a natural and rational and *literal* explanation of the account in Genesis, we must, I think, accept his interpretation. The scientific proofs, however, which Prof. Winchell adduces in support of "Preadamitism" are much more cogent than the Biblical evidence, but space does not allow me to give even the barest outline of those evidences, and I have merely cited a few of his arguments, in the hope that

---

* "Preadamitism," pp. 188–'95.

those who have not read his book may get it. My own opinion is this: If we would read the first few chapters or verses of Genesis as literal history, we would better adopt the theory of "Preadamitism"; but if we consider those accounts (as I do) *poems* on creation, etc., written by some religious seer or poet, in Chaldea, about 2000 B. C., we need not trouble ourselves with the question of "Preadamitism." "Adam," according to this view, would be considered not a specific name, like "Smith" or "Jones," but simply a *generic* term, applied by the poet to the *first human being;* it really means simply "The Man." "Eve" would be used to denote "the mother of all living" (Gen. iii, 20). "Cain" would stand as the representative or "father" of the agricultural tribes. "Abel" would be the progenitor of the pastoral tribes; the conflict between the two brothers would mean the invasion of "Abel's" territory by "Cain," which would result in the conversion of the latter into the wandering warrior, the builder of cities, etc. "Seth" would be the "Father of the Faithful"— the first preacher. Some such view as this seems to be suggested by what is said of "Jabal," "Jubal," and "Tubal-cain" (Genesis iv, 20–22); and it seems preferable, *considering what we know of the origin of Genesis*, to either the theory of "Preadamitism" or to the view of Ewald and others, who see in Genesis nothing more than legends, like those of heathen nations, about the origin of the world, "the golden age," etc.* This view obviates all the difficulties involved in any attempt to treat Genesis as literal history, while it preserves all the great moral and spiritual truths which it was evidently

---

* Ewald, "History of Israel" (English translation), i, pp. 256–277.

designed to teach. No one would read Milton's account of creation or Bunyan's "Pilgrim's Progress" as literal history, and yet he might learn many valuable lessons from these writers. Why, then, attempt to make their great Chaldean prototypes speak in the prosaic tongues of the historian and scientist of the nineteenth century A. D. ?

CHAPTER V.

MAN'S PRIMITIVE HOME AND CONDITION.

"DISTANCE lends enchantment," says the proverb, and so the home of our childhood as it recedes in the past is surrounded by imagination with delights it never really possessed. May not this inborn tendency of the human mind have given rise to the beautiful stories of a "golden age," an "Eden," long past, which we find in circulation among the various nations of the earth? At any rate, prosaic science and history unite in asserting that the "golden" or "Edenic" age of man is not in the past but in the *future*.

It is interesting to note that many, mistaking poetry for prose, or allegory for fact, have sought for the *locality* of "Eden," not only in every part of the world, but even outside of it; for from the second to the tenth century not a few of the Fathers, and after them others, "held that it was the same as the Paradise of which the New Testament speaks, and lay in secret remoteness, half on earth and half in heaven."* "These fond dreamers," as the writer quoted calls them, came nearer the true meaning of the story of Eden than their condemners; and, since there have been so many even fan-

---

* Geikie's "Hours with the Bible," I, chap. viii.

tastical opinions expressed by theologians concerning the locality of Eden, it would be far more modest in them not to ridicule, as some of them have done, the Evolutionist's "imaginary" being ("the connecting link") in an imaginary continent—Lemuria." Since both Theology and Science confessedly can not point to the exact abode of the first human beings, and say, "Behold, there it is!" even the *conjecture* of a learned scientist is worthy of consideration, especially since certain facts strongly support such conjecture. An English ornithologist located Lemuria, the primeval abode of humanity, in the Indian Ocean; and Prof. Alexander Winchell summarizes the facts upon which this conclusion rests thus: 1. "We have the direction of *known* movements of migration over the earth. These, it is true, concern chiefly the nations of the Mediterranean race; though to a considerable extent, also, tribes and peoples of the Mongolian and even the African stocks. Most of the movements of the white and brown races have been from central and southern Asia. 2. A large proportion of the animals and plants (except forest growths) which have become useful to man are known to have had their origin in the Orient." Hence, we must believe that such plants and animals have been raised in the Orient longer than they have been in the Occident; in other words, man existed in those parts before he did in these. 3. "Man, as an animal, is unclothed and possessed of a delicate skin. All naked land-animals are natives of warm countries; and man similarly, it may confidently be argued, made his advent in a region where the elements did not oppose his coming. *Primitively he was a tropical animal*, and only wandered into colder zones as he had learned to protect himself by artificial coverings. 4. The mammalian fauna (or animal kingdom) of the *Oriental world is highest and most approximated to the type of man;* and hence it should be inferred that man is not only a tropical but an Oriental animal. The four great continental regions, as has been often remarked, presents a graduated succession in the rank of their mammalian faunas. Australia is lowest; South America is next in rank; North America stands third; the Orient stands highest.

"Now, that the event has shown man to have been the destined culmination of organic improvement, it becomes apparent that the Orient was the birthplace of the human species." After discussing the arguments in favor of the existence of "the hypothetical continent of Lemuria," he concludes: "When we examine the soundings of the Indian Ocean, we find that the graduations in depth are entirely consonant with the hypothesis of a primitive but now wasted continent. Lemuria lies in the region indicated by the facts of geographical distribution of Carnivores (flesh-eating animals) and higher Primates as the quarter of the world reserved for the first appearance of the human being. *It is now generally admitted that Man's birthplace was in a region covered at present by the waters of the Indian Ocean.*" *

Having thus learned, at least approximately, *where* the first human beings lived, we will now consider the vexed question of their original condition, physical, intellectual, religious, etc. It is well known that there are two radically different and mutually destructive

---

* "Preadamitism," pp. 354–361.

theories on this subject: one holding that man's primitive condition was a state of "utter barbarism"; the other, that it was a highly civilized condition. The late Dr. Charles Hodge states the latter and popular view thus: "That the primitive state of our race was not one of barbarism from which men have raised themselves by a slow process of improvement, we know, first, from the authority of Scripture, which represents the first man as created in the full perfection of his nature; secondly, the traditions of all nations treat of a golden age from which men have fallen. These widespread traditions can not be rationally accounted for, except on the assumption that the Scriptural account of the primitive state of man is correct. Thirdly: The evidence of history is all on the side of the doctrine of the Bible. Egypt derived its civilization from the East; Greece from Phœnicia and Egypt; Italy from Phœnicia and Greece; the rest of Europe from Italy. Fourthly: The oldest records, written and monumental, give evidence of the existence of nations in a high state of civilization in the earliest periods of human history. Fifthly: Comparative philology has established the fact of the intimate relation of all of the great divisions of the human race." *

In reply to all this, it may be said, first, that "the authority of Scripture" on the question at issue *is the very point to be proved*. Of course, any one who believes that Genesis is verbally inspired of God must accept its "authority," but we have already seen that this dogma rests on a very slender foundation; we have no more reason to believe that our Genesis is inspired

---

* Hodge's "Systematic Theology," II, p. 93.

than we have to believe George Smith's "*Chaldean Genesis*" is; they both came from the same region, and were evidently the result of the speculations of Chaldean sages on the origin of the world and man. Secondly: Even if we grant the inspiration and consequent "authority" of Genesis, its *meaning* is by no means so clear as Dr. Hodge would have us believe. For instance: he says that "Man was originally created in a state of maturity and perfection," and "this perfection, as to his body, consisted not only in the integrity and due proportion of all its parts, but also in the perfect adaptation to the nature of the soul with which it was united. It is commonly said by theologians that the body was created immortal and impassable. With regard to its immortality, it is certain that if man had not sinned he would not have died; but whether the immortality which would then have been the destiny of the body would have been the result of its original organization, or whether after its period of probation it would have undergone a change to adapt it to its everlasting condition, is a matter to be subsequently considered." Looking through the subsequent pages, I find that the doctor, in treating of the resurrection of the body and discussing St. Paul's remark that "flesh and blood can not inherit the kingdom of God" (II Cor. xv, 50), says, that "our bodies as now organized, consisting as they do of flesh and blood, are not adapted to our future state of being, and that everything in the organization or constitution of our bodies designed to meet our present necessities will close with the life that now is." *
Since the doctor, of course, believes that man originally

---

* "Systematic Theology," II, p. 92; and III, p. 780.

consisted of flesh and blood, he must also believe that the human body would have been changed to adapt it to its everlasting condition even if Adam had not sinned; but he is not (as his class is not) very clear on this subject. Hence, we see that both the *inspiration* and the *interpretation* of Genesis remain to be established; and, although our author attempts to show that the account of Man's Fall "is neither an allegory nor a myth, but a true history," * yet he well knows that some of the most saintly clergymen in the Church—men occupying the highest positions—consider it an allegory. Thus, Canon Row tells us that the present Bishop of London and the late Archbishop of Canterbury held this view.† And hence "the authority of the Scriptures" on this subject is by no means so clear as "orthodox" theologians would have us believe, while their views are refuted by the most indisputable facts. We have seen that Dr. Hodge himself admits that "man as concerns his body belongs to the animal kingdom." ‡ If so, Dr. Hodge's remark, that "it is certain if man had not sinned he would not have died," is false, for it is absolutely indubitable that for ages before his appearance those animals to whose kingdom he "belongs" died; and there is, therefore, no shadow of reason to suppose that man would have proved an exception if he had not sinned. Hence we see what absurd contradictions and insuperable difficulties the literal interpretation of Genesis involves. Thirdly: Dr. Hodge thinks that "the wide-spread traditions of a golden age, from which men have fallen, can not be rationally ac-

---

* "Theology," II, p. 123.   ‡ *Supra*, p. 75.
† Canon Row's "Future Retribution," p. 149.

counted for except on the assumption that the Scriptural account of primitive man is correct." Does any one believe that the *Golden Age of Greece* ever really existed in the sense here defined? No; and it is most perilous to appeal to such traditions to confirm an "inspired" record, for we might rationally believe that both the traditions and the record have the same origin —an origin which Science, if not Theology, can and does explain. The third and fourth reasons which our author assigns for believing that Genesis is literally true are essentially the same, and are no reasons at all, for all Science recognizes the high state of civilization in Egypt and elsewhere, but Archæology shows that such civilization was *not primitive, but a development from a lower state.* Finally, " Comparative Philology," as we shall see, so far from confirming the popular doctrine, shows that language itself has been a slow development, and so refutes the common view.

We are now free to consider the scientific view of primitive man.

" However imperfect the relics of prehistoric men may be," says Prof. Huxley, " the evidence which they afford clearly tends to the conclusion that, for thousands of years, before the origin of the oldest known civilizations, men were savages of a very low type. They strove with their enemies and their competitors; they preyed upon things weaker or less cunning than themselves; they were born, multiplied without stint, and died for thousands of generations alongside the mammoth, the urus, the lion, and the hyena, whose lives were spent in the same way." * " Human life," says Dr.

---

* " Popular Science Monthly," April, 1888. p. 736.

Tylor, "may be roughly classed into three great stages, savage, barbaric, civilized, which may be defined as follows: The lowest or *savage* state is that in which man subsists on wild plants and animals, neither tilling the soil nor domesticating creatures for his food. Savages may dwell in tropical forests where the abundant fruit and game may allow small clans to live in one spot and may find a living all the year round, while in barer and colder regions they have to lead a wandering life in quest of the wild food which they soon exhaust in any place. In making their rude implements, the materials used by savages are what they find ready to hand, such as wood, stone, and bone; but they can not extract metal from the ore, and therefore belong to the Stone Age. Men may be considered to have risen into the next or *barbaric* state when they take to agriculture. With the certain supply of food which can be stored till the next harvest, settled village and town life is established, with immense results in the improvement of arts, knowledge, manners, and government. Pastoral tribes are to be reckoned in the barbaric stage, for, though their life of shifting camp from pasture to pasture may prevent settled habitation and agriculture, they have from their herds a constant supply of milk and meat. Some barbaric nations have not come beyond using stone implements, but most have risen into the Metal Age. Lastly, *civilized* life may be taken as beginning with the art of writing, which, by recording history, law, knowledge, and religion for the service of ages to come, binds together the past and the future in an unbroken chain of intellectual and moral progress.

"This classification of three great stages of culture is practically convenient and has the advantage of not describing imaginary states of society, but such as are actually known to exist. So far as the evidence goes, it seems that civilization has actually grown up in the world through these three stages, so that to look at a savage of the Brazilian forests, a barbarous New-Zealander or Dahoman, and a civilized European, may be the student's best guide to understanding the progress of civilization ; only he must be cautioned that the comparison is but a guide, not a full explanation." * These last words express the main principle which anthropologists adopt in their consideration of the rise of civilization—the principle, namely, that " the condition of primitive man is represented by the condition of the lowest race of modern times." " I know of no method," says Prof. Winchell, " of avoiding this conclusion." † But Dr. C. Geikie, among others, decidedly objects to this principle. " It is the mode of this school (the evolutionist)," says Geikie, "to collect all the most degraded and savage customs and usages of any people, and assume that they are traces of the original condition of the race. But such a course is utterly unphilosophical, for it may with equal force be urged that they are illustrations of the decay of a primitive civilization." Yet he accepts this very principle in the second chapter of his work. " It is hard," he there says, " to carry ourselves back to the infancy of the world and think aright of the childhood of the human mind. . . . *The simple fancies of savage tribes at the present day were then, in fact, the sober belief of all races.*" ‡ If

---

* Tylor's " Anthropology," pp. 23-25.

† " Preadamites," p. 413.

‡ " Hours with the Bible," I, pp. 16, 164.

we are to take the intellectual status of "savage tribes at the present day" as representative of primitive man's intellectual condition, it is hard to see why we should refuse to accept their "customs and usages" as typical of primeval customs and usages, for these are only outward and visible signs of an inward and spiritual condition. Hence Prof. Winchell's conclusion seems valid.

Applying this principle, Mr. Spencer and others give us a more or less complete picture of primitive man—physical, emotional, intellectual, social, and religious. "*Physically*," says Winchell, "the men of the Palæolithic Epoch, judging from the few skulls and skeletons discovered in Belgium and England, were of rather short stature." *

Spencer also thinks that the primitive man was smaller in stature, less powerful, more callous and phlegmatic than man now is. †

"*Socially and intellectually*," continues Winchell, "Palæolithic man, in the regions in question (Europe), seems to have existed in a most primitive condition. Dwelling in wild caverns, he hunted beasts with the rudest stone implements and clothed himself in their skins. We find no evidence of the use of fire, though probably known, and there are some indications that he made food of his own species. Few attempts at pottery have been discovered, and in these the product was rude, hand-made, and simply sun-dried." This assertion that "we find no evidence of the use of fire" in the Palæolithic Period, is contradicted by M. Joly, among others, who says: "It can not be denied that

---

* "Preadamites," p. 413.
† "Principles of Sociology," i, chap. v.

the use of this element was known to the earliest quaternary men. Numerous hearths, ashes, cinders, bones partly or entirely carbonized, fragments of rude pottery blackened by the smoke, etc., have been found in caves belonging to the age of the cave-bear, etc. With fire prehistoric men burned the bodies of the dead," etc.*

In the sixth and seventh chapters of his " Sociology " Mr. Spencer considers the emotional and intellectual characteristics of primitive men. He thinks that they were impulsive, improvident, unsociable, self-satisfied, caring nothing for the approbation of one another, and brutal toward women. They could form no " conception of general facts," no " abstract ideas," only limited " associations of ideas," no notion of natural law or " uniformity of Nature," and possessed simply " a *reminiscent*, not a *constructive* imagination." It is interesting to contrast this view of primitive man with that which was held in past years. "As to knowledge, our first parent," says Dr. Geikie, " has been supposed to have excelled all men since. It was a favorite mode of stating this, among Christian writers before the Reformation, to say that the great master Aristotle was *almost* as learned as Adam." † Dr. Geikie apparently does not believe that our forefather was quite so learned as this, yet, if he believed the creed which the doctor, following a German rabbi, formulates as " the religious belief of our first parents," he certainly must have surpassed Aristotle in knowledge and faith.

"*Æsthetically*," Prof. Winchell thinks, " Palæolithic

---

* " Man before Metals," p. 193; and Tylor's " Early History of Man," chap. ix.
† " Hours with the Bible," i, p. 91.

man had advanced no further than the use of necklaces formed of natural beads, consisting of fossil foraminifera from the chalk. Some flints from the river-drift of St. Acheul present rough sketches which, it has been conjectured, may have been prompted by the artistic feeling. Some of them bear remote resemblances to the human head in profile, three-quarter view, and full face; also to animals, such as the rhinoceros and mammoth." * Did primitive man possess *Language?* "There was a time," answers Prof. W. D. Whitney, "when all existing human beings were as destitute of language as the dog." † But, if we hold, with this writer, that language is "everything that bodies forth thought and makes it apprehensible," ‡ we must claim language for our progenitors.

Prof. Whitney agrees with Dr. Tylor that "there are various ways in which men can communicate with one another. They can make *gestures*, utter *cries*, speak *words*, draw *pictures*, write *characters* or *letters*." It is well known that Tylor believes that gestures constituted the primitive language of man, or at least that it is the lowest form of communication. The next step consists of "emotional cries," as "ah!" "oh!" "ur-r-r," "puh!" etc. Then "imitative signs" follow, such as a deaf and dumb child's imitating the act of washing the face, etc. The union of "gesture-actions and gesture-sounds forms what may be called a Natural Language," which language "really exists." This natural language "is half-way between the communications of animals

---

* "Preadamites," p. 416.
† "Encyclopædia Britannica," article "Philology."
‡ "Life and Growth of Language," p. 1.

and full human speech," and how the latter was developed Dr. Tylor shows very satisfactorily in his admirable little work on "Anthropology," and in his "Early History of Mankind." *

M. Joly believes that primitive man "had at least the power of creating language." He indorses Sir John Lubbock's remark that " Languages are human in the sense that they are the work of man; divine in the sense that man, in creating them, made use of a faculty with which Providence had endowed him. . . . We believe that languages themselves are organisms which have their life in embryo—their infancy, their ripe age, their changes, their distant and repeated migrations, their decadence and death." He thinks that " quaternary man expressed his feelings by cries resembling interjections, his most vivid perception by onomatopœia"—i. e., imitative sounds. He agrees with Whitney and others that there was no "single parent language whence all others are derived." † "The original formation of language," says Tylor, "did not take place all at once, but was a gradual process extending through ages, and not absolutely stopped even now," and hence "it is not a hopeful task to search for primitive languages." It is hoped that the reader may consult the works of these authors on this intensely interesting and important question; and having, I trust, made it clear that primitive man possessed a very low form of lan-

---

* Compare Dr. Romanes's admirable work, "Mental Evolution in Man," chaps. v to xv, inclusive; Lubbock's "Origin of Civilization," chap. ix; Max Müller's "Lectures on Language," etc.; Tylor's "Anthropology," chaps. iv to vi; and "Early History of Mankind," chaps. ii to iv.

† "Man before Metals," pp. 312–320.

guage, consisting, probably, of gestures and emotional cries, which gradually developed into full human speech, I pass to a consideration of the most important question of all concerning our forefather, viz., his *religious* condition. The popular view, it is well known, holds that he was created absolutely *pure and perfect*, was placed in a paradise, where he was tempted in some mysterious way, so that he was finally induced to eat the "forbidden fruit," and thus partially or totally corrupted his nature, and was consequently banished from Eden; the ground and all other creatures were cursed for his sake, and so on.

Dr. Geikie, as already stated, formulates a creed for Adam. He thinks our forefather believed:

1. "That God alone created the universe. That He existed of necessity before creation, and must exist forever without change, which would imply that He is Immaterial and Eternal.

2. "That harmony prevails throughout creation; ... and hence the great Master of the Whole was One, Only, and All-Wise.

3. "That this Great Being made the world from nothing; that the existence of all creatures depends absolutely on his will; that He interrupts the course of Nature, that is, works miracles, when he thinks fit; that He is, therefore, Supreme and Almighty.

4. "That all that has been or is owes its first source to Him, and has been and is upheld directly by Him—that is, He is Omnipresent.

5. "That He created man as to this soul in His own image; that is, spiritual, free, and immortal. Hence He must love virtue and hate vice, or, in other words, He must be a Holy God.

6. "That the lot of man is often found to correspond with his conduct, thus showing the Righteousness of God. But, the fact that this is not always realized here, is an absolute proof that our conduct and our lot will be brought, hereafter, to correspond. Hence Adam must have believed in a Future State.

7. "That God watches with an all-embracing Providence over all things; especially over man at large, and each individual in particular, and thus must be the All-Good.

8. "That man is weak and wrought upon by impulses from within and temptations from without; that when he sins, God pardons him, on seeing and repenting of his faults. Thus Adam must have believed in the Tender Pity and Mercy of the Heavenly Father.

9. "That God demands, not on His own account, but for the good of man himself, our homage and obedience to His sovereign Will, not only in the most secret thoughts, but also outwardly; and that He has hence given us Commands and Prohibitions—some of abiding force, others for particular circumstances and times.

10. "He had a trust in the mysterious promise of a Future Deliverer—the 'Seed of the Woman,' who should bruise the head of the Serpent, and undo the ruin of the Fall."

No wonder, then, that the doctor should add, "It is impossible, indeed, to conjecture how much may have been disclosed to one who stood in such unique relations to his Maker." * If Adam possessed all this knowledge of and faith in God, he not only surpassed

---

* "Hours with the Bible," I, pp. 93-95.

an Aristotle and a Bishop Butler, but his knowledge and faith equaled that of the Deliverer of the Sermon on the Mount.

It is hardly necessary to add that Science takes an absolutely different view of primitive man's religious condition, and all its facts disprove this theory.

Thus, Sir John Lubbock thinks that "the first great stages in religious thought may be regarded as—

1. "*Atheism;* understanding by this term not the denial of the existence of a Deity, but an *absence of any definite ideas on the subject.*

2. "*Fetichism;* the stage in which man supposes he can force the deities to comply with his desires.

3. "*Nature-worship, or Totemism;* in which material objects—trees, lakes, stones, animals, etc.—are worshiped.

4. "*Shamanism;* in which the superior deities are far more powerful than man, and of a different nature. Their places of abode also are far away, and accessible only to Shamans (priests).

5. "*Idolatry, or Anthropomorphism;* in which the gods take still more completely the nature of men, being, however, more powerful. They are still amenable to persuasion; they are a part of Nature, and not creators. They are represented by images or idols.

6. "In the next stage the Deity is regarded as the Author, not merely a part, of Nature. He becomes for the first time a really supernatural being.

7. "The last stage is that in which morality is associated with religion."[*]

Mr. Spencer treats this question quite fully in the

---

[*] "Origin of Civilization," chapters v–vii, inclusive.

first volume of his "Sociology." He there discusses the primitive man's ideas of animate and inanimate nature, of sleep and dreams, of death and resurrection, of souls, ghosts, spirits and demons, of another life and supernatural agents, of inspiration, divination, sorcery, etc., of ancestor-worship, animal and plant worship, and Nature-worship. He thinks that primitive man got the notion of "soul" as distinct from "body" from the dream, during which he supposed his "other-self" wandered off from his body. Having got this idea of a double self, he naturally inferred that in swoon, death, etc., the "other-self" had merely gone away on a longer journey than when he slept.

This simple idea, Mr. Spencer shows, leads to all those views of inspiration, resurrection, a future life, etc., which prevail among savages, and to ancestor-worship, which he considers "the root of every religion." No synopsis of his views can adequately express them and so the reader should consult the work itself.* "It was partly through political circumstances," says Prof. Fiske, "that a truly theistic idea was developed out of the chaotic and fragmentary ghost-theories and Nature-worships of the primeval world. This Nature-worship and ancestor-worship of early times was scarcely theism." Man originally personified all physical phenomena, and in all this personification "our prehistoric ancestors were greatly assisted by that theory of ghosts which was perhaps the earliest speculative effort of the human mind. . . . The mass of crude inference which makes up the savage's philosophy of nature is largely based upon the hypothesis that every man has

---

* " Principles of Sociology," i, chapters viii–xxv.

another self, a 'double,' wraith, or ghost. This hypothesis of the 'other-self,' which serves to account for the savage's wanderings during sleep in strange lands and among strange people, serves also to account for the presence in his dreams of parents, comrades, or enemies, known to be dead and buried. The other-self of the dreamer meets and converses with the other-selves of his dead brethren, joins with them in the hunt, or sits down with them to the wild cannibal banquet. Thus arises the belief in an ever-present world of ghosts, a belief which the entire experience of the uncivilized man goes to strengthen and confirm. It was in accordance with this primitive theory of things that the earliest form of religious worship was developed. In all races of men, so far as can be determined, this was the worship of ancestors." * It thus appears that Prof. Fiske agrees with Mr. Spencer. "It can not be denied" says M. Joly, "that God has always revealed Himself to man in His works, but the conception of a Divine Being, of a Supreme Cause, was of slow progressive development in primitive man, advancing almost imperceptibly by an instinctive and spontaneous movement. Just as the knowledge of our Ego (Self or Soul) and of the exterior world was not acquired spontaneously, without effort, reflection, or experience, so the idea of the existence of God, at first embryonic, so to speak, has need, in order to attain its complete development, of slow and successive efforts of the human mind which has conceived it.

"The idea of God is at first individual, infinitesimal, sometimes strange and childish—it grows purer

---

* Fiske's "Idea of God," pp. 62-80, inclusive.

and larger with the growth of the natural intelligence and acquired instruction of him who conceives it. Then, from being individual, it becomes collective; and finally, passed from one to another, it progresses gradually, until it attains to this formula—'Power, Love, and Wisdom, united, yet divided, compose His being.'

"Man, then, as he came from Nature's hands, was endowed with too weak an understanding to enable him to attain at once to a clear and precise knowledge of the Divinity."* In short, he was endowed with the *capacity of learning about God*, which capacity was gradually developed by the various means already noted, until it could formulate the great principles of Monotheism and Christianity.

Now, the main reason why theologians object so strongly to this theory of man's primitive condition, is its inconsistency with the popular doctrine of man's fall and depravity in Adam.

It is claimed that man was created perfectly pure in every part and faculty of soul and body, but that, by an act of disobedience, he fell, and thereby so corrupted his nature that the mission of the Saviour was rendered absolutely necessary to his salvation from sin here and hell hereafter. The necessity of the Atonement or of the Saviour is thus supposed to rest on the fact of Adam's Fall, and it is now my purpose to refute this popular error. In doing so I shall quote those whose words ought to carry conviction throughout the Church. In the seventh chapter of his able work on "Future Retribution," Canon Row, of England, discusses this subject in a masterly manner. He shows:

---

* "Man before Metals," pp. 327–329.

1. "That from the third chapter of Genesis to the last of Malachi the Fall of Man is not once mentioned or even referred to by the sacred writers." The apparent exception in Job (xxxi, 33) "disappears in the alternative marginal rendering of the Revised Version."

2. "The Fall of Man is not only never affirmed by our Lord to have been the foundation of His divine mission, but it is not once *directly referred to* by Him in the whole course of his teaching."

John viii, 42–44, is an apparent exception, but, even if it be a reference to the Fall, it by no means involves the conclusion that without it Christ would never have come into the world—that His mission to man would have been unnecessary.

3. "No reference to the Fall is to be found either in the Acts of the Apostles, in the Epistle to the Hebrews, in those of St. Peter, St. James, St. John, St. Jude, in nine of St. Paul's Epistles, nor even in the Revelation, except in its identification of the old Serpent 'with the Devil.'"

"It will doubtless be urged," says the Canon, "by those that hold the popular theories on this subject, that all these writings *presuppose* it, though they do not directly refer to it. To this I answer:

"First. It is incredible, if they presuppose it as the foundation on which their teaching rests, that all direct, and even indirect, reference to it should be entirely wanting.

"Secondly, In investigating a subject like the present we have nothing to do with presuppositions and assumptions, which really mean nothing more nor less than reading into the sacred page, for the purpose of meeting the exigencies of our own theories, what is not to be found therein. By this practice it is easy to make Scripture say anything which the commentator or the reader wishes."

4. "The references to the third chapter of Genesis in the remainder of St. Paul's Epistles are four in number, viz. (1) I Cor., xv, 21, 22; (2) II Cor., xi, 3; (3) I Tim., ii, 12–15; and (4) Rom., v, 12–21." The first three passages may be set aside at once, for no one would be so foolish as to maintain that they prove the popular doctrine of Adam's Fall. I mean, while they refer to Adam's *sin*, they neither prove that his sin totally corrupted his nature nor that it was the basis of Christ's mission to man; this is the point at issue. Indeed, the classic passage in Romans does not prove this. It is, confessedly, a most difficult and obscure passage, but, notwithstanding all obscurities, "its general purpose (as Row says) is sufficiently clear." The writer intended to "affirm that the evil which has resulted from Adam's (Man's) transgression has not only been repaired by the work of Jesus Christ, but that the mischief which has been occasioned by the one stands to the good effected by the other, in what may be called a *ratio of greater inequality*—i. e., that the work of Jesus Christ wrought *far more good than the transgression of Adam has wrought evil.*"

Observe: This is only a *matter-of-fact statement*. Not one word is said about Adam's Fall being the *sine qua non* of Christ's mission—that without which He would not have come to earth. We heartily believe what St. Paul says. We believe that Adam, whoever he was, wherever and whenever he lived, *sinned*—i. e., freely violated Divine, Moral Law. We believe that corrupt habits are acquired and hereditarily transmitted. And we believe that Jesus, by what he taught, did, and suffered, has more than repaired the evil which resulted from the First Man's transgression. We believe that the third chapter of Genesis, like Bunyan's "Pilgrim's Progress," contains profound moral and spiritual truths, but we *do not* believe that the popular view of man's primitive condition is either scripturally, scientifically, or philosophically correct. The proposition that a being created perfectly pure and in direct communion with God, the Holy One, should disobey Him, is utterly irrational. All his inclinations would be *toward* the good, and it would be morally *impossible* for him to do evil. I have read many attempted solutions of this problem, but none was satisfactory. The evolutionary theory, whatever its difficulties may be, does not involve any such philosophical absurdities; it is, at least, more credible.

"Evolutionists say that, if wrong-doing is easier than right-doing, it is because wrong-doing implies a *falling back* on the more deeply implanted primitive (animal) instincts, and right-doing the exercise of more recently acquired and morally higher instincts." *

This is at least more intelligible than the theory which holds that the first man was perfectly pure, and yet did such evil as to corrupt his own nature and that of all his descendants. "Reversion," as the writer just quoted remarks, "is generally, if not always, an easy process; the difficult thing is to add something to the ancestral inheritance." If man was originally only a little above the anthropoid apes, we can understand why many persons are still brutal; their development is im-

---

* "Popular Science Monthly," December, 1887, p. 269.

perfect; their moral and spiritual faculties are dull and weak. "But, if so," the "orthodox" theologian would reply, "then *education*, not *atonement*—a professor of moral and physical science, not a redeemer—is what is needed." When I treat of "Evolution and the Atonement" I shall discuss this point more fully; meanwhile I may say: First, the word "atonement" is used in so many senses that it is necessary to *define* it very carefully before one can speak of its necessity, etc. But, secondly, even if we hold the popular view on this subject, viz., that Christ's death was the *penalty* of man's sin—that he was the victim chosen instead of the sinner to bear his punishment—we may yet adopt the evolutionist's theory of man's primitive condition. Let us grant that man was originally a savage scarcely raised above the level of the anthropoid ape, who very slowly acquired power to conquer and subdue his animal passions. *The moment he acquired such power he became a responsible being, and although his will was not absolutely free then, as, indeed, it is not now,*[*] *yet he might have resisted the evil, and, as he did not do so, he ought to suffer the consequences*—the punishment. Hence, if a Saviour is needed to bear such punishment at all, he is so needed on the evolutionary view. In a letter to the author on this subject the Bishop of Carlisle, England (Dr. Goodwin), says: "I am not sure that any particular scientific theory of the origin of man makes the doctrine of our relation to God through the Incarnation (for that I conceive is ultimately what is meant by the doctrine of the *atonement*) more difficult than it would be if we put such scientific theory

---

[*] See "Present Day Tracts"—Tract xxx, by Canon Row.

altogether out of the question. The great fact which we have to deal with is the *rebellion of the will of man against the will of God;* this, I take it, express it as you will, is the basis of sin; this is what separates the condition of man in relation to God from that of any other creature. The book of Genesis represents the *beginning* of this rebellion in a very simple, striking, and picturesque way. But suppose the book of Genesis had been lost, and we had begun (so to speak) with the New Testament; suppose (which is quite conceivable) that the Incarnation had taken place *without* all the preface which we find in the Old Testament, and Christ had declared that he came to 'make an end of sin,' such as the experience of the world showed to exist, would not this revelation have fitted in equally well with any scientific knowledge as to the origin and descent of man? For my part, I wonder how man ever came into existance at all; Darwin (even granting all he tells us in the 'Descent of Man' to be true) seems to me only to magnify the marvel of his existence. If Julius Cæsar and Alfred the Great and Washington were legitimate descendants of minute Ascidians, no words can express the miracle of the transformation; '*but there man is*'; the Scripture says that he is there because God willed him to be. Mr. Darwin says he was evolved from something which existed previously; grant that this second view is true, it does not change the fact that, when man came to be what he is, he differed from other creatures in having an independent will and that sometimes he has misused his independence. Therefore, if the highest life of man consists in union with God, man's highest destiny calls for *at-one-ment* with God; it calls for reconciliation, for the realization

of what Holy Scripture calls 'an adoption' as sons."
This ought to satisfy the most ardent traditionalist that
Evolution, by exploding the popular doctrine of man's
fall, does not destroy the need of the Saviour.

Instead of looking for the basis of the Atonement in
the third chapter of Genesis, we should look for it in the
great book of experience, and by basing its necessity on
the *fact of sin* rather than on a document, we make it
coextensive with mankind.

I have thus stated as clearly and as candidly as I
could what after a careful and unbiased consideration
of the facts of the case seems to me to be the true view
of man's origin, antiquity, and primitive condition. I
need hardly add that I have not aimed either at origi-
nality or completeness, but have merely tried to suggest
lines of thought which every student of these great
problems may follow out for himself. This is the
foundation; in the next part I shall rear the superstructure, or rather the framework, of a system of theology which alone seems to be tenable in the light of
modern research.

PART II.

INTRODUCTION.

THE DOCUMENTS.

In considering the origin of Christianity, the first question to be answered is, When and by whom were the books of the New Testament written?

The day has long since passed when thinking persons will rest satisfied with the assurance, come whence it may, that the Bible says thus and so, and, being an inspired book, its *ipse dixit* is conclusive.

Whatever else the Bible may be *proved* to be, it is a book, and like all other books it must submit to a critical examination. Its contents may have proceeded from minds which were divinely illuminated; but we must know first of all who were its authors, when they lived, and what reason we have for believing that they were specially gifted on religious subjects. Such questions are not suggested by a diabolical spirit, but by the most intensely religious and earnest spirit. Religion is too important a subject to rest in a state of uncertainty or on untested authority. Bishop Butler says a *man is responsible for the use of his understanding.* Our reason and conscience are given us of God to use, and if we fail to use them, or if we misuse them, we shall certainly be held responsible for the same. Such a responsibility is an awful fact, but it *is* a fact, and we may as well realize it.

We dare not ignore it, and, if we recognize it, we must question every professed revelation on every subject, and must satisfy our reason and conscience that it is true. "We have no other faculty than reason to judge of revelation itself" (Butler).

It is not necessary to my purpose to consider the origin of all the books of the New Testament, and so I shall confine my attention to ten of the Epistles ascribed to St. Paul, the book of Revelation, the Four Gospels, the Acts of the Apostles, and the Epistle to the Hebrews, from which we may gather all the facts which it is absolutely necessary we should know in order to understand the rise of Christianity.

In considering the authorship and authenticity of a book there are two sources of evidence available, namely: first, the references to or use of said book by contemporary and immediately subsequent writers; and, second, the contents of the book itself, which should fit in with what we know from authentic history of the times in which it was professedly originated. It is plain, therefore, that the student of Christian origins must know something about the early Christian writers who were the associates and immediate successors of the Apostles and traditional authors of the books of the New Testament.

Fortunately, the English reader is enabled, through the services of "The Christian Literature Publishing Company," of New York, to familiarize himself, with comparatively little effort, with the writings of the "Christian Fathers," as the early writers of the Church are called. The first volume of "The Ante-Nicene Fathers," published by the aforementioned company, will give him the facts at first hand which he should know in order to understand the time and circumstances that saw the birth of Christianity. If he have not the books in question and do not care to buy them, he should borrow them from some clergyman who has them, for it is absolutely necessary that he go to the root of this matter for himself. So many learned and apparently equally honest writers have reached diametrically opposite conclusions on some of the questions at issue that there is only one course open to the student—he must use their works mainly as guides to the discovery of the facts of early Christian literature and history, and from those facts draw his own conclusions. But I would here protest, once for all, against the inferences which certain "orthodox" writers of our day draw from the differences of opinion which prevail among the (so-called) "advanced critics." Indeed, the common answer given to the arguments of these critics is that they are mutually destructive. But there is hardly a half truth in this assertion. The critics do, indeed, differ among themselves, as "orthodox" theologians differ, on certain points. But they are agreed on the general point at issue. Thus they may differ as to the particular *date* or *mode of origin* of a certain book, but they are all quite agreed that the Gospels, for instance, were of so *gradual and slow formation as to allow the insertion of unhistorical matter.* This is the great point at issue, and it should ever be kept clearly in mind. I am sure that he who will study the writings of the "advanced critics" with an unbiased mind, and examine for himself the early Christian authors to whom they refer, will feel after such study that, however great may be their differences on minor points, yet they are not sufficient to destroy the common conclusion of the critics, namely, that the New Testament literature was of so gradual a formation, it originated so long after the events referred to are said to have occurred, and in such a manner, that unhistorical matter may very readily have been inserted. The principal Christian fathers whose writings the reader ought to consult are :

1. Clement of Rome, the third bishop of that Church, who lived and wrote between A. D. 30 and 100. His *Epistle to the Corinthians* was so highly esteemed in the early Church as to be publicly read in the congregations along with the Epistles of St. Paul, etc.

2. Polycarp, Bishop of Smyrna, who lived and wrote between 65 and 155 A. D. His *Epistle to the Philippians*, and an *Encyclical Epistle* issued by the church of Smyrna on the occasion of Polycarp's martyrdom, have reached us, and throw some light on the subject in hand.

3. Ignatius, Bishop of Antioch in Syria, has left us seven short epistles, which are generally considered genuine and authentic, and were issued about the year 100 or 105 A. D.*

4. Papias, Bishop of Hierapolis, a city in the province of Phrygia, in Asia Minor, lived and wrote between the years 70 and 155 A. D. "He was a hearer of the Apostle John, and was on terms of intimate intercourse with many who had known the Lord and His Apostles. From these he gathered the floating traditions in regard

---

* The author of "Supernatural Religion," Part II, chap. ii, among others, denies the Ignatian authorship of these epistles, but on insufficient grounds.

to the sayings of our Lord, and wove them into a production divided into five books," the greater portion of which has been lost, but a few invaluable fragments have reached us.

5. Justin, commonly called "the Martyr," was a Gentile philosopher, but was born in Samaria, near Jacob's Well. He was well educated; had traveled extensively; and, finally, after trying the philosophy of Socrates and Plato, "he climbed toward Christ," and became the first Christian apologist, or defender of the faith. He flourished between the years 110 and 165 A. D. His first "*Apology*" was addressed to the Roman Emperor, Antoninus Pius, who reigned for twenty-three years from the year 138 A. D. The second "*Apology*" was addressed to the Roman Senate. The only other work of Justin which we need notice is his "*Dialogue with Trypho*," a Jew, which "is the first elaborate exposition of the reasons for regarding Christ as the Messiah of the Old Testament, and the first systematic attempt to exhibit the false position of the Jews in regard to Christianity." These three works are "unquestionably genuine."

6. Irenæus, Bishop of the Church of Lyons, in Gaul (France), lived and wrote between 120 and 202 A. D. His celebrated work, "*Against Heresies*," in five books, "is one of the most precious remains of early Christian antiquity. It is devoted, on the one hand, to an account and refutation of those multiform Gnostic heresies which prevailed in the latter half of the second century; and, on the other hand, to an exposition and defense of the Catholic faith." *

---

* " Ante-Nicene Fathers," vol. i, Introductory Notices.

Other writers may be referred to in the following pages, but it will then be time enough to give their dates and location, and the six writers mentioned are the most important witnesses, since they lived contemporaneously with or immediately after the Apostles. The reference to "Gnostic heresies" suggests a most important question, viz., the nature of Gnosticism and its influence on early Christian thought, to which we must devote a few pages. "Gnosticism" is derived from the Greek word *gnosis* (γνῶσις), which means "*knowledge*," and was applied to the tenets of an early sect, who claimed to have superior knowledge in matters religious. The word "Agnosticism," so familiar to modern thought, is the exact opposite of "Gnosticism," and means "*without knowledge*," and Prof. Huxley, the originator of the word, tells us that "it came into my (his) head as suggestively antithetic to the 'gnostic' of Church history, who professed to know so much about the very things of which I (he) was ignorant." *

The sources of Gnosticism are to be found in various forms of religious and philosophic speculation antecedent to Christianity, especially in the teachings of a celebrated Jewish philosopher, *Philo* by name, who flourished at Alexandria, in Egypt, between the years B. C. 20 and A. D. 50, and, again, in the influences flowing from the old Persian religion and the Buddhistic faiths of India and the East.

"The fundamental questions with which Gnosticism concerned itself are the same which in all ages have agitated inquiry and baffled speculation, viz., the origin of life and the origin of evil—how life sprung from the

---

* "Popular Science Monthly," April, 1888, pp. 763-765.

Infinite Source—how a word so imperfect as this could proceed from a supremely perfect God. The Oriental notion of matter as utterly corrupt is found to pervade all Gnostical systems, and to give so far a common character to their speculations. It may be said to be the ground principle of Gnosticism.

"Setting out from this principle, all the Gnostics agree in regarding this world as not proceeding *immediately* from the Supreme Being. A vast gulf is supposed to separate them. In the general mode in which they conceive this gulf to be occupied they all agree. The Supreme Being is regarded as wholly inconceivable and indescribable—as the Unfathomable Abyss—the Unnameable. From this transcendent source Existence springs by emanation, in a series of spiritual powers. It is only through these several powers or energies that the Infinite passes into life and activity, and becomes capable of representation.

"To this higher spiritual world is given the name Pleroma ($\pi\lambda\acute{\eta}\rho\omega\mu a$ = Fullness), and the divine powers composing it, in their ever-expanding processes from the Highest, are called Æons.

"So far a common mode of representation characterizes all Gnostical systems. All unite in this doctrine of a higher emanation-world."

But the Gnostics had many and various theories concerning the passage from the higher spiritual world to the lower material one, into which we need not enter. Christ is recognized by them "as a higher Æon, proceeding from the kingdom of light for the redemption of this lower kingdom of darkness." Gnosticism reached its full and systematic development during the first quarter of the second century, and then its influences issued from two main centers, viz., Antioch in Syria and Alexandria in Egypt. It was "in the air" long before, and we shall soon see how it affected (or is supposed to have affected) Christian thought, as expressed in the New Testament.*

Philo, the Jewish philosopher of Alexandria, who lived between the years B. C. 20 and A. D. 50, has been mentioned, and we must glance at his teaching, since it is also believed to have affected the writers of the New Testament, especially the "Gospel according to John" and the Epistle to the Hebrews. According to Philo, God is "a Being better than all goodness, holier than all holiness, more beautiful than all beauty," who "is absolutely separated from this corrupt world, and of whom man may know that *He is*, but not *what* He is." But if God is such a Being, so pure, so holy, so lofty, that He could not come in contact with the corrupt, material world, how was the world created? To bridge over the vast abyss between the two, Philo brings forward his doctrine of the "Word" (λόγος = Logos), who was the instrument of all creation, the first-born, the Son of God, who ruled over a world of subordinate "words" or "æons."

The word Logos (Word) has two meanings, Reason and Speech. Philo uses it sometimes in one and sometimes in the other of these senses, but predominately in the former. When he wishes to distinguish between them, he calls Speech "*uttered* Reason," and Reason "*immanent* Speech." The Reason, he says, is like a fountain, and utterance flows from it. The seat of reason is the ruling and spiritual sphere of human na-

---

* "Encyclopædia Britannica," article "Gnosticism."

ture; the seat of speech is the vocal organs. Hence "the Divine Logos" is the manifestation of God; and "the Sacred Logos" is used for the Scriptures; and the "True Logos" is the rule of life, namely, "to live in accordance with the highest nature."* Remembering that such teaching as this was circulating in the regions where "John's Gospel" was produced, we can readily understand the peculiar form of the following passage: "In the beginning was the Word, and the Word was with God, and the Word was God. The same was in the beginning with God. All things were made by him; and without him was not anything made that was made. . . . And the Word was made flesh, and dwelt among us (and we beheld his glory, the glory as of the only begotten of the Father), full of grace and truth" (John i, 1–15).

The person who wrote those lines was influenced by Philo's philosophy; at least so say many learned critics, and we shall consider this opinion further on.

The apostles and early disciples were primarily preachers, and only secondarily writers, and so they did not, immediately after our Lord's death, sit down and write his biography, but went forth into all the world to preach the Gospel to every creature, and hence the books of the New Testament were called forth by circumstances.

The first writings thus produced were not the "Gospels," as an uninformed person might imagine from

---

* Farrar's "Early Days of Christianity," vol. i, pp. 265–279; Keim's "Jesus of Nazara," i, pp. 276–297; "Encyclopædia Britannica," article "Philo."

their position in the New Testament, but the Epistles of St. Paul. There are four epistles, viz., those to the Corinthians, Romans, and Galatians, which even the most radical skeptics acknowledge to be the works of the Apostle. The *First Epistle to the Corinthians* was written by St. Paul at Ephesus about the year 57 A. D. The following are the most ancient witnesses to its genuineness, and they are quite sufficient. Clement of Rome says: "Take up the Epistle of the blessed Apostle Paul; what did he write to you at the time when the Gospel first began to be preached? Truly under the inspiration of the Spirit, he wrote to you concerning himself and Cephas and Apollos, because even then parties had been formed among you." * Ignatius, in his Epistle to the Ephesians (chapter ii) quotes the tenth verse of the first chapter of I Corinthians, saying, "It is befitting that you should in every way glorify Jesus Christ, who hath glorified you, that by a unanimous obedience ye may be perfectly joined together in the same mind, and in the same judgment, and may all speak the same thing concerning the same thing." This is only one of many of his quotations from this Epistle of St. Paul.

Polycarp also asks, "Do we not know that the Saints shall judge the world, as Paul teaches?" Again, "Neither fornicators nor effeminate, nor abusers of themselves with mankind, shall inherit the kingdom of God," etc. (I Cor., vi, 2, 9, 10).†

Justin Martyr writes, "There shall be schisms and

---

* Clement's "Epistle to the Corinthians," chap. xlvii, "Ante-Nicene Fathers," vol. i.

† Polycarp's "Epistle to the Philippians," chaps. xi and v.

heresies" (I Corinthians, xi, 19).* Irenæus says, "Paul was not ignorant of it (the destruction of the world) when he declared, 'For the figure of this world passeth away.'" And again, "Paul declares, 'We know in part, and we prophesy in part, but when that is perfect is come, the things which are in part shall be done away" (I Corinthians, vii, 31; xiii, 9, 10). "But this also," he adds more plainly, "Paul has declared in the Epistle to the Corinthians when he says, 'Brethren, I would not that ye should be ignorant how that all our fathers were under the cloud, and were all baptized with Moses in the sea,'" etc. (I Corinthians, x, 1, etc.). And in many other passages this writer quotes copiously from this epistle.† The *Second Epistle to the Corinthians* was written by St. Paul soon after he wrote the first, and is likewise so well attested that no one doubts its genuineness.

Thus, among the many quotations from this epistle in the writings of Irenæus, we find this: "Paul said plainly in the *Second Epistle to the Corinthians*, 'In whom the god of this world hath blinded the minds of men that believe not'" (II Corinthians, iv, 4). ‡

The *Epistle to the Galatians* was written from Corinth about the year 58 A. D., and is quoted by Clement of Rome, who says: "Jesus Christ our Lord gave his blood for us by the will of God; His flesh for our flesh, and His soul for our soul." # Although this reference is doubtful, it is considered by many skeptical

---

* "Dialogue with Trypho," chap. xxxv.

† "Against Heresies."

‡ "Against Heresies," Book III, chap. vii; Book IV, chaps. xxviii, xii, iii, ix, etc.

"Epistle to Corinthians," chap. xlix.

critics as being based on Galatians, i, 4. Ignatius says, "Which bishop, I know, obtained the ministry for the public, not of himself, nor by men, nor out of vainglory, but by the love of God the Father and the Lord Jesus Christ," etc. (Galatians, i, 1). This allusion is also uncertain. Irenæus is the first writer who expressly refers the epistle to St. Paul: "Paul . . . says, in the Epistle to the Galatians, 'Then fourteen years after I went up again to Jerusalem with Barnabas,'" etc. (Galatians ii, 1, 2).* And many of his contemporaries ascribe it to St. Paul.

"The early heretics were also acquainted with the epistle, ascribing it to its true author. It was in Marcion's Canon, though he is said to have omitted an important passage and interpolated two words in another. Both charges are false, though Tertullian makes them." †

The *Epistle to the Romans* was written from Corinth after the Epistle to the Galatians, in the same year, and its genuineness is unquestioned. Clement, Polycarp, and others quote it or refer to it, and Irenæus says: "Paul, when writing to the Romans, has explained this very point: 'Paul, an Apostle of Jesus Christ, predestinated unto the Gospel of God,' etc. And again, writing to the Romans about Israel, he says, 'Whose are the fathers,' etc." ‡ But since such radical skeptics as Baur, Davidson and others admit the genuineness of these four epistles it is unnecessary to discuss it.#

---

* "Against Heresies," Book III, chap. xiii, § 3.
† Dr. Samuel Davidson, "Introduction to New Testament," vol. i, p. 86.
‡ "Against Heresies," Book III, chap. xvi, § 3.
\# Davidson, *ut supra;* Baur, "Church History," vol. i, pp. 56, 61, 66, etc.

In addition to these four epistles, there are *six* others which many of the advanced critics attribute to St. Paul, viz., the epistles to the *Thessalonians* to *Philemon*, to the *Colossians*, to the *Philippians*, and at least part of the *Epistle to the Ephesians*. With regard to the Epistles to the Thessalonians and Philippians, Renan, the well-known French skeptic, says: "The difficulties which certain ones of modern times have raised against them consist in those slight *suspicions* which it is the duty of criticism to express freely, but not to dwell upon when more cogent reasons oppose. These three Epistles possess a character of authenticity which overcomes every other consideration."* To this conclusion Dr. Davidson assents. " Too much importance," he says, " is attached by Baur to *uniformity* of ideas and expressions as evidence of Pauline authorship. He takes four epistles unquestionably authentic and forming a group by themselves as the standard of measurement for groups of later and earlier origin. By this means little room is left for *growth* in the Apostle's mind ; nor is there latitude for the influence of the wide variety of circumstances through which he passed, of the persevering opponents he had to encounter, or of the local diversities of peoples." The *First Epistle to the Thessalonians* was written from Corinth about the year 53 ; the second was written about 69. The Epistle to the Philippians was written from Rome, " near the end of the Roman captivity " of Paul—i. e., A. D. 69 or 70.†

---

* Renan's "St. Paul," p. 11.
† Davidson's " Introduction to New Testament," i, pp. 4–16, 156–176, and 336–351.

Davidson answers all of Baur's objections to these three epistles, and also gives quotations of, or references to, them from the Fathers which prove their genuineness.

Both Renan and Davidson accept the *Epistle to Philemon* as the work of St. Paul, and it was probably written about the year 60 or 61.* The Epistles to the Colossians and the Ephesians are more doubtful. The external evidence in favor of the Pauline authorship of *Colossians* is as good as that supporting *Galatians*, etc., but Davidson rejects it on internal grounds. He thinks it is tainted "with gnostic influence," and, as "the stage is not an advanced one," he places the date "about 120 A. D. in Asia Minor, perhaps in Phrygia." † "Nothing in all this, however," says Renan, "is decisive. If the Epistle to the Colossians is the work of St. Paul (*as we believe it to be*), it was written in the latter part of the Apostle's life, at a period in which his biography is very obscure." ‡

Davidson rejects the Pauline authorship of the *Epistle to the Ephesians*, although he says, "Antiquity is agreed in assigning the epistle to Paul." He thinks it, like Colossians, "originated in the Gnostic period between 130 and 140 A. D." # But Renan thinks that, although Paul himself did not write or dictate this letter, yet "it was composed while he was yet alive, under his eyes, in his name"—or, at least, this "is not to be declared improbable. Paul, a prisoner at Rome, might commisson Tychicus to go and visit the churches of

---

* Davidson's "Introduction," i, pp. 149-155.
† Ibid., vol. ii, pp. 170-194.
‡ Renan's "St. Paul," pp. 11-13.
# Davidson's "Introduction," ii, pp. 195-230.

Asia, giving him several letters, the Epistle to the Colossians, the note to Philemon, and the Epistle, now lost, to the Laodiceans.

"He might also give him copies of a sort of *circular letter*, with the name of the church left blank, which would be the so-called Epistle to the Ephesians. In going to Ephesus, Tychicus might show this unsealed letter to the Ephesians, and we may suppose the latter took one copy of it, or transcribed its contents." *

Thus, then, it appears that according to all the ablest and most radical critics we have at least four epistles which are the real works of St. Paul, while six others are accepted as the Apostle's productions by many of the advanced critics, and even those who reject them as St. Paul's works admit that they were written in or near his time, and contain the real apostolic tradition, and this is all-sufficient for our purpose.

It is not necessary to discuss in this connection the other epistles, save that to the Hebrews, which is undoubtedly not the work of St. Paul. Both external and internal evidences prove this. "The writings of the Apostolic fathers are silent on this point," and " the epistle was not considered apostolic till the fourth century, when it first obtained a canonical position and was assigned to Paul." The internal evidence against the Pauline authorship is thus summarized by Dr. Davidson:

1. It has no title. "The name of the writer does not appear, contrary to Paul's method." 2. "The manner in which the Old Testament is quoted differs from the Pauline." 3. "The writer betrays an imper-

---

* Renan's "St. Paul," p. 18.

fect knowledge of the tabernacle and the temple—a thing that could not be asserted of Paul, who lived in Jerusalem for a considerable time." 4. According to ii, 3, the writer was not an Apostle; but had received the gospel from early witnesses." 5. "The hermeneutical principles of the epistle differ from Paul's. In allegorizing the Old Testament, the author goes much further than the Apostle." 6. "The doctrinal system of the Epistle to the Hebrews, though based upon Paulinism, is worked out in a different way, and assumes another form." 7. "The phraseology and style of the epistle are different from Paul's." He thinks, with Archdeacon Farrar, that Apollos was the author, and "the letter was probably written A. D. 66." *

I have included this epistle in my enumeration and discussion of the New Testament books, because it gives the correct view of the Atonement, as we shall see, and, although not the work of St. Paul, it is a production of the Apostolic age, and is just as truly inspired as it would be if St. Paul had written it.

The Book of Revelation is almost universally ascribed to St. John the Apostle. Baur says: "Not long after the Apostle Paul left the sphere of his labors at Ephesus, we meet the Apostle John at the same place. The Apocalypse (Revelation) was written, according to its own statement, at or near Ephesus," and by St. John.†

Dr. Davidson gives us a good summary of the external evidence in proof of the Johannine authorship of this book, the most satisfactory of which is Justin Mar-

---

* Davidson's "Introduction," ii, pp. 177-289; Farrar's "Early Days of Christianity," i, pp. 247-480—especially chap. xvii.

† Baur's "Church History," i, pp. 86, 153.

tyr's testimony to it. "There was a certain man with us," he says, "whose name was John, one of the Apostles of Christ, who prophesied by a Revelation that was made to him, that those who believed in our Christ would dwell a thousand years in Jerusalem" (Rev., xx, 4, 5).* "It is an undoubted fact," adds Davidson, "that from the middle of the second century, several distinguished fathers connected with the church in Asia Minor, who had excellent opportunities of knowing the prevailing traditions there, received the work as an authentic document of John's."

But he goes on to ask—and here I quote him at length—"Does *internal* evidence coincide with the external as regards authorship? In four places John calls himself the author (i, 1, 4, 9; xxii, 8). He speaks of himself like Daniel, 'I, John.' He treats of the Apostolic age, when Jewish ideas prevailed and the expectation of Messiah was fresh in the general mind. A book bearing his name, and composed thirty years before his death, would have called forth a contradiction (if it had not been his), and such contradiction would have reached us from the circle of his disciples through Irenæus." The contents of the book agree with the assumption that it proceeds from an apostolic man:

1. Its *Eschatology*, or "doctrine of the last things," is apostolic. "The idea of their Lord's speedy coming (to judgment) had made a deep impression on the minds of the Apostles." And this idea is present in the Apocalypse, although "John puts a wide interval between the manifestation of Messiah and the end of the world—the space of a thousand years."

---

* "Dialogue with Trypho," chap. lxxxi.

2. In like manner the *Christology* (doctrine concerning Christ) of the Apocalypse "contains apostolic elements."

3. "The conception of *Antichrist* also harmonizes with apostolic times. The name of this power does not appear in the book, but the idea is found in a concrete form."

4. "The *Pneumatology* (doctrine concerning spirits) of Revelation agrees with that of the apostolic writings. The power of the devil in relation to the kingdom of Christ is presented under the same aspect in the Apocalypse and Paul's Epistles. . . . As far as the individuality of John is reflected in the New Testament and tradition, it is in harmony with the contents of the Apocalypse. The sons of Zebedee were impetuous spirits, whose feelings led them easily into excess or revenge. They wished to call down fire from heaven to consume the inhabitants of a Samaritan village, and begged the chief places in the kingdom of heaven. John forbade one who presumed to cast out devils in the name of Jesus (Luke, ix, 54; Matthew, xx, 20-24; Mark, ix, 38). He was a Boanerges, or 'Son of Thunder,' with a decided individuality and an ardent disposition requiring checks (Mark, iii).

5. "As far as he appears in the *Acts* and Pauline *Epistles*, his mind is somewhat narrow, unemancipated from national prejudice." He observed Easter on the day of the Jewish Passover, and tradition says that "he was a priest and wore the sacerdotal plate." This agrees with the priestly particulars in the seven epistles (Revelation, ii, 3). "After removing to Asia Minor, he is described as indignantly contending against false teachers, both Jewish and Gentile. Irenæus states from

Polycarp that the Apostle, going into a bath on one occasion, discovered (the heretic) Cerinthus there, and leaping out of it, hastened away, saying he was afraid of the building falling upon him and crushing him with the heretic.* These traits are faithfully reflected in the book before us, which betrays an impassioned spirit full of rage against the despisers of God and his Anointed, with images of dragons, murder, blood and fire, vials of wrath. The souls of martyrs invoke vengeance on their persecutors; and all heaven is summoned to rejoice over the downfall of Babylon." Both Baur and Davidson think that St. John belonged to the Jewish party that opposed St. Paul so strongly (Galatians, ii, and Acts xv), and verse second of chapter second (Revelation), which speaks of "them which say they are apostles and are not," is supposed to refer to St. Paul. Various other arguments are advanced by these authors to prove that St. John was the author of the Revelation, and wrote it "between" June, A. D. 68, "when Nero (Roman emperor) died, and January, A. D. 69, when Galba was murdered," and these arguments seem conclusive.†

We come now to the most difficult and the most important question of this section, namely, the origin of the *Gospels*.

The first fact which must be clearly and fully grasped is that *our Gospels are only four of many accounts of our Lord's life which were produced, but most of which are now lost.* The author of the third Gospel assures us that "many" had taken in hand to set forth in or-

---

* "Against Heresies," Book III, chap. iii, § 4.
† Davidson, "Introduction," i, pp. 240–301. Cf. Farrar's "Early Days of Christianity," vol. ii, Book V, pp. 103–335; "Supernatural Religion," vol. ii, pp. 388–409.

der a declaration of those things which were believed among the disciples, and so it seemed good to him also to write what had been delivered unto him from the beginning by eye-witnesses and ministers of the word (Luke, i, 1–3). Of these "many" narratives we have at least fragments preserved in the writings of the early fathers, the most notable of which is that called the "*Gospel of the Hebrews.*" "The Gospel of the Hebrews," says Dr. Keim, "the existence of which at the end of the second century is attested, and traces of which are to be found at least as far back as the middle of that century, runs remarkably parallel to our first Gospel. Coming a hundred times in contact with the latter, written in Hebrew, tenaciously adhered to by the believing and tradition-observing Jews as the true and only Gospel, rather as the genuine Gospel of the Apostle Matthew, it has from the time of Jerome (fourth century) downward to Lessing, Baur, and Hilgenfeld, often been regarded as, or conjectured to be, the true original Matthew. On the other hand, and especially by modern criticism, this view has been combated and the work has been shown to be a later production derived from our existing Matthew." *

"Several fragments of a '*Gospel of the Egyptians*' have been preserved, chiefly by Clement of Alexandria, and in the second Epistle of Clement of Rome; † it must, therefore, have existed tolerably early, at any rate as early as the middle of the second century. The Gospel of the Egyptians is the work of a gloomy, self-

---

* Keim's "Jesus of Nazara." vol. i, pp. 40–44.

† "Ante-Nicene Fathers," vol. ii. pp. 392, etc.; Clement's "Stromata," iii, chap. ix.

mortifying ascetic, and the early Church rejected it on account of its asceticism and its obscure mysteries." *
Then there are the Apocryphal or spurious Gospels,† which are merely corrupt and perverted versions of our Gospels. The most important of these are: "*The Gospel of James*," the "*Gospel of Thomas*," and the "*Acts of Pilate*," which date back to the second century. "*The Gospel of James*" narrates the two miraculous births, that of Mary herself, and that of Jesus, in a medley of beautiful and revolting fancies.‡

"Thomas" unfolds the miraculous world of the childhood and boyhood of Jesus, who, in this book, altogether ceases to be human. # "The Acts of Pilate," following our Gospels, John inclusive, narrates the condemnation of the Innocent One, for whom Pilate and the Roman ensigns, the sick who had been healed, friends and foes, all plead; then come the resurrection and the ascension, the reality of which occurrence is attested by witnesses of every kind, even by Annas and Caiaphas. ‖

The *Gospel of the pseudo-Matthew*, which appeared in the time of Jerome, and "*the 'History of Joseph the Carpenter,'* bring us down much later—at the earliest, in the fifth century." △

Now, when we consider that the age immediately succeeding that of the Apostles—i. e., the second century —saw the birth of so much spurious literature; when we remember, further, that even in the apostolic age, according to Luke, "many" accounts of the Master's life were written, we are at once forced to the signifi-

---

* Keim, *ut supra*. † "Ante-Nicene Fathers," vol. viii.
‡ Ibid., vol. viii. pp. 361-367. # Ibid., vol. viii, pp. 395-398.
‖ Ibid., vol. viii. pp. 416-458.
△ Keim, "Jesus of Nazara," vol. i, pp. 46, 47.

cant conclusion that our four Gospels are mere "survivals of the fittest," *according to the judgment of that age*. They are the result of a process of sifting and selection from a great mass of materials more or less corrupt. But, not only are they simply four of "many" Gospels; they were not gathered into one volume or Canon until the *latter half of the second century*. Up to that time the various books of the New Testament were preserved by the different congregations and "sects" to whom they were addressed or who had secured them; and it is hard to say on what *principles*, if any, the originators of the Canon proceeded: circumstances ruled. In the second half of the second century there was a "Canon of the New Testament," consisting of two parts, called *the Gospel*, and *the Apostle*.

The first was complete, containing the four Gospels alone; the second, which was incomplete, contained the Acts of the Apostles, and Epistles—i. e., thirteen letters of St. Paul, one of Peter, one of John and the Revelation. How and where this Canon originated is uncertain.* Possibly the birthplace was Asia Minor, but this is by no means certain. It is a fact, however, that Irenæus and other fathers had a Canon which they considered Apostolic. Even in the fourth century the Epistles of James and Jude, the second of Peter, and the second and third of John were not universally received as canonical works.† But slowly they were all adopted by various councils.

It thus appears that each one has to review for himself the external and internal evidences in favor of

---

* "Encyclopædia Britannica," article "Canon."
† Eusebius, "Ecclesiastical History," Book III, chap. xxv.

the genuineness and authenticity of the books of the
New Testament, and accept or reject them according
to the strength or weakness of such evidences. It may
be said just here, "The men of the time of Irenæus
ought to know better than we what were genuine and
authentic writings and what were not." But obviously
we must consider their *critical powers* and know *why*
and *how* they were led to adopt such and such opinions.
Unfortunately, they are known to be men of very weak
judgment, who accepted the miraculous as a matter of
course, and attributed writings to the Apostles on very
slender grounds. Thus Irenæus, in an oft-quoted passage, says: "It is not possible that the Gospels can be
more or fewer than they are. For, since there are four
zones of the world in which we live and four principal
winds, while the church is scattered throughout all the
world, and the pillar and ground of the church is the
Gospel, it is fitting that she should have four pillars
breathing out immortality," etc. "Now" (Strauss long
ago remarked) "this strange mode of proof is not
indeed to be understood in the sense that the circumstances so stated constituted the reason why Irenæus
adopted neither more nor fewer Gospels; on the contrary, these four had already achieved a position of preeminent credit in the circles of the Catholic Church,
striving as it was after catholic unity, and it was this
position, thus already given which Irenæus sought to
justify according to the spirit of his age; but it is precisely in this explanation that we recognize a *spirit*
entirely alien to that of our own time—to that of intelligent or reasonable criticism."* Surely men permeated

---

* Strauss's "Life of Jesus," English translation, vol. i, p. 57.

by a spirit which could entertain such fancies were most uncritical. But, however much we may suppose that men in their position *ought* to have known, yet there is ample reason to suspect their knowledge.

As a matter of fact (and this is a third point even more important than the fact that the Gospels are "survivals of the fittest," selections from "many" gospels, which assumed their present shape about the end of the second century), we know that *none of the fathers before Irenæus explicitly refers to our Gospels, and attributes them to the persons whose names they bear*. Let us examine the so-called "Apostolic Fathers" in order:

First, We find in the writings of Clement of Rome, Polycarp, Irenæus, and Barnabas, composed during the first quarter of the second century, many references to and some plain quotations from *some* documents or traditionary accounts of our Lord's life, but none of these fathers *explicitly* attributes such documents to Matthew, Mark, Luke, or John.

Second. Papias, who probably wrote his "Exposition of the Oracles of the Lord" between 125 and 150 A. D., is the first one who explicitly attributes any writings to Matthew or Mark. He says: "Mark having become the interpreter of Peter, wrote down accurately whatsoever he remembered. It was not, however, in the exact order that he related the sayings or deeds of Christ, for he neither heard the Lord nor accompanied Him. But afterward, as I said, he accompanied Peter, who accommodated his instructions to the necessities of his hearers, but with no intention of giving a regular narrative of the Lord's sayings. Wherefore Mark made no mistake in thus writing some things as he remembered them. For of one thing he took especial care, not to omit anything he had heard, and not to put anything fictitious into the statements."

Of Matthew this father says: "Matthew put together the oracles (speeches) of the Lord in the Hebrew language, and each one interpreted them as best he could." * This passage can be better understood in connection with other quotations from later fathers. Irenæus tells us: "Matthew issued a written Gospel among the Hebrews in their own dialect, while Peter and Paul were preaching at Rome and laying the foundation of the Church. After their departure (decease), Mark, the disciple and interpreter of Peter, did also hand down to us in writing what had been preached by Peter." † This is plainly a repetition of Papias's opinion, and all subsequent notices are the same; but it is noteworthy that Irenæus and later fathers say that Mark wrote his Gospel *after* Peter's death; while Papias gives us to understand that he wrote it during the Apostle's *lifetime*. Indeed, some of the later fathers say that Peter authorized Mark's Gospel. But Dean Alford— a most conservative writer—unhesitatingly rejects this statement, "because no such authorization is apparent," and "had such been the case we should have found it called the Gospel according to *Peter*, not according to Mark." He thinks that the only inference that may be fairly drawn from this general tradition is "that Mark, from continual intercourse with and listening to Peter, and possibly from preservation of many of his narratives entire, may have been able, after his death,

---

* "Ante-Nicene Fathers," vol. i, p. 155.
† "Against Heresies," Book III, chap. i.

or at all events when separated from him, to preserve in his Gospel those vivid and original touches of description and filling out of the incidents which we now discover in it. Further than this (he adds) I do not think we are authorized in assuming, and even this is *conjecture only.*" *

Owing to the great varieties of the tradition concerning Mark's Gospel, I think we can not attach much importance to it. Dr. Davidson's estimate of it seems just. " A careful examination of Papias's testimony (he says) shows that it does not relate to our present Gospel, nor bring Mark into connection with its author. All we learn from it is, that Mark wrote notes of a Gospel which was not our Canonical one." Papias says Mark related the sayings of Christ "*not in order.*" " The opposite of 'not in order,' " says Davidson, " is *arrangement.* But this statement is not applicable to our present Gospel of Mark, for every one sees that Mark *did* write an arranged work, like Matthew's and Luke's. The difficulty of reconciling this testimony with the condition of the present Gospel is therefore palpable." †
Hence we conclude that the earliest tradition concerning Mark's writing a Gospel shows at most only that *he made notes of Peter's sermons which were subsequently worked over by an unknown author and incorporated into our present Gospel which was attributed as a whole to Mark.* What Papias says about Matthew does not prove that he wrote our "Matthew," for two cogent reasons:

---

* Alford's Greek Testament, vol. i, Prolegomena, chap. iii, § 2, pp. 34, 35.
† Davidson's " Introduction," pp. 533-584.

First, he merely states that Matthew " put together the *speeches* of the Lord," probably the Sermon on the Mount and such like (Matthew v–vii, etc.), but our present Gospel contains many *narratives* as well as speeches.

Secondly, Papias, says "Matthew wrote in the *Hebrew* (i. e., Aramaic) language," but our Gospel is written in *Greek*, and even Dean Alford does not believe that it is a translation of the Hebrew Matthew. The passage in Irenæus about Matthew is also a mere repetition of Papias, as are the other early patristic traditions.

" The earliest Apostolic Fathers have no quotation from the *Gospel according to Luke*, nor any express allusion to it. In Clement's *Epistle to the Corinthians* (chapter xii), a place resembling Luke vi, 36–38 in some respects, differs from it and all the gospel parallels so much, that it seems to have been taken from tradition. Hermas contains no allusion to it; and Papias does not seem to have been acquainted with it. The Ignatian Epistles show no trace of acquaintance with our Gospel. The *Epistle of Polycarp to the Philippians* has one passage (chapter ii), " Remembering what the Lord has taught us, saying, ' Judge not, and ye shall not be judged; forgive, and ye shall be forgiven; be ye merciful, and ye shall obtain mercy; for with the same measure that ye mete withal it shall be measured to you again,' in which both Matthew and Luke's Gospels may have been used, the former more closely than the latter." * We come now to the testimony of Justin Martyr, middle of the second century. In his writings

---

* Davidson's " Introduction," vol. i, pp 443, 444.

there are numerous quotations from and references to either our Gospels of Matthew, Mark, and Luke, or to their originals, and he explicitly mentions " memoirs which were drawn up by the Apostles and those who followed with them." * He also says that these memoirs were " called Gospels," but he does *not* say that Matthew, Mark, and Luke wrote them. True; when he speaks of the memoirs having been composed " by Apostles and those who followed with them," we, believing that Mark and Luke followed with Apostles, naturally think of them, and yet we may be utterly mistaken. For, while Justin *may* have referred to our present Gospels, it is obvious that he may have referred to *their originals*—to the " notes " of Mark, " the speeches " recorded by Matthew and other apostolic or post-apostolic traditions or narratives. This opinion is strengthened by the fact that Justin evidently had other documents before him when he wrote the " Dialogue " and " Apology," which he considered of equal authority with the " Memoirs." Thus, he tells us that Jesus was born in a *cave*, which contradicts Luke ii, 12, 16; that when He was baptized, " a fire was kindled in the Jordan "; and, finally, that he was in the habit of working as a carpenter when among men, making plows and yokes." †

These statements are all entirely different from the Gospel notices of the same events, and indicate a different source; and Strauss's opinion that they are taken from the " Gospel to the Hebrews " seems quite credible. Hence we seem forced to the conclusion that, if

---

* " Dialogue with Trypho," chap. ciii, First Apology, chap. xvi, etc.

† Ibid., chaps. lxxviii, lxxxviii.

Justin used our Gospels, he also used other documents which he considered of equal authority with them, but it is more probable that he used the originals of our Gospels. At any rate, he does not *explicitly* ascribe the Gospels to those whose names they bear, and this is the important fact to be remembered. We may attempt, with Canon Westcott and others, to show that he did not do this because of the peculiar circumstances under which he wrote; but the *fact* remains that neither Justin nor any other of the Apostolic fathers explicitly ascribes our Gospels to Matthew, Mark, and Luke.*

We seem, therefore, to be driven to this conclusion: While the Gospels contain much of the real apostolic tradition about Jesus, yet we do not and can not know exactly who wrote that tradition, and the Gospels assumed their present shape so slowly and gradually that some unhistorical elements *may* have been incorporated in the narratives. The oldest part of the Gospels is doubtless that which is common to them all—that which has been aptly called "the Triple Tradition." This probably includes the "speeches" recorded by Matthew, the "notes" of Mark and Luke, and other traditions which were circulated among the early disciples. Those parts which are peculiar to each Gospel as it now stands were additions of the later or latest *rédacteurs*. The opinion I hold, then, is that the authors of our Gospels drew what is common to them from the same source; but whether that was a written document, or an oral tradition *stereotyped in a certain form*, or *both*, I do

---

* See Westcott on the Canon—part referring to Justin; and Dr. George P. Fisher's "Grounds of Theistic and Christian Belief," p. 191, etc.

not know, and it is not necessary to stop to consider. It thus appears that the earliest and most important external evidence is *not sufficient to prove* that Matthew, Mark, and Luke wrote the Gospels which bear their names; the most it can do is to create a *probability* that these evangelists made certain " notes " on our Lord's life and teaching, which formed the basis of our present Gospels which were finally ascribed as a whole to these evangelists.

The *internal* evidence leads to the same conclusion. Dr. Davidson points out that, in " Matthew," "some things are put in a wrong order, and are therefore chronologically incorrect"; "things are related in a way which shows a mixture of later traditions"; "certain events, for instance the feeding of the five and the four thousand, are doubled, as the facts are substantially the same, the minor circumstances alone being different"; and, finally, " it contains unhistorical and mythical elements. The most palpable example of this is in chap. xxvii, 52, where we are told that, at the expiration of Jesus the graves were opened, and many bodies of the saints who slept arose, came out of their resting-places after the resurrection of their Lord, and even went into the holy city, where they appeared to many. The apocryphal nature of this account is apparent." *

The author, in these last words, expresses the real characteristics of the Gospels which throw suspicion upon their historical value; and M. Renan takes the straightforward course when he unhesitatingly declares that "it is evident that the Gospels are in part legendary, since they are full of miracles and the supernatu-

---

* Davidson's " Introduction," i. pp. 386-392.

ral."* All minor objections to their historical character, such as the reduplication of events, the contradictions in the genealogies, etc., might receive more or less satisfactory answers;† but the great difficulty lies in the narratives of miracles. Undoubtedly, if we were to find such narratives in the Sacred Books of India—in any *other* documents than our Bible—we should unhesitatingly set them aside as legends; but, having been taught that the Bible is the infallible word of God, that Christ was God, and that "with God all things are possible," we accept without question the narratives of miracles found in this Book. But our age insists that the very same objections apply to the Bible-miracles that are applicable to other miracles; in other words, *all* miracles must be proved by unimpeachable evidence before they can be accepted, and all narratives of miracles must be subjected to a most rigid examination, *while the very fact that they narrate miracles casts suspicion upon their historical character.* We demand the same sort and amount of external evidence to prove the authenticity of documents narrating miracles that we require to prove miracles themselves. This is what our age insists upon, and there is no use in denouncing those who hold this view; there is no use in accusing them of being influenced by a false philosophy or immoral motives, for the latter charge is certainly false in many cases, while the former is hardly less so, since the question is, What is false philosophy? Is that a false philosophy which insists on treating all documents alike before they are proved to be different in origin and na-

---

* Renan, "Life of Jesus," p. 17.
† Alford, "Greek Testament," i, Prolegomena, chap. i, § 4, etc.

ture? Surely not; and this is all that Biblical critics do. They freely grant the *a priori* possibility of miracles, but they insist that any given case of miracle must be *proved*, and they further urge that it is simply a dictate of common sense that *an extraordinary event must be substantiated by an extraordinary amount of evidence.* Can this be done in the case of all the Gospel miracles? This question will be answered later on. Meanwhile I may remark that it is now evident why it is so important to know who wrote the Gospels, when they were written, and under what circumstances. If we had sufficient evidence to show that *eye-witnesses* wrote the narratives of miracles found in the Gospels; if we knew that such witnesses were men of acute *critical* powers, who could not easily be deceived; and, finally, if we were shown that the miracles were of such a character that *no cause recognized by natural science could explain them*, then we might not hesitate to accept the narratives as authentic. To make myself sufficiently clear, I will add: If the earliest Fathers—Clement of Rome, Polycarp, Barnabas, Papias, and Justin—had told us that eye-witnesses of the miracles wrote the Gospels, and if they had also given us a sketch of their intellectual and moral characters, showing them to be men of acute critical powers, who accepted the said miracles only after thoroughly examining their nature and cause, I would consider such evidence " sufficient," at least for myself; but it must be plain, from the foregoing sketch of patristic testimony, that these Fathers do *not* furnish us such evidence. It rather appears that it is quite possible, at least, that the narratives of miracles, for the most part, are after-additions to and embellishments of mere "notes" which Matthew, and probably Mark and Luke—the latter at second-hand—made upon our Lord's life; which " notes," so far as we know, did not contain accounts of miracles. *This possibility is itself sufficient to prevent us from insisting on accepting the miracles as an article of faith*, a *sine qua non of church-membership.*

It will be observed that I have not attempted to assign any definite *date* to either one of our first three Gospels. I have not done so—

First, because it seems impossible to ascertain the exact dates of these writings. Every author has his own estimate, and, where "doctors" thus disagree, it behooves us to hesitate.

Secondly, it is not at all necessary to my purpose to ascertain such dates. The Gospels were doubtless composed within a *century* after the death of our Lord; and it matters not whether any one of them was written before the destruction of Jerusalem or not, at least so far as the conclusions of this book are concerned. Probably Matthew made his "notes" before the year 70, and Mark and Luke made theirs some time between that disastrous year and the year 100 A. D. And subsequent *rédacteurs* may have filled up their outlines. At any rate, this is about the author's view; but, whether it be accepted or not, it is hoped that the slow and gradual formation of the Gospel narratives has been sufficiently proved, while it is absolutely certain that the traditional view rests on a foundation of sand.*

It will also be observed that I have thus far spoken of the first three Gospels alone, and have ignored the "*Gospel according to John.*" I have done this because

---

* See "Supernatural Religion," vol. i, part ii.

the latter differs in many respects from the former, and it is customary to consider this Gospel apart from the others. It would, of course, be folly to attempt, in this connection, a full discussion of the origin and authorship of this Gospel, for hundreds of volumes have been written on this subject. I must, therefore, merely express my opinion, giving three or four reasons only for such an opinion, and refer the reader to the large treatises which have been written on this question.

I think, then, after considering with an unbiased mind the arguments *pro* and *con*, that the Johannine authorship of the Fourth Gospel is "*not proven.*" In the first place, none of the earliest Fathers—those already quoted—ascribe the Gospel to John, and their alleged references to or quotations from it are not even so clear as those to the other Gospels. It is not expressly ascribed to John until between the years 160 A. D. and 200, when the Muratorian Fragment mentions it and Irenæus says, "John, the disciple of the Lord, who also had leaned upon His breast, did himself publish a Gospel during his residence at Ephesus, in Asia Minor." *

" The testimony of this Father is thought to be weighty because of his early relation to the Church of Asia Minor, and to Polycarp. It should be noticed, however, that he does not appeal to Polycarp as a voucher for the Johannine authorship of the Gospel, nor to any disciple of John. The relation of Irenæus to Polycarp and the Church of Asia Minor does not seem to have been intimate. He was only a *boy* when he listened to Polycarp's sayings relative to Christ, which were taken from Apostolic tradition." And the author

---

* "Against Heresies," Book III, chap. i.

just quoted shows that Irenæus made "mistakes" about John's writings, and "confounded his own notions and inferences with facts." †

Secondly, the author of the Book of Revelation (St. John) *could not* have written the fourth Gospel, *because the two books are absolutely contradictory in spirit and style.* We have seen that the author of the Apocalypse was a real "Son of Thunder," who breathes out threatenings and slaughter against "those who say they are apostles and are not"; while the key-note to John's Gospel and Epistles is, "My little children, *love* one another." In the one book the Apostle appears as he did in real life—a Boanerges, calling down fire from heaven upon the enemies of the Lord; in the other, he appears as the "Disciple of Love," leaning on the Master's bosom and exhorting his fellow-Christians to love one another. It requires no specially acute critical powers to perceive this very striking contrast between the Apocalypse and the Gospel. The ordinary lay reader will observe it. But it may be said that the Apostle's nature may have undergone a *development* in grace during the interval between the writing of the Apocalypse and the Gospel. *If so, such a development was simply miraculous.* The Apostle must have been past middle life—perhaps sixty years old—when he wrote the Revelation, and a man's style is so thoroughly settled at this time of life that it would be a psychological impossibility that he should change as profoundly as the Apostle must have changed if he wrote the Gospel during the short period of fifteen or twenty years which are supposed to have intervened

---

* Davidson's "Introduction," ii, p. 389.

between the composition of the two books in question. The more one considers this argument, the more thoroughly convinced will he become that the author of the Revelation and the author of the Gospel are not the same person.

Thirdly, there is at least one story in this Gospel which St. John could never have written—which is clearly a later addition—viz., the story of the resurrection of Lazarus. Of all the miracles which Jesus is said to have wrought, this is unquestionably the greatest, and yet *neither " Matthew," " Mark," nor " Luke " has one word to say about it.* Why this remarkable omission? the thoughtful reader must ask. Surely this miracle was a greater display of superhuman or divine power than any other which Jesus is said to have wrought—than the raising of the boy at Nain, for instance, and yet neither of the first three Gospels mentions it. The various attempts of commentators to remove this difficulty are thoroughly unsatisfactory.

Thus M. Godet, one of the ablest defenders of the old view, holds that the omission was due, first, to the *gradual* formation of the Gospel-tradition; and, secondly, to consideration of the feelings and position of the family at Bethany. According to this author, there were three streams of tradition, which united to form the Gospels: First, "that started by the Apostles themselves, and this probably constituted the permanent and universal stock of oral evangelization and passed in a tolerably uniform manner into the written tradition, into our synoptic Gospels." Secondly, " other stories were started by those members of the church who had either been subjects or witnesses of the facts. These coming more or less accidentally to the knowledge of the writers of the Gospels, formed the special treasure of each of our synoptics." Finally, other stories " were purposely and at first withdrawn from public narration, or were only included in it with a certain reserve of names and things." The resurrection of Lazarus, M. Godet claims, belonged to the third class of stories. "There was a feeling that the home at Bethany, that sanctuary still inhabited by the family into whose intimacy the Lord had been received, should be respected in public teaching and in the preaching of the gospel within the churches." It seems incredible that M. Godet should have been able to persuade even himself that such an explanation is tenable; for, in the first place, it was *impossible* that so marvelous an event as this should have been kept a secret, and, according to the narrative itself, numbers flocked from Jerusalem to Bethany to see the resurrected Lazarus (John, xii, 9). It would seem, therefore, that the notoriety and danger of the family could not have been much increased by the writers of the Gospels recording this event some thirty or forty years after its occurrence. Secondly, as just intimated, even if the alleged reserve had been possible and necessary during the first few years of apostolic preaching, it was certainly *not* necessary when the synoptic Gospels were written, for the home at Bethany was then probably completely broken up. While, therefore, " the mention or omission of a single miracle performed by the Lord is," in most cases, " too accidental a circumstance " to be specially noticed, yet the omission of *such* a miracle by the earliest narrators, when there was every reason why it should be recorded, is wholly inexplicable, and proves conclusively that they knew nothing about it. And since this is so;

since Matthew—who, according to the popular view, wrote the first Gospel, and must have been among the disciples who witnessed the resurrection of Lazarus (John, xii, 6, 8, 16), or at least must have heard of this event from those who were present if it ever happened—since this Apostle, as well as "Mark" and "Luke," has said nothing about this wonderful event, why should John? It is incredible that the first three Evangelists should have ignored this miracle if it were ever wrought. Their silent protest against the truth of this story, as well as its apostolic authorship, is fatal. But, if the writer fabricated this narrative, surely we must hesitate to trust him implicitly in other narratives.

Hence we conclude that the fourth Gospel was written many years after St. John's death, and merely attributed to him by tradition, in order to give it authority in the Church.

Finally, the fourth Gospel is a peculiarly *doctrinal* and not an historical treatise, as is evidenced not simply by its opening words, but by its general tone—the sixth chapter, and so on. And its doctrines about the "Word" indicate its source. It was evidently written by a philosopher who belonged to the school of Philo. He may have been a disciple of St. John, who, after the Apostle's death, became to him what Plato did to Socrates—an expounder of his master's doctrines in his own language and style; but this exposition almost amounts to a *perversion*, since he makes the bigoted Jew, who wrote the Revelation—who was a "pillar" of Jewish orthodoxy and narrowness (Galatians, ii, 9)—talk most liberally about "other sheep, not of this (Jewish) fold" (x, 16, etc.), and so on. The catholicity—the Gentilism—of the author of John's Gospel equals that of

St. Paul, if it does not surpass it. But the main indication of the authorship is to be found in the doctrine of "the Word." This is merely an advance—but it *is* an advance—on Philo's doctrine; and hence while this Gospel may have been written by an elder or member of the Ephesian Church, who claimed to set forth St. John's doctrines in a philosophic form, yet it "could not have been written by John, or even read aloud to him after it had been written." *

Of course, all the foregoing arguments, as well as others, against the Johannine authorship of the fourth Gospel, have been considered by such writers as M. Godet, Dr. Fisher, etc. Godet's argument, especially, in favor of the traditional view, is quite conclusive against *special* theories of certain critics; but, after considering his argument carefully and candidly, I am forced to say that it does not seem to me to affect the main contention of the critics. While he proves very clearly, for instance, that the date of the composition of the Gospel which Baur or even Hilgenfeld assigns (A. D. 160-170 and 130-140 respectively) is too late; while he shows that it was in *existence* at least as early as the middle of the second century (this, of course, does not prove that St. John wrote it); while he even proves that *too much* stress has been laid by different critics on alleged non-Johannine characteristics, the Logos-idea, etc.—yet his attempted refutation of the foregoing (four) arguments is not conclusive, and nothing he says prevents one from holding that a Philonic disci-

---

* Rev. H. R. Haweis's "Christ and Christianity, Story of the Four," p. 103, etc—an eloquent and, on the whole, a satisfactory work.

ple of St. John may have written this Gospel between the beginning and the middle of the second century.*

But, lest any one should think that the establishment of the non-apostolic authorship of the Gospels is *necessary* to the main argument of this book—especially the discussion of miracles which follows—I shall quote and comment upon a very pregnant sentence of Prof. Huxley's which was called forth during his controversy with the Rev. Dr. Wace. He expresses an anxiety to "get rid of the common assumption that the determination of the authorship and of the dates of these works" (the Gospels) "is a matter of fundamental importance. That assumption is based upon the notion that what contemporary witnesses say must be true, or at least has always a *prima facie* claim to be so regarded; so that if the writers of any of the Gospels were contemporaries of the events (and still more if they were in the position of eye-witnesses), the miracles they narrate must be historically true. . . . But the story of the 'Translation of the Blessed Martyrs Marcellinus and Petrus' (to which endless additions might be made from the fathers and the mediæval writers) yields, in my judgment, satisfactory proof that, where the miraculous is concerned, neither considerable intellectual ability, nor undoubted honesty, nor knowledge of the world, nor proved faithfulness as civil historians, nor profound piety, on the part of eye-witnesses and contemporaries, affords any guarantee of the objective truth of their statements, when we know that a firm belief in the miraculous was ingrained in their minds, and

---

* See "Supernatural Religion," vol. ii, Part III.

was the presupposition of their observations and reasonings." *

For such reasons I said above: "If we had sufficient evidence to show that eye-witnesses wrote the narratives of miracles found in the Gospels; if we knew that such men were of acute critical powers who could not easily be deceived; and, finally, if it were shown that the miracles were of such a character that no cause recognized by natural science could explain them, then we might not hesitate to accept the narratives as authentic." To draw out my meaning more fully, let us suppose that the Gospels were written by their traditional authors, and that Matthew and John, at least, were eye-witnesses of the events they record, then how many of the miracles they narrate would we be obliged to accept as really supernatural events?

Let it be remembered that the disciples were by no means "men of acute critical powers," so well versed in natural science that their testimony must be accepted as that of experts, who accepted the miraculous character of the events they record only after the most rigid and scientific examination of their nature and causes which precluded all confounding of natural and supernatural causes. They were simple Jews and Galileans, believing in the common occurrence of miracles, and judging every extraordinary event to be a miracle.

Hence I remark, first, we need not, as I shall show more fully in the next chapter, accept any of the *healings*, save perhaps one, as miracles, for medical science has long recognized natural causes which might have

---

* "Popular Science Monthly," August, 1889, pp. 457, 458; cf. September number of same review.

wrought them.* The exception alluded to is the cure of the man said to have been born blind (John ix). The sudden healing of the blind is quite common; † but the cure of one *born* blind by the methods said to have been adopted would be truly miraculous. Still, only those who believe in the *verbal* inspiration of Scripture need be troubled by the details given in this story—the parents' testimony, etc. If St. John wrote this account, a long time intervened between its original production and the production of the oldest manuscript we now possess—some two or three hundred years; and it is not unreasonable to suppose that a blind man was cured by Jesus, and that St. John recorded the fact, and that his account has been somewhat embellished by a later copyist.

It is well known, and admitted by all, that additions have thus arisen. For instance, John v, 4, even Alford grants, is a spurious later embellishment of the narrative; chapter xxi is also confessedly a late addition (Godet, Alford, etc.); and hence we need not be particularly troubled by minute details, but emphasize only the general facts, and, if so, the above explanation of the cure of the blind man is quite rational and credible. ‡

---

* See Tuke's "Influence of the Mind upon the Body," Part IV, etc.

† Tuke, ibid., pp. 446–449, etc.

‡ One of the most remarkable additions by a later copyist to an ancient manuscript is the well-known passage I John v, 7. "The spuriousness of that verse," says Archdeacon Farrar, "is as absolutely demonstrable as any critical conclusion can be"; and he gives facts and reasons which sustain his assertion. See his "Early Days of Christianity," vol. ii, p. 458, and other commentaries. Since, then, early manuscripts were so freely handled, it is hardly allowable to build whole pyramids of apologetics on a few words.

But, of course, this explanation gains strength when it is shown, as has been done, that the apostolic authorship of this Gospel is highly doubtful.

Secondly. Supposing the Gospels to have been written by their traditional authors, we are not obliged to accept the alleged *raisings of the dead* as truly miraculous events. In the case of Jairus's daughter the account itself (Matthew ix, 24) explicitly says that the maid was not dead but only asleep—i. e., in a trance or swoon. In the case of the boy at Nain (Luke, vii, 2–17) we have a story confessedly written by one who was not an apostle and an eye-witness, and we may rationally suppose that the same thing happened here as in Jairus's home. Even the resurrection of Lazarus need not be accepted as unquestionably a miraculous event— except, of course, by the verbal inspirationist—for in this case, also, it is, at first, said, "Lazarus sleepeth" (John, xi, 11), which, however, is subsequently explained (xi, 13, 14) to mean that he was really dead. But without by any means accepting M. Renan's disgusting account of the origin of this story, we might believe, supposing John to have written it, that Lazarus really did fall into a sleep or swoon, and remained so for two or three days; was buried in one of the rock-hewn sepulchres of the time (not in a grave dug in the ground, as among us); and was, like Jairus's daughter, awakened out of this trance by his Friend.

This story, as well as that in chapter ix, may have been slightly embellished by a subsequent copyist of St. John's manuscript. But, as stated above, I think that the silence of the other Gospel writers concerning this alleged event is utterly fatal to the truth and apostolic authorship of the story, and hence much suspicion is cast upon the whole Gospel narrative. But if St. John did witness and record this event, it certainly is not irrational, in view of the facts stated, to explain it as has been done.

Hence it appears, thirdly, that even granting the traditional authorship of the Gospels, the only miracles which necessarily bear a really supernatural appearance are the so-called *nature miracles*, such as the stilling of the tempest, the feeding of the five and the four thousand with the few loaves and fishes, and the conversion of water into wine; for although, as Prof. Huxley says, such a thing as turning water into wine is easily effected by scientific men, yet the simple Galileans at Cana were not scientists. If these events really happened, and were witnessed by the writers of the stories, it is very difficult, if not impossible, to give a natural explanation of them. But I shall offer in the next chapter a few considerations which I think explain the origin of these stories, without supposing the occurrence of such wonderful events. I have necessarily anticipated somewhat, because the question of the authorship of the Gospels is so intimately connected with the truth of the narratives of miracles which they contain, and the great importance of the subject must be my apology for such anticipation.

The *Acts of the Apostles* is generally attributed to Luke, but the following facts disprove this view:

1. The earliest (alleged) references in the writings of the Fathers are quite insufficient to prove that this book, at least as it now stands in the New Testament Canon, was written by Luke. The most satisfactory witness on this subject is, as in other cases, Justin Martyr, but not only does he fail to ascribe it expressly to Luke,

his alleged references to the *Acts* are more than doubtful.

The first Father who plainly asserts that Luke wrote the third Gospel and the Acts is Irenæus, close of the second century. The *existence*, however, of both the Gospel and the Acts, in substantially their present form, before this time—perhaps before the time of Justin—is satisfactorily established; but we are now more especially concerned with their *authorship*, and any one who will carefully examine the writings of the earliest Fathers must admit that the Lukan authorship of the books in question can not be proved from them.

2. The *internal* evidence indicates that the Gospel and the Acts were written after Luke's time. Whatever we may think of Baur's celebrated theory that Christianity arose according to the great "*law of development by antagonism*," yet we must admit that, as a matter of fact, two parties existed in the Apostolic Church—one, the Gentile party, headed by St. Paul, the other, or Jewish party, headed by Peter, James, and John—and between these two parties there raged an unceasing conflict over the observance of the Ceremonial Law of the Jewish Church. This is conclusively proved by the Epistle to the Galatians and the Acts. It is upon this fact that many modern critics base their view of the origin of Acts. They claim that it is plainly the work of one who wished to *conciliate* the two parties. Peter is made to speak like Paul, and Paul makes great concessions to Peter. Thus Peter preaches to the Gentiles, and defends his conduct in real Pauline language, before the "brethren" at Jerusalem (Acts, x, and xi, 19).

In the council which met to consider the question

of circumcising the Gentiles, we observe especially the conciliating spirit (Acts, xv). Peter opposes the imposition of "a yoke upon the neck of the disciples which neither the fathers nor they were able to bear"; and James, "the pillar" of Jewish orthodoxy, speaks to the same effect; while Paul is represented as deferring greatly to the judgment of "the pillars"; indeed, all through the Acts Paul is represented as a faithful Jew, who visits the holy city regularly, and by no means condemns the Ceremonial Law in unmeasured terms. He circumcised Timothy "because of the Jews" (Acts, xvi, 13); he purifies himself at Jerusalem, and pays the expenses of four Nazarites' offerings, lest he scandalize "the thousands of Jews" (Acts, xxi, 17–27). In short, Paul, the Apostle to the Gentiles and the strong opponent of Jewish ceremonies, in this book is made to "act as a pious Jew—nay, his relations with Jewish Christianity are of the friendliest sort. Immediately after his conversion he joins the disciples at Jerusalem, speaking boldly in the name of the Lord Jesus.

"He receives special commendation from the church of the metropolis and their chiefs when he goes thither the third time. At his fourth visit he salutes the Jerusalemite Church, and at his fifth he has a friendly reception, though prejudices are strong against him. His hostile relations toward Jewish Christians are passed over. Titus is unmentioned, though the Apostle had a dispute at Jerusalem on his account (Galatians, i, 3–5). In like manner Peter's appearance at Antioch and public rebuke are unnoticed (Galatians, ii, 11–21). It is impossible to suppose that this silence is other than intentional. A pious observer of the law could not be a strong opponent of Judaizing practices without obvious inconsistency. It is true that St. Paul became as a Jew to Jews (I Corinthians ix, 20); but that expression does not imply that he performed legal duties without a pressing necessity, or that he refrained from acting in accordance with his intense conviction of the law's invalidity. It does not consist with his performing or allowing circumcision, as the book of Acts represents him, because he himself makes circumcision incompatible with salvation by Christ" (Galatians v, 2). In other words, although St. Paul became "all things to all men," yet he never sacrified a *principle* in his lenient treatment of others. Hence, while the author of Acts rests his statements concerning our Apostle on one of his characteristics, he seems to have gone too far; he used this only as a clever mediator would use it.*

What, then, shall we think of the authorship of the third Gospel and of the Acts?

First. They were certainly written by the same person, as is proved not only by the opening words of Acts, but also by the fact that the diction and style of both are identical.

Secondly. He belongs to the Pauline party, as is evident from the great space which he devotes to St. Paul's history, and yet he was kindly disposed toward the Petrine or Jewish party, and desired the union of the two.

Thirdly. He was probably a Gentile of Asia Minor, for "a special interest in Asia Minor is betrayed in the Acts, inasmuch as apostolic persons of importance in the

---

* Davidson's "Introduction." vol. ii, pp. 86, 87, etc., and Zeller's "Acts of the Apostles," two vols.

traditions of Asia Minor are brought before us in the narrative of the Acts—as, for instance, John along with Peter (iii, 1; viii, 22); the evangelist Philip (vi, 5; viii, 5 *et seq.*; xxi, 8 *et seq.*) and Joseph Barabbas (i, 23); and, further, the Acts shows itself well informed respecting the political state of affairs here (and in Greece); and, finally, the scene of the greatest part of the narrative, precisely where the interest is principally of a geographical nature (xiii, 1; xxi, 16, the sketch of Paul's journeys) is laid in the regions of Asia Minor." * " Everywhere there is a wide sympathy with the Gentiles. The future of the Church is felt to lie with them. The author's respect for the Roman officials and the Roman government is quite Pauline. Gallio, the Corinthian town-clerk, the Roman soldiers, the Roman governors, even Felix and Agrippa, appear to advantage.

The Roman police and officers are kind to Paul, the judges are indulgent and conciliatory. One hears him gladly, another wishes to set him at liberty, a third wants a little bribe, but means no harm to Paul.†

All this points to a Gentile author, perhaps a native of Asia Minor. The *date* of the composition of the Acts can not be precisely ascertained, but it was written some time after the death of St. Paul and St. Peter, when the two parties had begun to long for unity and peace—i. e., some time between the years 75 and 125 A. D. This approximate date is all-sufficient for our purpose. Critics may fight about more exact dates. It remains to account for the ascription of these books to Luke, the comparatively obscure companion of St.

---

* Zeller's " Acts of the Apostles," vol. i, p. 77.
† Haweis, " Story of the Four," p. 132.

Paul. The explanation is probably to be found in the fact that Luke made certain "notes" on St. Paul's missionary journeys which the author of Acts used as the basis of his work. There are certain passages in the Acts (viz., xvi, 10-17; xx, 5-15; xxi, 1-18; xxvii, 1; xxviii, 16) in which the author speaks in the first person; "we" did thus and so, he says, and that pronoun "we" is supposed, by most writers, to prove that the author of the whole book was a companion of St. Paul, but obviously it can only prove that the author of the "*we-sections*" was a companion of the Apostle. He was doubtless Luke, and the author of Acts adopted and incorporated his "notes" into his work, which was ascribed as a whole to St. Paul's companion, and coming from such a source the book would of course have weight with both the Pauline and the Jewish party. M. Renan's remark that the author of a work so carefully prepared as the Acts evidently is would hardly have allowed the "we" to remain, is answered by the very fact that the Acts is a work "well prepared, composed with reflection, and even with art." The author *wished* his book to carry with it the authority of a companion of St. Paul.*

It is hoped that none will suppose that the foregoing sketch of the evidence of the genuineness and authenticity of the books in question pretends to be either original or exhaustive. Far from it! I have aimed merely to state briefly the conclusions of critical experts which seem to me to be valid, and to suggest lines of thought which the reader should follow out

---

* Renan, "The Apostles," p. 14.

by consulting such works as those appended to or quoted in this chapter.

The final result, then, of our consideration of the origin of the books of the New Testament—the conclusion that will be assumed as proved throughout this book—is that the ten epistles ascribed to St. Paul, especially those to the Romans, Corinthians, and Galatians, are his works; that the Revelation is St. John's; that the first three Gospels are *not* the works of Matthew, Mark, and Luke, but contain merely certain "notes" made by these disciples which were worked over by the authors of our Gospels some time between the years 70 and 125 A. D.; that the Gospel of John was written by a Philonic philosopher, probably a disciple of St. John at Ephesus, some time between the beginning and middle of the second century; that the Acts was written by a Gentile disciple in Asia Minor—perhaps at Ephesus—between the years 75 and 125 A. D., and was based on notes by St. Luke on St. Paul's missionary journeys.

Now, then, it may appear to some that this view completely destroys the *historic* value of the books in question. To which I would reply: Not at all; it merely destroys a false theory of inspiration—the verbal theory. It merely asserts that there may be some chaff mingled with the wheat which must be carefully separated from the wheat, but it declares emphatically that *the wheat is there.* Even the most radical skeptics admit that the books of the New Testament furnish us the *essential* facts of our Lord's life and teachings; that, notwithstanding the mist of legend which obscures the Sun of Righteousness, His form is clearly discernible by means of the glasses of criticism.

Thus Prof. Huxley says: "It may be said that critical skepticism carried to the length suggested is historical pyrrhonism; that if we are to altogether discredit an ancient or a modern historian because he has assumed fabulous matter to be true, it will be as well to give up paying attention to history. It may be said, and with great justice, that Eginhard's 'Life of Charlemagne' is none the less trustworthy because of the astounding revelation of credulity, of lack of judgment, and even of respect for the eighth commandment which he has unconsciously made in the 'History of the Translation of the Blessed Martyrs Marcellinus and Petrus.' The rule of common sense is, *prima facie*, to trust a witness in all matters in which neither his *self-interest*, his *passions*, his *prejudices*, nor that *love of the marvelous*, which is inherent to a greater or less degree in all mankind, are strongly concerned; and when they are involved, to require corroborative evidence in exact proportion to the contravention of probability by the thing testified." *

M. Renan says: "In nearly all ancient histories, even in those which are much less legendary than these (the Gospels), the details leave room for infinite doubt. When we have two accounts of the same act, it is extremely rare that the two accounts agree. We may say that among the anecdotes, the speeches, the celebrated sayings reported by historians, not one is rigorously authentic. Were there stenographers to fix these fleeting words? Was there an annalist always present to note the gestures, the manners, the feelings of the actor? Endeavor to arrive at the truth in regard to the manner

---

* "Popular Science Monthly," April, 1889, p. 758.

in which this or that contemporaneous event happened, you will not succeed. Two accounts of the same occurrence, by eye-witnesses, differ essentially. Must we, therefore, renounce all the coloring of narratives and confine ourselves to the general enunciation of facts? This would be to suppress history. Indeed, I do believe that if we except certain short, almost mnemonic, axioms, none of the discourses reported by Matthew are literal; our stenographed trials scarcely are. I willingly admit that this admirable relation of the Passion contains a multitude of approximations. Should we, however, write the life of Jesus, omitting those teachings which represent to us so vividly the physiognomy of his discourses, and confine ourselves to saying, with Josephus and Tacitus, that "he was put to death by the order of Pilate, at the instigation of the priests?" That would be, in my opinion, a species of inaccuracy worse than that to which we are exposed by admitting the details which the texts furnish us. These details are not true to the letter; but they are true with a superior truth. They are truer than the naked truth, in this sense, that they are truth rendered expressive and eloquent, raised to the height of an idea. To what would the life of Alexander be reduced were we to confine ourselves to that which is absolutely certain? Even the traditions which are in part erroneous contain a portion of truth which history can not neglect.*

"We too often forget," says Mr. Spencer, "that not only is there a soul of goodness in things evil, but very generally also a soul of truth in things erroneous. Even the absurdest report may, in nearly every instance, be

---

* Renan, "Life of Jesus," pp. 41, 42.

traced to an actual occurrence; and, had there been no such actual occurrence, this preposterous misrepresentation of it would never have existed." *

By applying this principle we may, notwithstanding all the difficulties raised by criticism, ascertain the essential facts of our Lord's life and teaching.

NOTE.—The following books, among others, may be profitably consulted on the subject of this chapter:

1. Advocates of the traditional view: Westcott, "Canon of the New Testament"; Godet's "Commentary on St. John's Gospel," three vols., and on the "Gospel of Luke," two vols.; Alford's "Greek Testament," Prolegomena; "Present-Day Tracts," No. xvi, by Dr. Wace (cf. Huxley and Wace controversy, "Popular Science Monthly" for April, May, June, July, and August, 1889); McCosh's "Christianity and Positivism," Lectures viii, ix, x; Dr. Fisher's "Grounds of Theistic Belief," chapters vi, vii, viii, xvii, xviii; Dr. Gregory, "Why Four Gospels?" These, I think, while they are only a few who have written in advocacy of the traditional view of the origin of the New Testament, are some of its ablest advocates—Westcott and Godet particularly, and, if they fail to convince, so will the others.

2. Opponents of the traditional view: Strauss, "Life of Jesus," English translation, vol. i; Baur's "History of the Christian Church," two vols, and his other works; Zeller's "Acts of the Apostles," two vols.; Renan's "Life of Jesus," "The Apostles," and "St. Paul"; Keim, "Jesus of Nazara," vol. i; Matthew Arnold's "Literature and Dogma"; Haweis, "Christ and Christianity—Story of the Four"; Davidson's "Introduction to the New Testament"; Greg's "Creed of Christendom"; and "Supernatural Religion," two vols. But it can not be too earnestly insisted upon that the student use these writers and all others simply as *guides* to the discovery of the facts for himself. He should not pay too much attention to the peculiar theories of any writer, but seek for the common facts upon which all profess to base their views. He should go to the early writers themselves, should study the age and the circumstances in which Christianity originated, the characters of those who originated it, etc., and draw his own conclusions.

---

* Spencer's "First Principles," p. 3.

CHAPTER I.

EVOLUTION AND MIRACLES.

In discussing this the most important question of the age it is absolutely necessary to earnestly impress upon the reader the fact that while the evolutionists deny the actual occurrence of many, if not all, given instances of miracles, none deny the *possibility* of such occurrences, and this for the simple reason that such denial would be utterly absurd. Where is there a man who would dare to say that he knows not only all the actualities but all the possibilities of nature—not only what has happened on this globe and all others, but also all that may happen throughout the coming future? If there be such a one, he is a fit subject for the treatment of a lunatic; yet the commonest charge which "orthodox" theologians bring against scientific theologians who question the authenticity of certain narratives of miracles is that they are influenced by a false philosophy which denies the possibility of the occurrence of (for instance) the resurrection of a dead body.

The chief "argument" against the views of Strauss, Baur, Renan and their school, which I heard advanced in the theological seminary which I attended, was that they denied on *philosophical*, not on *historical* grounds the occurrence of miracles. Strauss and Baur, it was said, were disciples of the Pantheistic Hegel, whose system of philosophy denied the possibility of miracles. I accepted this teaching until I read the works of these authors themselves, when, to my utter astonishment, I found that it was a most unjust and false charge. True, Strauss and Baur studied Hegel's philosophy, but this was not the real reason why they called in question the miracles recorded in the Bible. It was because they found the historical evidence adducible insufficient to prove these alleged events.

M. Renan distinctly says: "It is not in the name of this or that philosophy, but in the name of constant *experience*, that we banish miracle from history. We do not say, 'Miracle is *impossible*.' We say: 'There has been hitherto no miracle *proved*. None of the miracles with which ancient histories are filled occurred under scientific conditions. Observation, never once contradicted, teaches us that miracles occur only in periods and countries in which they are believed in and before persons *disposed* to believe in them. No miracle was ever performed before an assembly of men capable of establishing the miraculous character of an act. Neither men of the people nor men of the world are competent for that. Great precaution and a long habit of scientific research are requisite.'" *

The same unjust charge is brought against evolutionists who doubt the occurrence of miracles. It is urged that because they believe in "the uniformity of Nature"—i. e., *that natural forces are constant in their operation*—they deny the possibility of miracles; but the following quotation from Prof. Huxley certainly ought to refute this charge: "No one (he says) is enti-

---

* Renan's "Life of Jesus," p. 43, 44.

tled to say *a priori* that any given so-called miraculous event is impossible. Nobody can presume to say what the order of Nature must be : all that the widest experience (even if it extended over all past time and through all space) that events *had* happened in a certain way could justify, would be a proportionally strong *expectation* that events would go on so happening, and the demand for a proportional strength of evidence in favor of any assertion that they had happened otherwise. It is not, therefore, on any *a priori* considerations that objections to the supposed occurrence of miracles can be based," but only on " the inadequacy of the evidence to prove any given case of such occurrences.'' " Natural law," "the order and uniformity of Nature," and the like, are, according to this eminent scientist, mere *names* applied to certain phenomena ; but they do not, in the least, explain those phenomena—reveal their prime causes, etc.—and hence " these terms have no greater value or cogency than such as may attach to generalizations from experience of the past and to expectations for the future, based upon that experience." * This is precisely the view which Canon Mozley expresses in the second of his " Bampton Lectures on Miracles "; and hence the charge that the critics and scientists deny the authenticity of the Bible-miracles because they are influenced by a false philosophy, can be pardoned only on the ground of ignorance, "invincible ignorance." Those intelligent persons (and they are many) who make this charge are, to say the least, disingenuous.

It is freely granted, then, that any miracle is possi-

---

* "Popular Science Monthly," February. 1888, pp. 355, 356.

ble, but the real question is, *Has any miracle ever actually been wrought?*

Evolution replies, not by asserting the "uniformity of natural law," and the consequent impossibility of the occurrence of miracles, but by showing *how miracles are manufactured.*

The primitive man or savage has no idea of an "order of nature," or of what we call the "supernatural," but he has an idea of the *ghost-world*. "In every tribe, a death from time to time adds another ghost to the many ghosts of those who died before. Originally, these ghosts are thought of as close at hand, haunting the old home, lingering near the place of burial, wandering about in the adjacent bush. Continually accumulating, they form a surrounding population; usually invisible, but some of them occasionally seen. These multitudinous spirits are agents ever available, as conceived antecedents to all occurrences needing explanation." *

The Jewish belief that demons caused disease, etc., was of a piece with this philosophy. "The primitive man knew nothing of a *world* in the modern sense of the word. The conception of that vast consensus of forces which we call the world or universe is a somewhat late result of culture; it was reached only through ages of experience and reflection. Such an idea lay behind the horizon of the primitive man. But, while he knew not the world, he knew bits and pieces of it; or, to vary the expression, he had his little world, chaotic and fragmentary enough, but full of dread reality for him. He knew what it was to deal from birth

---

* Spencer's "Principles of Sociology," i, pp. 215–217.

until death with *powers* far mightier than himself. To explain these powers, to make their actions in any wise intelligible, he had but one available resource; and this was so obvious that he could not fail to employ it. The only source of action of which he knew anything lay within himself, was the human *will*, and in this respect, after all, the philosophy of the primeval savage was not so very far removed from that of the modern scientific thinker. The primitive man could see that his own actions were prompted by desire and guided by intelligence, and he supposed the same to be the case with the sun and the wind, the frost and the lightning. All the forces of outward Nature, so far as they came into contact with his life, he *personified* as great beings which were to be contended with or placated.

"As the phenomena of Nature were generalized, the deities or superhuman beings regarded as their sources were likewise generalized, until the conception of Nature as a whole gave rise to the conception of a single Deity as the author and ruler of Nature." *

This hypothesis of a ghost-world served to account for various diseases and mental states—epilepsy, insanity, inspiration, divination, exorcism, sorcery, etc.† The priest, the medicine-man, the warrior, the king, all great or extraordinary persons, were supposed to be possessed by a spirit; all wonderful phenomena were ascribed to the action of spirits. The Jews were no exception. We find the *teraphim*, or tutelar household gods (Genesis, xxxi, 19), the Nature-gods, Baal and Moloch and Astarte, worshiped among them. It is the

---

* Fiske's "Idea of God," pp. 63–65, 73, 74.
† Spencer's "Sociology," i, chaps. xvii, xviii.

plural *Elohim* who create the earth, and whose sons visit the daughters of men (Genesis i). Jehovah seems to be at first a tutelar deity, one of the Elohim (Genesis, ii), but gradually he became the chief among the gods, the national deity, and finally the Universal Father. *

With such facts before us, it is easy to understand at least most of the ancient accounts of miracles.

"Exorcism and sorcery," says Mr. Spencer, "pass insensibly into miracles. What difference exists refers less to the natures of the *effects* worked than to the characters of the *agents* working them. If the marvelous results are ascribed to a supernatural being at enmity with the observers, the act is sorcery; but if ascribed to a friendly supernatural being, the marvelous results are classed as miracles.

"This is well shown in the contest between the Hebrew priests and the magicians of Egypt. From Pharaoh's point of view, Aaron was an enchanter working by the help of a spirit antagonistic to himself; while his own priests worked by the help of his favoring gods. Contrariwise, from the point of the Israelites, the achievements of their own leaders were divine and those of their antagonists diabolical. Both believed that supernatural agency was employed, and that the more powerful supernatural agent had to be yielded to." † These views passed on down the stream of Jewish history to the time of Christ, and later, and hence, it is urged, *He* was regarded by admiring disciples as a Divine Being, and wonderful works were ascribed to

---

* Fiske's "Idea of God," pp. 74–77.
† "Principles of Sociology," i, pp. 243–247.

him. These narratives *may* rest on a narrow basis of fact; for, as we have seen, "the absurdest report may in nearly every instance be traced to an actual occurrence"; but in thus attempting to trace the Biblical narratives of miracles to their real source we must be extremely careful, and this is what such men as M. Renan, Dr. Theodor Keim, and others are doing. They are attempting to separate the wheat from the chaff, and the present writer would aspire to do the same. Let it be remembered, then:

First, that I do not deny the possibility of miracles. I believe in the existence of an infinitely wise and powerful Being, who created and governs all things, and upon this basis rests the possibility of miracles. A miracle, according to such philosophy, is *simply one mode in which the Infinite Spirit manifests himself*— literally an *extra*ordinary event.

Secondly, while I do not believe in the Bible miracles in the gross, so to speak, I do believe that really wonderful and, properly speaking, miraculous events are recorded in the New Testament, *but those events were different from what they are commonly supposed to be*. Mr. J. A. Froude truly says: "No sane man ever raised his narrow understanding into a measure of the possibilities of the Universe; nor does any person with any pretensions to religion disbelieve in miracles of *some kind*. To *pray* is to expect a miracle. When we pray for the recovery of a sick friend, for the gift of any blessing, or the removal of any calamity, we expect that God will do something, by an act of his personal will, which otherwise would not have been done; that He will suspend the ordinary relations of natural cause and effect; and this is the very idea of miracle.

The thing we pray for may be given us, and no miracle may have taken place. It may be given us by natural causes, and would have occurred whether we had prayed or not. But prayer itself in its very essence implies a belief in the possible intervention of a power which is above Nature. The question about miracles is simply one of evidence." * To this I heartily assent. I believe in prayer and Providence (both general and special), and hence I believe in miracles, or that God has actually wrought *extra*ordinary events—events, that is, which can not be properly called "natural," as the word is commonly used, and exactly what I mean will soon appear.

As already stated, Mr. Spencer's canon, that "there is generally a soul of truth in things erroneous," is the principle which I shall apply in this chapter. Indeed, Dr. Keim, among others, has already applied this principle, with very satisfactory results, to the Gospel narratives, and I can not do better than give a synopsis of his views, with such emendations and explanations as I deem necessary to fully express my own opinions; for, while I think Dr. Keim has come *nearer* the truth— especially on this subject—than Strauss, Baur, Renan, and others, yet I would not be understood as indorsing *all* that he says. I would not be called his "disciple."

In a letter to the author the Bishop of Carlisle, England (Dr. Goodwin)—a man of most liberal instincts, and one to whom I am indebted for much kind consideration—says: "Keim, like other German writers, begins with ignoring the possibility of anything occurring beyond what we call the natural order, and there-

---

* Froude's "Short Studies," vol. i, pp. 186, 187.

fore he has to make some desperate attempt to account for the facts which he finds and which he can not deny." In reply I said, and now repeat, that this is an unjust charge to bring against Dr. Keim; for, while he freely grants, or rather insists, that there are mythical elements in the Gospels—while he takes a *higher*, more *spiritual*, more *refined* view of the miracles there recorded, than that of popular orthodoxy, yet he asserts not simply the "possibility" but the actuality of many of those miracles—especially of the resurrection of Jesus. He divides the works of Jesus into three classes, viz.—1. Miracles of healing; 2. Raisings of the dead; 3. Nature-miracles.* In the third volume of his great work, "*Jesus of Nazara*," he devotes ninety-seven pages—152 to 249—to the *healings of the diseased*. After considering "the critical difficulties" in the way of accepting these narratives just as they stand, he then passes to "the fundamental facts."

First, he says: "The acts of healing of Jesus presuppose, in general, a certain disposition, and indeed a spiritual disposition, on the part of the sufferers. The sick eagerly seek him, press upon him, fall down before him, touch his clothes, beg for mercy, express *faith* in his power to help (Matthew, viii, 2; ix, 20, 27 *et seq.*; xx, 30; xiv, 36; Luke, viii, 45; Mark, i, 24, 34, etc.). Instead of the sick themselves, those who belong to them—fathers, mothers, sons-in-law, masters, bearers— often appeal to him, or bring the sick and place them immediately at his feet (Matthew, viii, 6; ix, 2, 18, 32; Luke, iv, 38; Mark, i, 30, etc.). This faith often

---

* Keim's "Jesus of Nazara," vol. iv, pp. 159, 166, and 178 (English translation).

betrays its uncommon *strength* (Matthew, viii, 5–13; Luke, vii, 1 *et seq.*). Sometimes the faith is not mentioned (e. g., Matthew, viii, 14; xii, 10), but the omission is often due to the *rapidity* of the narrative, or the faith is *taken for granted*. . . . The cures at a distance (Matthew, viii, 5–13; Luke, vii, 1 *et seq.*, etc.) totally shut out, of course, the personal contact of Jesus with the sick—a contact which in other cases is the rule. Cures at a distance do not in any way imply the exercise of faith on the part of the sick. Cures at a distance cut away all natural or half-natural explanations of the results. Nevertheless, it is not therefore necessary to believe in the purely miraculous 'healing of (for instance) the centurion's son or servant.' Doubtless the father had not taken the journey from Capernaum to Jesus without the knowledge and *faith of the son;* restorative power already lay in this highly wrought faith and expectation." The remark of "Matthew" (viii, 13), "His servant was healed in the self-same hour" that the command ("Go thy way," etc.) was given, may be a slight exaggeration. But the healing of those persons who were said to have been "possessed of devils"—i. e., those who *were diseased in mind and body* *—seems to present greater difficulties to this view, but "if faith on the part of the sufferer" was not possible in these cases, "faith on the part of the sufferer's friends" (says our author) "is not necessarily excluded; and in the narrative of the lunatic this faith is expressly represented as efficacious (Matthew, xviii, 14–21; Mark, ix, 23). But when this faith is altogether wanting, as in the case of

---

* See Dr. White's admirable articles in "The Popular Science Monthly" for February and March, 1889.

the Gadarenes (Mark, v, 1 *et seq.*; Luke, viii, 26-39; Matthew, viii, 28-34), and of the possessed man of Capernaum (Mark, i, 21-28; Luke, iv, 33), instead of it, a *spiritual excitement* on the part of the sufferers themselves is always assumed, and one might say this was the case here almost more visibly than with other sick persons. There is an anxiety, an alarm which seizes these persons as soon as they come in contact with Jesus. They have a mental perception of his greatness, and they recoil from him. But in the very act of recoil they are attracted; they cry to him involuntarily; they would be freed of his presence, would be alone, and yet can not conceal the interest with which they regard him; they beseech their tormentor to leave them, and yet they recognize his power, his just authority; they struggle in their beclouded consciousness to become clear as to his nature, and their position in relation to him, and then, with or without protest, yield themselves up to the menace or command which he directs toward them. Though all these movements of mind are in the sources ascribed immediately to the foreign 'spirit' in the man, and not to the man himself, this can not hinder us in the present day from finding room for more accommodated views, and—what is of most importance —from establishing the fact that the traces of spiritual processes in Jesus' works of healing extend as far as the province in which the result appears to rest upon the simple activity of Jesus, the simple passivity of the man healed." If any one fancy that such mental efforts as Dr. Keim here attributes to "the possessed" were impossible, he would perhaps have his doubts removed by a visit to some asylum for the insane, and by a study of its phenomena. On one occasion, while visiting such an asylum, the inmate whom my friend and I were calling to see, and who had been suffering for years from *dementia*, immediately recognized my friend (her uncle), whom she had not seen for nineteen years. And, besides, she recalled other persons and events in a most striking manner, while a moment afterward her mind wandered again into utter absurdities and nonsense. Surely she was as incapable of the mental processes ascribed by Keim to the possessed as any one could be, and yet she manifested them. But it would doubtless be urged: "There are instances of the cure of *incurable* diseases recorded in the Gospel, such as leprosy.* What shall we say of these?"

The case of the healing of the leper, mentioned by all three evangelists (Matthew, viii, 1–4; Luke, v, 12–16; Mark, i, 40–45), Dr. Keim handles in a masterly manner. He frankly admits that "the thrice-given report is not to be put aside as absolutely unhistorical," but he holds that "the cleansing which the sick man asked for may originally have been *nothing more than the declaration of cleanliness*, which in the very same words was reserved to the priests by the legislation of Moses (Leviticus, xiii, 6, 17, etc.), and the materializing mythical spirit, insatiable and prone to misconception, was only too near at hand to add this case to the many real works of healing, and to convert the declaration into an actual cleansing." †

It would be impossible to convey in a short and imperfect synopsis of his views the impression which Dr. Keim's able argument makes on one's mind, and it is

---

* "Encyclopædia Britannica," article "Leprosy."
† Keim's "Jesus of Nazara," vol. iii, pp. 152–249.

hoped that the reader will consult the work itself, even if he has to borrow it. In thus adopting Dr. Keim's opinion that the cures which Jesus wrought were "*mind-cures*" or "*faith-healings*," I would not be understood as indorsing all *modern* instances of such cures, though I do think that the manner in which certain people handle these cures is most unpardonable and unphilosophical. No really intelligent and educated person pretends to know *what or how great influence the mind may have on the body*, and there are well-authenticated cases of truly wonderful cures which deserve more thorough and careful consideration than has yet been given them. I know a most estimable woman— Miss Jennie Smith, missionary on the Baltimore and Ohio Railroad—who was bedfast for years, and was cured in a most wonderful manner—as she believed, by "faith." I have heard her story from her own lips, and also read the book which gives a full account of her recovery, including the testimonial of her physician to the effect that "a *psychical uplift*"—supernaturally or naturally, what matter about words?—was the cause of her cure, and I think whatever allowances may be made for unconscious additions, etc., yet her cure was quite as wonderful as some, at least, of the healings recorded in the Bible.*

"The chronicles of psychical healing as a phenomenon," says an able and brilliant writer on this subject, "are a fascinating study that may be pursued with both pleasure and profit, for the practice may easily be traced through the long epochs of authentic record to the time

---

* See "From Baca to Beulah," by Jennie Smith. Garrigues Bros., 608 Arch Street, Philadelphia, Pa.

when 'history and legend, meeting with a kiss,' lure the eager search into the myths and magic of remote antiquity. Medical books are filled with descriptions of unhoped-for, sudden, and prodigious cures, that would easily pass for miracles; the annals of prayer and faith-cure abound with well-attested cases; such cures frequently occurred during the earlier years of many Christian sects, as the Waldenses, Moravians, Huguenots, Covenanters, Quakers, Baptists, and Methodists; Jesus and his Apostles performed miracles of healing; the *sacred writings of all nations refer to mental healing as a common practice;* and mythology and folk-lore afford ground for a belief that, in prehistoric times, mankind may have been acquainted with no other mode of restoring the sick to health." *

In the fourteenth chapter of his valuable work on "Nature and the Supernatural," it is well known the late Dr. Horace Bushnell maintains that "miracles and spiritual gifts are not discontinued" even now, and gives cases of wonderful cures which it is much easier to sneer at than to explain. It is customary for a certain class of persons, on the one hand, to scoff at all such records of extraordinary and inexplicable events, and, on the other, to accept implicitly the cures mentioned in the Bible as real miracles. In other words, they attempt to *stake off* the Bible and the events it records from all other books and events—to make it a book *sui generis*—but this is impossible in our day. The Bible must submit to comparison and criticism;

---

* "Facts and Fictions of Mental Healing," by Charles M. Barrows; Carter & Karrick, Boston—an admirable and philosophic little book; and cf. Dr. D. H. Tuke's able treatise on "The Influence of the Mind upon the Body," especially Part IV.

and the events it records, however wonderful, must be shown to have, at least, a basis in fact and reason; they must be shown to be nearly allied to, if not of a piece with, other well-attested facts. In short, the Bible must be confirmed and illustrated by history and science, if thinking people are to accept it. But I hear some one say, "This is Rationalism." True, and it is because the author is firmly convinced that "the faith once delivered to the saints" must be shown to be *rational* that he writes on this great subject. In thus attempting to give "a rational" account of Christ's life and teachings we by no means deny the Divine element in that life. In attempting to explain his works of healing according to the well-recognized laws which govern the mind and body, we do not deny the Divine element in those cures; *we leave untouched the profound question as to the prime origin and cure of all disease.* As Miss Jennie Smith's doctor says: "God himself is doubtless *potentially in the means used.* I myself" (he adds), "in common with not a few students of Nature, prominent among whom is to be named Dr. Lionel Beale, fully accept this view, recognizing the truth expressed in the words of that eminent authority in science, that life, always and everywhere, is ultimately 'the operation of *immanent Deity*,' * and that in the use of proper means we have simply acted in the divine order, yet by no means limiting the Deity himself." †
In other words, those who call others "rationalists" and "enemies of the faith," because they use their God-

---

* According to the chapter on "God and Nature" (Part I), I hold, with many other students of Nature, that not only Life, but *all* the operations of Nature, are due to "immanent Deity."

† "From Baca to Beulah," pp. 214, 215.

given reason and conscience in the study of the Bible narratives of wonderful cures, have yet to learn what is meant by the Apostle when he says, "IN HIM we live and move and have our being." If so, then *all healing is ultimately due to this Power*, and it is not atheism or an anti-religious spirit which seeks to explain these phenomena of Jewish and Christian history. It may be well to add a couple of instances of remarkable cures—one a mental healing and the other a faith-cure—which may serve merely to illustrate the view of the New Testament miracles just set forth. Mr. Barrows tells us that Dr. Charles F. Taylor, whose reputation is well known to medical men, in a paper on "Bodily Conditions as Related to Mental States," read before the New York Academy of Science in 1879, gave many instances of mental cures, among which was the following:

A lady came to Dr. Taylor with a lame shoulder, which was drawn forcibly upward, firmly fixed in that position and very sensitive to handling. She explained that several years before, while reaching up to turn the slat of the shutters, she had felt a sharp pain in the shoulder, and since that time had been unable to move it. Supposing that it might be a spasm, and not wishing to treat it himself, he sent her to a brother physician, who gave her some liniments, and, when these failed to have the desired effect, a professional "rubber" was sent her, who used a great deal of disagreeable, violent, and painful manipulation. A year from her first visit, therefore, she reappeared before Dr. Taylor in a very sad plight. He immediately sought out his fellow-physician, who had thus far treated the case, and together they made an examination. They found the large pectoral (breast) muscle shortened and enlarged to twice its natural size, and the arm so firmly bound down that it was with difficulty that she got her clothing on. The two surgeons etherized the patient and made an unsuccessful attempt to stretch the contracted muscle by mechanical force. The lady was so prostrated by the operation that she was obliged to remain in bed for over a month. Then a consultation was held at her house, in Brooklyn, and, when the physicians had explained what they had come for, she got up, and, to their utter astonishment, the muscles completely relaxed, and the arm was perfectly free to move in any direction.

Three years later the patient's other arm became affected in the same way, and Dr. Taylor, supposing the cure to have resulted from the mechanical stretching, repeated the operation in this case, and the same result followed as in the first instance. The case was accordingly dismissed as cured; but a month later the doctor was requested to visit her, and found that no permanent benefit had been received, and the muscles and shoulder had relapsed into the same condition as before. After striving for weeks to find remedies for a state of things he could not comprehend, he finally took the hint which circumstances forced upon him, and administered *laughing-gas* to his patient! This was administered twice, with an interval of four days, when the muscles relaxed, motion was restored to the shoulder-joint, and there has been no recurrence of the condition described.*

This was a clear case of an abnormal bodily condi-

---

* Barrows, "Facts and Fictions of Mental Healing," pp. 134–143, etc.

tion produced by a mental disorder, and its cure by so simple a remedy reminds us of the New Testament accounts of healing paralytics, the man with the withered hand (Luke, vi, 6–11, etc.), the blind, etc., by a mere word or the application of clay, and so on.

Dr. Tuke gives numerous instances which furnish in all essentials even better parallels to the New Testament healings than this does, and it is earnestly hoped that the reader may consider such cases more carefully and candidly than is generally done.

Again, Dr. Bushnell, in the work referred to, after alluding to the wonders of Ignatius, Polycarp, Justin Martyr, Athenagoras, Irenæus, Tertullian, Origen, and other church fathers, to the dreams of Huss, the prophesyings of Luther, and Fox, and Archbishop Usher, the ecstasies of Xavier, etc., discusses the miracles of our own time, among which was the case of an English gentleman, whose faith in the gift of healing had been established by his own personal experience of it. "He was a man whose connections and culture, whose well-formed, tall, and robust looking person, whose beautifully simple and humble manners, and whose blameless, universally respected life among strangers not of the same faith, were so many conspiring tokens winning him a character of confidence that excluded any rational distrust of his representations." He had been an invalid for a long time, with only a slender hope of recovery, but after his conversion "it became a question with him whether, as he had been healed spiritually, he ought not also to expect and receive the healing of his body by the same faith. After a hard struggle of mind he was able, dismissing all his prescribed remedies, to throw himself on God, and was immediately and permanently made whole. At length one of his children he had with him, away from home, was taken ill with scarlet fever. 'And now the question was,' said the father, 'what was to be done? The Lord had indeed healed my own sickness, but would he heal my son?' I conferred with a brother in the Lord, who, having no faith in Christ's healing power, urged me to send immediately for the doctor, and dispatched his groom on horseback to fetch him. Before the doctor arrived, my mind was filled with revelation on the subject. I saw I had fallen into a snare, by turning away from the Lord's healing hand, to lean on medical skill. The doctor arrived. My son, he said, was suffering from a scarlet fever, and medicine should be sent for immediately. When he was gone, I called the nurse and told her to take the child into the nursery and lay him on the bed. I then fell on my knees, confessing the sin I had committed against the Lord's healing power. I also prayed most earnestly that it would please my Heavenly Father to forgive my sin, and to show that he forgave it by causing the fever to be rebuked. I received a mighty conviction that my prayer was heard, and I arose and went to the nursery, and on opening the door, to my astonishment, the boy was sitting up in his bed, and on seeing me, cried out, 'I am quite well, and want to have my dinner.' In an hour he was dressed and well, and eating his dinner. Next morning the doctor came and was amazed to find the boy well, but said, after feeling his pulse, 'Yes, the fever is gone.'"* This is only one of several remarkable cures which Dr. Bushnell cites, but it must suffice.

---

* Bushnell's "Nature and the Supernatural," pp. 479-481.

Two thoughts are suggested by these facts: First, a most effectual way of arousing prejudice against such views as are here advocated is to say, "Oh, this is classing *Christ* with modern physicians and miracle-mongers." And some critic, aiming at temporary success in argument, rather than at the truth, will doubtless resort to this method of refuting an argument which it is difficult to answer. Hence, I anticipate his "refutation" by saying, *I make no classification whatever, but merely cite facts of history and ask that they may be considered.* I would be the last one to class our Lord with inferior persons, but I do believe that the cures he wrought may be illustrated and confirmed by those which have been performed by others. Where is the atheism or infidelity in holding that *all disease is healed by the same Power—probably a spiritual force not generally recognized—and that the cures wrought by the Saviour were, therefore, only extraordinary examples of what commonly happens?* There is no infidelity in such a view; but granting that the so-called " mental healings " and " faith-cures " of ancient and modern times have been the result of the operation of a Spiritual Power not usually recognized, it becomes more than probable that some Great Physician should arise who, relying on such means of healing, would perform wonderful cures.

Secondly, it may be said that such men as that one referred to by Dr. Bushnell are religious fanatics, and hence there is no parallel between his cure and that of the blind, the lame, the deaf, etc., spoken of in the New Testament. But what proof have we that those who were healed by Jesus and his Apostles were not religious enthusiasts? They were probably just such persons—Mary Magdalene, for instance, certainly was. And it is vain to point to the narratives of the said cures and to attempt to show from them that there is no parallel between modern faith-cures and New Testament healings, since we know not how much those narratives have been *embellished* by later hands. The fundamental facts, then, which gave rise to all the stories about Christ's performing miracles were certain mental and spiritual healings, to which were gradually added other and more wonderful events. Those events were of two kinds—raisings of the dead and Nature-miracles.

Among the former Dr. Keim considers the raising of Jairus's daughter,* and the raising of the widow of Nain's son.† In explanation of the first miracle he adopts the rationalists' view that the words of Jesus, "The maid is not dead but sleepeth," are literally true, and hence she was merely aroused from "a lethargic faintness," or *swoon*, by Jesus' vigorous taking hold and lifting up of the patient. This fact was seized upon by the writer as a repetition of the miracles performed by Elijah and Elisha (I Kings, xvii, 17, and II Kings, iv, 8 *et seq.*), and wrought out in its present form. At any rate, the verbal utterance of Jesus ("The maid *is not dead*," etc.), Keim emphatically insists, "mocks every attempt to establish the decisively miraculous view." But he rejects *in toto* the story of the raising of the widow of Nain's son, who, he thinks, "was really dead." "The genuine histories" (he says) "of the life of Jesus do not compel us to have this belief (that the dead was really revived), but only the *later* authors. Nor should we overlook the fact that it is

---

* Matthew, ix, 18-26, etc. † Luke, vii, 11-17.

only *one* later author who is acquainted with this incident. This miracle, known (according to the narratives) throughout all Judea, remained entirely hidden from the other Evangelists, who, if they had known or believed it, would have eagerly registered it as an occurrence of the first importance." Hence we are to regard this as simply a legend which grew up later and was based, probably, on Elijah's raising the woman of Zarephath's son.* In a similar way our author disposes of the resurrection of Lazarus. "This enrichment," he says, " is no history, but the destruction of history."

"These journeys (of John's Gospel), these deeds and miracles, these addresses, these murderous attacks, are unhistorical." He thinks that the author of John's Gospel merely desired to set forth Jesus as the Resurrection and the Life, and hence chose the parable of the Rich Man and Lazarus as the basis of a *picture-miracle* which shadowed forth this truth.† At any rate, owing to the uncertain authorship of this Gospel, and to the fact that this gigantic miracle was not known to the earlier Evangelists, we dare not insist upon its reality. We come now to the great *nature-miracles* ascribed to Jesus, namely, the stilling of the storm on the Lake of Galilee,‡ the feeding of the four thousand and the five thousand by multiplying the loaves,# the turning the water into wine at Cana ∥ and the draught of fishes.ᴀ

As to the first miracle, Keim thinks that a storm may have occurred while the disciples were crossing the

---

* Keim's "Jesus of Nazara," vol. iv. pp. 149–178.
† "Jesus of Nazara," vol. v, pp. 72–87.
‡ Luke, viii, 22–25, etc.   # Luke, ix, 10–17.
∥ John, ii, 1–11.   ᴀ Matthew, iv, 18, etc.

lake, with Jesus asleep in the ship, and that his "action consisted merely in the interposition of a purely human power, in his pious courage, imparting calm and decision, or in a *petition to God for help, in answer to which help was given or appeared to be given.*"

The latter view is doubtless the true one.

"The regal miracle" of feeding the four thousand or five thousand with a few loaves and fishes, our author thinks, "did not take place in a literal sense, and, as in the case of the storm, a higher interpretation spontaneously forces itself upon every one. We think of the spiritual bread (John, vi) which Jesus dispenses and which he distributes by means of his Apostles, making even the deserts green and pleasant, and with one loaf satisfying a thousand men, as five loaves did five thousand. We think of the heavenly treasure unexhausted by distribution—so that to each of the twelve Apostles, the missionary successors of Jesus, there remains in the twelve baskets more for giving away than had at first been at the disposal of Jesus and themselves." Keim speaks favorably of the view of Paulus and Ewald that in the wilderness, Jesus, having first by his words lifted the minds of his hearers above earthly necessities, evoked from those who were prepared to make sacrifices a grand exhibition of hospitable brotherly love— men who possessed the means helped those who were in need.* Thus every want was supplied with limited resources, first the spiritual wants, but next also the physical. "Such a basis," he adds, "is not to be denied." He thinks that our Lord's words to Peter and

---

* Ewald, "History of Israel," vol. vi, pp. 249-252 (English translation).

Andrew, "Follow me and I will make you fishers of men" (Matthew, iv, 19), gave rise to the tradition about the miraculous draught of fishes. The story is therefore a "mere *picture of an utterance* of Jesus drawn for the eyes of babes"; it is due to a misunderstanding of this reported utterance.

The miracle of turning water into wine at Cana is disposed of thus: "In the case of so pronounced and *unattested* miracle it is useless to attempt to lay hold of a definite historical fact. The Evangelist has portrayed an utterance of Jesus in a picture, and has visibly signalized the *début* of Jesus in that utterance and picture.

According to the earlier Gospels, Jesus certainly had spoken words appropriate to this narrative: "The sons of the bride-chamber can not mourn so long as the bridegroom is with them," and "new wine is not put into old wine-skins, which tear, but into new ones, and both are preserved" (Matthew, ix, 14–17).

"From this and from the actual joyous and friendly feasts which Jesus held with his disciples and with the publicans, could easily be derived the picture of a wedding festival at which Jesus was, naturally, not the bridegroom, but the bringer of joy for the guests and particularly for his disciples, and thus in a higher style the bridegroom." * If, now, these explanations seem far-fetched and irrational, I would ask the reader to remember two facts:

1. This is but a most imperfect exposition of Dr. Keim's views, and a careful study of his great work would effectually remove any such impression.

2. It must not be forgotten that Eastern people

---

* "Jesus of Nazara," vol. iv, pp. 203–210.

were endowed with especially *vivid imaginations*, while the "Gospel of John" is peculiarly a *doctrinal* work (see Introduction); and therefore the author's conception may have been fitted into a material framework somewhat as St. John chose the earthly Jerusalem as the framework of his vision of the new Jerusalem (Revelation, xxi).

At any rate, whatever may be thought of the foregoing explanation of the Christian miracles, it must be acknowledged, from what has been said in the introductory chapter, that these miracles, especially the Nature-miracles and the raisings of the dead, are not substantiated by evidence which any body of scientific men, who were unbiased by preconceived theories, would accept. We do not and can not know when or by whom the narratives of these miracles were composed, and hence we must explain them as best we can. It has been said, ever since the time of Hume, that "it is more probable that men should deceive or be deceived than it is that such miracles as those in question should be wrought," and this is true. It may also be said that, considering the origin of the Gospels, almost *any* explanation of the miracles is more probable than that which attempts to accept them just as they stand recorded.

This, then, is the view which seems to be the most probable: Jesus was a great Prophet, and, as such, it was quite natural that he should have wrought miracles of healing. "It would have been a miracle if he had not wrought miracles" among such religious enthusiasts as the Jews were, and at the time when the national expectation of the Messiah was at its height. These faith-cures and mind-cures formed the basis of many and various stories, more or less exaggerated, which gradually grew up around the life of this wonderful Person, and were incorporated in our "Gospels." "But," it would be urged right here, "the interval between the death of Christ and the formation of such fabulous stories is not *long* enough for the growth of these myths." * Now, we will not stop to discuss the question *how* long is that period, for we can not ascertain its exact length, but let us say it was only *fifty* years (and this is certainly a most liberal concession to the advocates of the traditional view), yet, as Renan truly observes, "The legend of Alexander (the Great) was complete before the generation of his companions in arms was extinct; that of Francis d' Assisi commenced *while he was yet alive*." † If this is so, it is quite credible that the life of so great a Person as Jesus of Nazareth was, should, within fifty years, be surrounded with all sorts of legendary stories.

The real reason why the efforts to explain, or explain away, if you please, the alleged miracles of Christian history are so distasteful to most people, is, not their intrinsic weakness—not because they are based on an assumption of impossible or improbable facts—but rather the false notion that they and they alone can prove the *divine* character of Christ. In refutation of this silly notion, I would ask the simple question, Did the miracles of Elijah or Elisha or the Apostles prove their divinity? No! The divinity of Christ, as I hope to show later, rests on a more solid foundation than that of miracles; these would merely prove that he was

---

* Canon Row's "Jesus of the Evangelists," chap. xvi.
† Renan's "Life of Jesus," p. 40.

endowed with superhuman power; and, indeed, even if the narratives of the miracles be altogether false, still the very existence of such stories as those in the New Testament—the very fact that such legends about Jesus grew up at all—proves that he must have been a truly wonderful person. No ordinary person (John the Baptist, for instance) would ever have called forth such a train of legends. Hence all (or nearly all) that miracles would prove concerning Jesus is proved by the New Testament, even if it be a collection of myths. If " there is a soul of truth in things erroneous," surely we have a soul of truth in these narratives; back of all the clouds of fable we discern the divine form of the Man of Nazareth standing like a beautiful, shining beacon of God, a "light to lighten the Gentiles and the glory of His people Israel." "But," it will be asked here, "what are you going to do with the Virgin-Birth and Resurrection of Jesus?" I am going to aim to get at the kernel of truth which lies imbedded in the husky narratives of these two wonderful events, and this I shall do in a spirit of the profoundest reverence.

First, then, let it be distinctly understood that the *possibility* of a virgin's bearing a child is not denied. We know, in fact, that "parthenogenesis" (virgin-birth) actually occurs among lower animals—for instance, bees and wasps—and it is not impossible, therefore, that parthenogenesis should happen in the human family, although there is no instance of this known among *vertebrates*.* But the *improbability* of the occurrence of so

---

* This has been denied; and it has been alleged that "out of a great number of virgin eggs a chick is occasionally hatched." Of course, not being a practical scientist myself, I am no authority on this difficult question. I may quote one, however, who is a very high

wonderful an event can be destroyed only by the most *overwhelming evidence*. Have we such evidence in favor of the parthenogenetic conception of Jesus? It seems almost useless to answer this question, so notoriously weak is the historical evidence on this subject. We have no proof, worthy of the name, that the "speeches" recorded by Matthew, or the "notes" of Mark and of Luke, contained any reference to the virgin-birth. On the contrary, the *nature* of these writings precludes the supposition that they contained an account of this alleged event. The Epistles of St. Paul likewise contain no evidence on this point—in short, all the earliest narratives of our Lord's life and teachings fail to furnish us even approximately satisfactory proof of the virgin-birth; but the evidence adducible rather seems to favor the view that Joseph was the father of Jesus, for the question is frequently asked, "Is not this Joseph's son?" (Luke, iv, 22; John, i, 45; vi, 42, etc.), which would lead us to believe that Jesus, during his lifetime, was considered by his acquaintances the son of Joseph as well as of Mary. It is obvious that only one person—

---

authority on such subjects. Prof. Joseph Le Conte tells me that "one is peculiarly liable to mistake in the case of chickens, from this cause: A hen will lay fertile eggs at least *two weeks after union with a cock*. The sperm is *retained in an active condition in crypts in the upper part of the oviduct*, at least so long, and perhaps much longer. The egg, coming down from the ovary, *is fertilized in the oviduct*, even though there has been no contact with the cock for two or three weeks." This seems a satisfactory explanation of alleged instances of parthenogenesis among chickens; but, however this may be, no instance of virgin-genesis among *human* beings is known to scientists, and they would not believe so improbable an event, unless it were proved by the most conclusive *scientific* evidence, which is certainly not possible in the case before us.

namely, Mary herself—could know that Jesus was parthenogenetically conceived, and when we remember that only the *later* narratives of our Lord's life give us the story of the virgin-birth, without telling us whence it came, we must hesitate to accept this wonderful story. Add to this two other facts: First, the birth of Jesus was precisely the event which the fabulists laid hold of and magnified, as the "Apocrypha" amply shows;* and, secondly, the writer of the account bases his narrative on the prophecy of Isaiah: "Behold, a virgin shall be with child, and shall bring forth a son, and they shall call his name Immanuel, which, being interpreted, is God with us" (Isaiah, vii, 14). This gives us the clew by which to unravel the legend of the virgin-birth, and to get at "the soul of truth." The origin of great men, especially in the ancient world, was wont to gather around it clouds of mystery and legend. The Messiah of the Jews, prophecy had said, would be born of a "virgin," and, although Isaiah evidently meant by this word simply a *young woman,* as every scholar must admit, yet the Greek version translated the Hebrew word (*almah*) by a word (*parthenos*) meaning "virgin," and, as this version was used by our Evangelists, it was natural that they should understand it literally, and thus originate the story of the virgin-birth. Hence the simple question here is, Shall we interpret this story *literally,* or shall we consider it the *poetic garb which enshrines a great fact?* Shall we accept *Isaiah's* meaning or that of his *later interpreter* (or, rather, misinterpreter)? *Considering the uncertainty of the authorship of this story,* I think we must at least hesitate to accept the literal in-

---

* See "Ante-Nicene Fathers," vol. viii, "Gospel of Thomas."

terpretation, and I for one believe it to be merely a poetic description of a great fact. I hold, with Keim and many of the evolutionists, that as great a miracle was wrought at the birth of Jesus as was wrought when Life, or Self-Conscious Mind, was introduced on our globe: a distinct "leap" was made in the process of spiritual evolution at His birth, whereby the goal toward which Humanity is moving was reached in one case. Jesus was therefore "the possibility of the human race made real." This view rests not on a few uncertain passages of the New Testament, nor is it an attempt to wriggle out of a dilemma to which criticism reduces us, but it is based on, first, the *whole career* of Jesus (for that career, notwithstanding all critical difficulties, may, I think, be clearly enough made out to justify this inference); and, secondly, *on the general law* of evolution.*
It is believed that the primitive form of force—that which first manifested itself—was what we call "gravity"; next, "chemical affinity" appeared, and this was a distinct *advance* upon gravity; then came life in its lowest forms, which was an advance (however originated) on chemical affinity; this was followed by mind in the lower animals, which was likewise an advance on life; and, finally, self-conscious mind appeared, at first in a low degree, in man; † but why should the process *stop* here? Why should not spiritual evolution reach *perfection?* We believe it did in the person of Jesus of Nazareth. He was the crown—the cap-stone—of that long column of spirituality of which Abraham, Moses, Isaiah, Buddha, Socrates, and others were the

---

* Keim, "Jesus of Nazara," vol. ii, pp. 38-101.
† See below, chap. ix.

bases. But, whether this view be accepted or not, it is sufficient to point out, as has been done, the unsatisfactory character of the traditional view. The story of the Virgin-Born, as it stands in the Gospel, is so improbable, and the evidence supporting it is so uncertain, that criticism can not accept it, yet it is comparatively easy to understand how such a story should originate concerning so great a person as Jesus was.

Even if we accept the traditional authorship of the Gospels, it is not necessary to accept the popular idea of the Birth. Only two of the Evangelists record this event—Matthew and Luke—but we do not know on what authority their accounts rest. It is generally assumed, for instance, by the Bishop of Carlisle, that the Evangelists learned the facts from Mary herself, the only one whose testimony on this subject would be valid; but it must be remembered that this is a pure *assumption*, incapable of proof, for the writers themselves do not say that Mary authorized their narratives, but, on the contrary, it appears that other considerations influenced them in their writing. St. Matthew writes with the avowed purpose of showing that Jesus was the Messiah of the Jews, and it was, therefore, the most natural thing imaginable that he should apply to Jesus Isaiah's prophecy (vii, 14; applied Matthew, i, 22, 23) about the virgin-born. Being a devout Jew, who accepted the infallibility of the prophets, he would not stop to inquire into the facts, but take it for granted that Isaiah's statement was applicable to Jesus. And, besides, even if there had been any inclination on his part to question the accuracy of the prophet, he could not, when he wrote his Gospel, have done so very satisfactorily, for by that time (A. D. 68 or 69) Mary was probably dead. But the decisive fact is that he writes from a *dogmatic* motive, and applies prophecy accordingly. However, it must be remembered that we have no satisfactory evidence to show that the Apostle Matthew wrote this story; and it is more than probable, it is well-nigh *certain*, that it is a later addition by some dogmatist to his account of the Lord's "speeches." The Bishop of Carlisle, in a recent work on "The Foundations of the Creed," lays much stress on St. Luke's testimony because he was a physician, and because he says that he "had perfect understanding of all things from the very first." But it must be remembered that St. Luke was a Gentile (Colossians, iv, 11, 14), who was familiar with stories of God-descended persons, and wrote his Gospel some time after Matthew, doubtless in foreign parts, and confessedly got his materials from tradition. It is quite reasonable to believe, therefore, that such a person would accept the stories afloat about Jesus as authoritative, but we are at liberty to question their authority. Great stress is laid on the fact that St. Luke was a physician, and that the third Gospel contains many medical terms. But physicians of that day were not so free from superstition as are those of our day; indeed, they were probably, in some cases at least, even more superstitious than many of their contemporaries; while "the medical language" of this Gospel can not prove its Lukan authorship—unless, indeed, Luke was the only physician among the early disciples who could write! Doubtless the *rédacteur* of Luke's notes on St. Paul's missionary journeys was also "a beloved physician"; at least such a supposition is by no means incredible, and nullifies the force (?) of this "argument." But again I must ask the reader to remember that the evidence alleged in proof of the Lukan authorship of this Gospel as it now stands in the earliest known manuscripts, is by no means satisfactory. The radical defect of the Bishop of Carlisle's exposition of this article of the creed is its twofold assumption: first, that the traditional authorship of these stories is true; and, secondly, that the authors were infallible and their testimony, therefore, irrefutable. It were much better for the cause of religion to frankly acknowledge the meagerness and weakness of the evidence adducible in support of the traditional views, and to offer an explanation which, while it robs the Birth of the supernatural drapery, yet retains the great fact that an *avatar* of God was born of Mary and Joseph.

The Resurrection of Jesus is the best attested miracle in the history of the world, and therefore deserves the most careful consideration. In giving it this, let it be remembered:

First. That the popular view of the resurrection is intimately connected with other doctrines of the Christian creed, especially with the doctrine of the ascension, of heaven and hell, and of our own resurrection. If we believe that the body which was crucified on Calvary rose from the grave and ascended into the heavens, we must believe that it now occupies some place (or space) somewhere in the universe; and, if this be so, the question at once forces itself upon the mind, *Where is that place?* Is heaven to be found in Mars, or Venus, or Jupiter, or some other planet? Very few, if any, intelligent theologians believe that heaven and hell are *places*. They rather hold that they are *states—spiritual condi-*

tions — consisting respectively in happiness and misery.*

Again, science proves as clearly as it proves anything (e. g., the revolution of the earth around the sun) that this universe of ours is *wearing out* and must finally end in utter ruin and chaos;† and hence the continuous existence of material bodies is precluded.

Second. It must be admitted that the resurrection of a dead body is so wonderful an event that only the most overwhelming evidence can prove it. Whether we agree with one skeptic that " we would not believe to-day the testimony of *millions* to the effect that a dead body had been raised to life," or not, yet I think the more moderate skeptics who urge that such a miracle must be proved by the testimony of *scientific experts* who could not possibly be deceived are quite reasonable in their demands.

Now — and this is the third point — is the resurrection of Jesus *so* attested ? In answer, we must summon the earliest and most reliable witnesses, and these are unquestionably the Epistles of St. Paul — especially those to the *Corinthians*. In the fifteenth chapter of *First Corinthians* (3–8) we are told that " Christ was seen of Cephas (Peter); then of the twelve. After that he was seen of above five hundred brethren at once; of whom a greater part remain to this present " (i. e., to the time when St. Paul wrote this letter). " After that he was seen of James; then of all the apostles. And last of all he was seen of me (Paul) also." This account

---

* Farrar's "Eternal Hope," Sermons I and II; Martensen, "Christian Dogmatics," § 276. etc.

† See Stewart and Tait, " Unseen Universe "; Fiske's " Unseen World "; A. Winchell's " Religion and Science," pp. 373–379, etc.

St. Paul confessedly gives at second hand (v. 3); he was not one of the twelve or one of the five hundred, and hence he only tells what they told him they had seen. The important question is, What is meant by this narrative? St. Paul himself, I think, gives us the key to its interpretation when he says, "last of all Christ was seen of me also." He classes the post-mortem appearances of Jesus to the other disciples with that to *himself*, and we know from his *Epistles to the Galatians* (i, 2–17) as well as from the *Acts* (ix; i, 22; xxvi, 1–23, etc.) that this was a *spiritual*, not a *bodily* manifestation. Hence we seem forced to this conclusion: The earliest tradition concerning Christ's resurrection simply teaches that it was a spiritual appearance—he showed himself in spirit to the apostles. And this was not a subjective hallucination of theirs, but a *real objective* manifestation of the spirit of Jesus from the unseen sphere. Around this kernel gradually grew the husky narratives of the Gospels, whose authorship is so uncertain; whose conceptions are so grossly materialistic; so inconsistent with the conceptions of the unseen sphere which scientific theology forces upon us, that we must set them aside as valueless. A popular question is, What became of the body of Jesus if it was not raised from the grave? This question is based on the details about the grave, etc., given in the Gospels; but *since they are unreliable, late additions*, the question has no force. The body doubtless crumbled into dust somewhere, and the disciples who saw Jesus alive in the spirit would care little about the body. It is absurd to ask a question which implies, as this does, the acceptance of the very narratives whose authority is in question. While we, therefore, frankly admit that the story of the resurrection of Jesus, as it stands in the Gospels, can not be accepted, yet we accept this great fact as stated in St. Paul's epistle just quoted. However, even if, *for the sake of argument*, we accept the traditional authorship of the Gospels, we can readily explain their accounts of the Resurrection. First, the facts stated about the risen Jesus appearing with the prints of nails in his hands and feet, and a lance-wound in his side, are easily accounted for when we find such a man as Mr. Alfred Russel Wallace accepting " the materializations " of spirits, which modern Spiritualism adduces. If a man of his high scientific standing can be so wofully deceived, it is certainly not irrational to believe that the simple peasants of Galilee and Judea should be deluded. This opinion gains great force when we accept the view of the Resurrection advocated above— that Jesus really *did* appear in spirit after death to his disciples. Granting this, we have only to believe that some one—the gardener possibly, or some one else— removed the body from the tomb, and soon after the manifestations began which so completely satisfied the disciples that they sought no further for the body. They saw, as many a devout and honest spiritualist in our day sees, the bodily form of their dear departed Friend. All this, let it be remembered, is simply said to show how one who accepts the traditional authorship of the Gospels may yet offer a credible explanation of their accounts of the Resurrection; but to one who, like the author, believes that the details of this event thus given are late additions by unknown *rédacteurs* of " notes " by Matthew, Mark, Luke, and John, such details, of course, offer no difficulty, need no explanation, since they are merely grossly materialistic embellishments of St. Paul's spiritual conception of the Resurrection. We accept his account, for the following reasons:

First. Granting that there *is* a God (and we believe this) who is interested in his creatures, and granting that the human spirit is immortal, it is *antecedently probable* that our God would give us some *positive* assurance of the life beyond the grave by sending back from the Beyond one of those messengers whom He has sent into this world to teach His moral law to man, and of all the instruments which might be chosen for this purpose Jesus of Nazareth was pre-eminently *the* one whom we might expect to be selected.

Secondly. When we find this antecedent probability supported by the evidence which the New Testament as a whole furnishes us, we do not hesitate to accept the spiritual manifestation of Jesus to his disciples after death.

There can be no shadow of a doubt, as even the most radical skeptics confess, that all the early disciples *believed* that they saw Jesus after his death, and all those theories which teach that these visions were *purely* subjective delusions are unsatisfactory, for, while great delusions have existed and produced wonderful results, yet the deep enthusiasm and hope of heaven which animated the apostles, especially St. Paul, together with the latter's positive testimony to the manifestation of the risen Jesus, point to a real, objective event.

Third. The view of the resurrection thus set forth is not liable to the *scientific* objections which may be urged against the old view, but true science rather confirms it. Physiology utterly fails to identify the spirit with the body; the two *coexist*, but they are *not one;* and if the spirit of man can *thus* manifest itself through matter, it is quite credible that it should manifest itself after it has been separated from its "tenement of clay," and the only question that can be raised in any case is, What evidence have we that this has happened?

We believe that in the case of Jesus we have sufficient evidence of his *post-mortem* manifestation; but we by no means indorse all alleged instances of such spirit-phenomena.* *Spiritualism has not yet proved its main point.* But while spiritualism has not yet proved its main point, namely, that the spirits of the departed manifest themselves to men in the flesh, yet it has proved more clearly than was hitherto shown the extraordinary power of the human spirit. Ignoring the various spiritualistic newspapers, the journals of the English and American Societies for Psychical Research teem with phenomena which prove at least the *semi-independence* of the mind and its *possible* manifestation in this world after its separation from the body. To cite only one instance: Prof. F. W. Barrett, in a paper read before "The English Society for Psychical Research," states it as his "conviction that at any rate some of the simpler phenomena of spiritualism are inexplicable by any cause at present recognized by Science." Various experiments with *private* " mediums," by whom tables were moved *when no hand was on them*, and in full daylight, led him to the conclusion that "*mind, occasionally and unconsciously, can exert direct influence upon lifeless matter.*" † If so, then mind must be at least *partially* independent of the material body,

---

* Keim, " Jesus of Nazara," vi, pp. 192–383.
† "Journal of the English Society for Psychical Research," 1886, pp. 24–44.

and the proposition that a disembodied spirit should exist independently of matter and should make itself known to an embodied spirit (man in the flesh) becomes less incredible.

The late Prof. Balfour Stewart, who was also a member of the English society in question, regarded Prof. Barrett's hypothesis as "a very sagacious one," and in his comments upon it he adds these important words: "Of late years miracles have come to be regarded, not as breaks of law, but as phenomena embracing a *higher law*—a doctrine which is a great advance upon its predecessor. Now, the question naturally arises, If there be this higher law, may there not be *occasional traces* of it to be met with in the world even at the *present time?* It is, I think, exceedingly unfortunate that a large class of theologians have attempted to decide this question in the negative." * Such hints as these from men like Stewart and Bushnell have led me to hunt for indications of the said "higher law" in the New Testament records, and for "traces" of the same law in the "mind-cures," "faith-cures," and "spirit manifestations" of modern times. In the case of the former I have been forced to set aside certain events—e. g., the resurrection of Lazarus—not as impossible, but as insufficiently attested events; while others, such as the healings of our Lord, have been accepted and classed as superior, indeed, but essentially similar to other cures of ancient and modern times; and, finally, the stories of the Virgin-Birth and of the Resurrection of Jesus have been *interpreted* somewhat differently

---

* "Journal of the English Society for Psychical Research," *ut supra*, pp. 43, 44.

from what most people interpret them, but they have been accepted as pointing to the most remarkable instances of the operation of that "higher law" which Prof. Stewart, among others, accepts. Of course, I expect this chapter to give offense, on the one hand, to the Materialists, and on the other, to the Traditionalists and Literalists, who assume their own infallibility. But I trust that there are a few independent thinkers who will give the opinions expressed a fair hearing, and even find in them an escape from the crudities and absurdities of false philosophy and traditional theology into an atmosphere of freedom and lofty spirituality.

NOTE.—Among the books which may be consulted on the subject of this chapter are: 1. Advocates of the popular view—Mozley's "Bampton Lectures on Miracles," Row's "Bampton Lectures on Miracles," and "Jesus of the Evangelists"; Fisher's "Grounds of Theistic Belief," chapters iv and vi; Christlieb's "Modern Doubt and Christian Belief"; Bushnell's "Nature and the Supernatural"; Trench "On Miracles," etc.

2. Opponents of the popular view—Strauss, Baur, Renan, Keim, Davidson, Huxley, Ewald, Zeller, "Supernatural Religion," two vols.; Longmans & Co., London, 1874; Greg, "Creed of Christendom"; John Fiske's "Unseen World," chapters iii, iv, v; Carpenter's "Mental Physiology," *passim*; Dr. Carpenter's and Tuke's works should be specially consulted on the question of mental healings.

CHAPTER II.

EVOLUTION AND INSPIRATION.

ARCHDEACON FARRAR, in the seventh lecture of his admirable work on "The History of Interpretation" (Bampton Lectures for 1885), gives us a graphic sketch of the decadence of rational Biblical interpretation and of the rise of that Bibliolatry which has, like the upas-tree, spread itself over the Lord's vineyard and is to-day poisoning everything with its deadly shade. All those who fancy that the free and easy handling of the Scriptures which has thus far characterized this work is sacrilege, ought to read this able work, and especially the lecture referred to, for they would then be able to distinguish between slavery to tradition and reverence for the Bible.

The post-Reformation epoch, Dr. Farrar tells us, "was retarded and its labor vitiated by a threefold curse: the curse of tyrannous confessionalism; the curse of exorbitant systems; the curse of contentious bitterness. It was the age of creeds, symbols, confessions, theological systems, rigid formulæ." The natural result was twofold: First, a dogmatic inflexibility, unsoftened by Christian love, which led to the most deplorable contentions and dissensions among Christians; and, secondly, a Bibliolatry which, while it professed to honor Holy Scripture by its irrational worship, really dishonored it by treating the Bible as a talisman and a fetich. We read such superstitious phrases as that "the writers of Scripture are amanuenses of God, hands of Christ, scribes and notaries of the Holy Ghost; not even instrumental authors, but only *living and writing pens.* Holy Scripture is described, not as the record of revelation, but as revelation itself. Christianity, which existed so many years before a single Gospel or Epistle had been written, was robbed of its power. In defiance of every historic fact, the inspiration of the Apostles was regarded as the annihilation of their proper individuality. This sort of dogmatism became more and more pernicious. God's presence and providence in the history of the world were practically ignored. The Bible was spoken of as 'a divine effluence,' 'a part of God.'" * The real cause of this Bibliolatry is clearly stated by Mr. Matthew Arnold. "Taunted by Rome with their divisions, their want of a *fixed authority*, like the Church, Protestants," he says, "were driven to make the Bible this fixed authority; and so the Bible came to be regarded as a thing all of a piece, endued with talismanic virtues. It came to be regarded as something different from anything it had originally ever been, or primitive times had ever imagined it to be." † It came to be considered "a book let down out of the skies, immaculate, infallible, oracular," and yet this notion of the Bible can be historically traced to *heathenism.* "We read in one of the historical books of the Jews (II Maccabees, ii, 13) that Nehemiah found-

---

* Farrar's "History of Interpretation." p. 373. etc.
† Matthew Arnold's "Literature and Dogma," preface, p. xxv.

ed a library and gathered together the writings concerning the Kings and of the Prophets, and the (songs) of David and Epistles of Kings concerning temple gifts." "This formation of a national library was really the germ out of which grew the Old Testament. It was a purely civic act by a layman, but it expressed the honor in which the national writings were coming to be held. It is coincident with this that we find a priestly movement to draw a sacred line around the more important writings of the nation. Tradition has credited Ezra, the priestly coadjutor of Nehemiah, with the first formation of the Old Testament Canon. The two traditions express one and the same fact from the secular and ecclesiastical point of view. In the exile (at Babylon in the sixth century B. C., II Kings, xxv, Ezra, etc.) the stricken nation came to value and honor its national heritage as never before. Its literary sense was quickened by close contact with the civilization whose great library constituted one of the chief treasures of the central city. It was natural that on their return to their native land the Jews should gather their race-writings and found a national library. A large part of these writings, and that part largely drawn from very ancient times, was composed of judicial decisions, legislative codes, etc., around which veneration properly gathered. This veneration was heightened by the popular traditions which assigned to Moses the bulk of their legislation, and traced it through him to Jehovah himself. During the exile a remarkable priestly development, which had been running on through two centuries at least, culminated in a completely organized hierarchy and an elaborate cultus.

"In the process of this final development in Babylonia

the legislation and histories of the nation were worked over by priestly hands, in the priestly spirit. The law of Moses was now for the first time completely set before the people, and on the restoration to Judea, was made the law of the land. It became, therefore, in a new sense sacred. The fresh, free inspirations of the prophets—inspirations most real and divine—died out in the exile, smothered partly by this priestly development.

"When no living prophet arose to make men hear the voice of God, men had to hearken for that voice in the words of the dead prophets. In the synagogues or meeting-houses which developed during the exile, when the holy temple was in ruins, and which, having been found useful, were continued in the restoration, the writings of the prophets were read each Sabbath. The true writings of the chief prophets had, therefore, to be indicated. Thus came the Canon of the prophets.

"The process of exaltation was at work, and continued thenceforth through the national history, increasing as the life of the nation ebbed. It was the period immediately following the destruction of Jerusalem by the Romans (A. D. 70), which busied itself in closing the Canon of Jewish Scriptures. Death bound up the Bible. No new chapters could be added, because there was no more life to write them. In its dotage this noble nation became known by its superstitious reverence for the law as 'the people of the book.' Learned doctors gravely taught their pupils that 'God himself studies the law for the first three hours of every day.'" *

---

* Dr. Heber Newton, "Right and Wrong Uses of the Bible," pp. 29-32; Ewald, "History of Israel," vol. v; Dr. William Smith, "Old

After the formation of the Old Testament Canon, thus briefly sketched, a hedge was built about the law by the Pharisees, Scribes, and Rabbis, that sprang from the great Synagogue of Ezra, and a most deplorable Bibliolatry resulted. But, although we read in I Maccabees, xii, 9, of the "Holy Books of Scripture," yet we do not find a rigid *theory* of inspiration until we come to the writings of Philo Judæus. He "is the first who seeks to give a theory of inspiration, and he does so by bringing the reflections of Plato upon the pagan inspiration (or $\mu\alpha\nu\iota\alpha$) to explain the Jewish doctrine. Following Plato, Philo says that inspiration is a kind of "ecstasy," and he seems to imply that the degree of inspiration is greater in proportion to the unconsciousness or at least the passivity of the man inspired."

The prophet, he says, "does not speak any words of his own, he is only the instrument of God who inspires and speaks through him"; but he says "that there are degrees of inspiration, and that all portions of Scripture are not equally inspired or at least have not the same *depth* of inspiration." *

Thus, the superstitious reverence for the Sacred Books, which was begotten by the Babylonian Exile, ultimately developed into "a recklessly invented theory of mechanical inspiration" in the hands of Philo, *who borrowed it from Heathen Philosophy*. This theory passed on from one generation to another, and, finally, in the post-Reformation epoch, it completely triumphed. I say "completely," for during the preceding ages there

---

Testament History," chap. xxv, and "New Testament History," Book I.

* "Encylopædia Britannica," article, "Inspiration;" Farrar "History of Interpretation," p. 153, etc.

had been more than one noble though spasmodic reaction against this heathen dogma. Since, then, we can thus historically trace the theory of verbal dictation to heathen philosophy—since it can be shown to be of a piece with those notions which the various heathen nations entertain concerning their Sacred Books—and, above all, since the Bible itself refutes it, surely we ought to be thanked rather than blamed for tearing down this human superstructure which has been built round the inviolable shrine of Holy Scripture. "For the first time in the history of Europe, Christian people have the knowledge by which they can correct their ideas about the Bible, in what may be called a Science of Comparative Bibliolatry."

By the labors of Prof. Max Müller and others, the Sacred Books of the East (India, Persia, etc.) are now within the easy reach of all, and any one may examine for himself these "Bibles of Humanity." We find precisely the same notions current in each race about its Bible that we have cherished concerning our own Bible. "According to the orthodox view of Indian theologians," says Prof. Max Müller, "not a single line of the Veda (the Hindu Bible) was the work of human authors.

"The whole Veda is in some way or other the work of the Deity; and even those who received the revelation, or, as they express it, those who *saw* it, were not supposed to be ordinary mortals, but beings raised above the level of common humanity, and less liable, therefore, to error in the reception of revealed truth. The views entertained of revelation by the orthodox theologians of India are far more minute and elaborate than those of the most extreme advocates of verbal inspiration in

Europe. The human element is driven out of every corner or hiding-place; and, as the Veda is held to have existed in the mind of the Deity before the beginning of time, every allusion to historical events, of which there are not a few, is explained away with a zeal and ingenuity worthy of a better cause. . . . But," he adds (and his words apply to our Bible), "let me state at once that there is nothing in the hymns (the Veda) to warrant such extravagant theories. In many a hymn, the author says plainly that he or his friends made it to please the gods," etc.* We find essentially the same notions current among the Mohammedans respecting their Bible—the Koran. "Mohammedan doctors of divinity divided into fiercely contesting parties over the question whether the Koran was created or uncreated, the latter theory, as most highly magnifying their Sacred Book, of course becoming the orthodox view." †

"Bibliolatry is pushed to a *reductio ad absurdum* in these pagan worships of their Sacred Books. Men will see their folly in the reflected light of these kindred follies, and another superstition will disappear from Christendom."

But not only is the theory of verbal inspiration heathenish; it is contradicted by the Bible itself. "The sacred writers thrust upon the attention of all those who are not blind the traces of human imperfection." "The Old Testament historians contradict each other in facts and figures, tell the same story in different ways, locate the same incident at different periods, ascribe the same

---

* "Chips from a German Workshop," i, p. 18.

† "Encylopædia Britannica," article "Mohammedanism," Part III, "Koran."

deeds to different men, quote statistics which are plainly exaggerated, mistake poetic legend for sober prose, repeat the marvelous tales of tradition as literal history, and give us statements which can not be read as scientific facts without denying our latest and most authoritative knowledge." Literary criticism, however imperfect it may yet be, has clearly shown "marks of a patient and noble literary workmanship" in all parts of Holy Scripture. "The historical books (Kings, Chronicles, etc.) are seen to be the work of many hands in many ages. They gather up the popular traditions of the race, carry down on their slow streams fragments from such far back ages that we have almost the clew to their story—glacial bowlders that now lie strangely out of place in the rich fields of later eras; songs of rude periods, Nature-myths, legends of semi-fabulous heroes, folk-lore of the tribes, scraps from long-forgotten books, entries from ancient annals, pages torn from the histories of other peoples to fill out the story; the whole worked over many times by many hands in many generations." The Pentateuch, or first five books of the Bible, commonly ascribed to Moses, are now shown to be the work of different hands, and by no means an infallible work.*

"The prophecies break up into fragmentary collections, in which the words of many different and obscure prophets are grouped under the name of some great prophet.† The Psalter (or Book of Psalms) separates

---

* See, for popular exposition of advanced criticism, "Encyclopædia Britannica," articles "Pentateuch," "Israel," and "Bible." Cf. Ewald, "History of Israel," vol. i; Kuenen, "Inquiry into the Origin and Composition of the Hexateuch," etc., etc.

† "Encyclopædia Britannica," articles "Isaiah," "Daniel," etc.

into several books of sacred song, dating from different periods. They repeat the same psalm, and divide one psalm into two, and join two into one, on principles by no means apparent to us." In short, "our critical glasses bring out, clear and strong, the fact of a human literary craft in these books, the signs on every hand of the labor of brain and skill of pen, through which the literature of a venerable nation, and of the infant church born of it, took slow shape into our Bible."*

Now, of course, the traditionalist would urge just here the common but fallacious "argument" against the advanced critics, namely, that they *differ* among themselves, and hence we can not trust their conclusions. To which we reply: Whatever may be the differences of opinion among the critics as to certain minor points, yet they have proved to demonstration that there are many numerical, historical, and even moral defects in the Bible, and so the theory of verbal dictation is utterly exploded. This is all-sufficient for our purpose. Each one must study for himself the writings of the various critics and accept or reject their views, according to the strength or weakness of the arguments advanced, but we may safely defy any one to prove the *literal infallibility* of the Bible, if any one familiar with the results of modern criticism could be so rash as to attempt this. Even readers of magazines, such as "The North American Review," etc., are familiar with "the mistakes of Moses," the prevalence of polygamy and slavery among the patriarchs—the inspired saints of Jehovah—wars of extermination under Joshua and others, and so

---

* Rev. Heber Newton, "Right and Wrong Uses of the Bible," chap. i, § III.

on. No thoughtful reader of the Psalms can fail to observe the purely human spirit in those bitter denunciations and invocations of God's wrath against his enemies which mar many portions of this otherwise beautiful and edifying bit of ancient poetry. And what thoughtful reader has not been deeply pained by the "Song of Deborah" (Judges, v) over the treachery of "Jael, wife of Heber the Kenite"? The thoroughly human spirit is here too evident to be denied, and yet this is only one of many such instances which might be pointed out were we disposed to do so.* But it is not necessary to do this. Enough has been said to show why we must reject the verbal infallibility of the Bible, and indeed it would hardly seem necessary to dwell on this point were it not a fact that, while many of our most conservative theological writers reject verbal inspiration, the majority of the laity, perhaps, accept it, or try to accept it.

There are various other theories of inspiration—modifications of the theory of verbal dictation—which are admirably dealt with by Canon Row in the last of his "Bampton Lectures," but it is not necessary to consider them, since my object is simply to refute the doctrine of verbal inspiration, and to enunciate what seems to be the only view which modern research will allow us to hold.

To begin at the beginning: The primitive man, as we have seen, had no such lofty ideas of God and the soul's nature and destiny as we have. He probably got his idea of the soul as distinct from the body from the dream; but, however this may be, when he did get

---

* Dean Stanley's "History of the Jewish Church," lect. xiv.

this notion it soon branched out into various ideas as to the operation of the disembodied spirit. Certain diseases—epilepsy, insanity, etc.—were supposed to be due to the presence of a foreign spirit which had taken possession of the subject. But "if a man's body may be entered by a wicked soul of the dead enemy, may it not be entered by a friendly soul? If the struggles of the epileptic, the ravings of the delirious, the self-injuries of the insane, are caused by an indwelling demon, then must not the transcendent power of marvelous skill, occasionally displayed, be caused by an indwelling beneficent spirit? . . . These questions the savage consistently answers in the affirmative.

"That manifestations of unusual will and strength are thus accounted for, we find proofs among early traditions."* And Mr. Spencer gives us instances of such ideas (familiar to all students of ancient history) from the Greeks (Homer), Egyptians, etc., which show that —to quote another writer—"artistic powers and poetic talents, gifts of prediction, the warmth of love, and the battle frenzy, were all ascribed to the power of the god possessing the man inspired." Philo, as stated above, borrowed Plato's views on this subject and so Heathenism and Judaism joined hands. "The early Christian Church seems to have simply taken over the Jewish views (thus heathenized) about the inspiration of the Old Testament; and, when the New Testament Canon was complete, the Fathers transferred the same characteristics to the New Testament writings also." Many of the most eminent fathers had been primarily heathen philosophers, and so it was natural

---

* Spencer's "Principles of Sociology," vol. i, chap. xviii.

that their philosophic views should influence their theology.*

Thus we may see how naturally the idea of divine inspirations may have arisen. Beginning with the notion that a foreign spirit—or "other-self"—took possession of a man, this opinion would be slowly differentiated into the idea of a superhuman being's ruling the man (for were not many of his words and actions superhuman?), and then this being would come to be worshiped as a god; and, finally, these "gods-many" would be consolidated, so to speak, into one God, to whom, of course, all thoughts and events would necessarily be ascribed. What shall we think of this philosophy? Shall we believe that men may be really possessed by foreign spirits? Surely not. Shall we reject the entire notion of divine inspiration? That, of course, depends on what is meant by "inspiration." If by this term we are to understand that a voice from the skies spoke to the inspired man, we shall hardly accept it. But if, with the Rev. Frederick Myers, we hold that the phrases "Thus saith the Lord" of the Prophets, and "The Lord said unto Moses," simply "signify a deep and true *impression* on the prophet's mind, that what he was saying was assuredly in accordance with the will of God" †—if this be inspiration, then we readily accept it. In short, the only view of inspiration which an enlightened philosophy will allow us to hold is that which considers it a "*functional endowment*." ‡ The spirit of man is a spark flashed forth from the Eternal Light—

---

* "Encyclopædia Britannica," article "Inspiration."
† Frederick Myers, "Catholic Thoughts on the Bible," p. 76, etc.
‡ Canon Row's "Bampton Lectures," p. 432, etc.

an "image" of the Divine Spirit—and as such it partakes of his nature. God sends great philosophers, like Aristotle, Socrates, and Newton, into the world; and poets, like Homer, Milton, and Shakespeare; and warriors, like Alexander, Cæsar, and Napoleon; and lawgivers, like Moses, Solon, and Lycurgus. All such men possess peculiar "gifts" which come from one and the same Divine Spirit (I Corinthians, xii, 4–11). They are pre-eminently endowed with the philosophic, poetic, military, and legal faculties or functions, and they speak with *authority* in their various spheres. Why, then, should we hesitate to believe that God specially endows certain men with the gift of religious insight—an Abraham, an Isaiah, a Paul, a Job, a Buddha, a Zoroaster, a Confucius, a Socrates? We should not hesitate to believe this, for such an endowment would be simply another instance of that "division of labor" (to use an economic term) which marks all creation. Even in the individual we have various organs to perform different functions—the eye does not do the work of the hand, nor does the memory discharge the functions of the will. How much more, then, should the different members of the social organism perform special functions! Of course, this view makes inspiration a "natural" function of the human spirit, but it is no less Divine in its origin—unless, indeed, we deny that Nature is of God. The theory which teaches that "the inspiration of Holy Scripture is of the nature of a miracle "* is either too vague for comprehension or it is not provable. The Rev. Brownlow Maitland, M. A., in an admirable little book entitled "Skepticism and

---

* Bishop Harold Browne, "Essay on Inspiration," p. 37, etc.

Faith,"* devotes a chapter to the discussion of the question "Is Revelation possible?" and the word "revelation" seems to be used as a synonym of "inspiration." The skeptic with whom the author argues says: "It is easy to talk in a general way of our receiving communications from without, and being able to discern whence they come to us. But when the person from whom they purport to issue is both unseen and unknown, you will, if you proceed accurately, according to the strict laws of induction, find yourself at a loss to *trace* those communications to their *real origin*.

"There are only two ways in which any conceivable revelation can be presented to our apprehension: it must come either direct to the mind or through the organs of sense. Suppose it to come direct to your mind. In that case your earliest knowledge of it will be in your consciousness of it in your thoughts. You find yourself thinking it; it is only as *your* thought, *your* idea, that you know it at all; from your own thoughts you can not disentangle it. *How you came* to think it you can not possibly know—whether it sprang up of itself in your mind, or were excited or infused from without; on the question of its origin it can give you no information.

"To assert, therefore, that it came to you from God would be to invent an hypothesis which is utterly incapable of verification. Or, suppose that the revelation is presented to you through your organs of sense. A voice strikes on your ear, or a visible phenomenon is exhibited to your eye. That is all that you are conscious of; a sensation, an impression on your senses, nothing

---

* New York, Pott, Young & Co., 1887.

more. What this means, or *what caused* it, can only be a matter of inference, of guess, on your part. The impression which you experience may be an illusive one, for aught you know, like the impressions experienced in hallucinations or dreams. Or, if it has a cause in some reality outside you, what that cause is you can not ascertain." Of course, the obvious answer to this latter mode of argument is, that it proves too much; it has no goal, as Mr. Maitland rightly observes, "short of universal skepticism." If we accept it, we can not know anything outside our own immediate circle of consciousness. Our only means of knowing of (even) the *existence* of one another are our organs of sense—sight, hearing, touch, etc.—and if we suppose that these deceive us, we are landed in absolute skepticism, and this it is practically impossible to accept. Hence we may rationally infer that a theory which involves a practical impossibility is false.

The real question, therefore, is, Have we sufficient *evidence* that God has spoken to man? I mean, of course, as we understand the word "speech." For instance: Can it be proved that St. Paul, on the way to Damascus, heard a Voice and saw a Form *outside* himself? Did a word really come to him from an objective spirit? Owing to the uncertain authorship of the *Acts*, and the ambiguous references to this "vision" in Galatians (ii, 16), we must, at least, admit that this question can not be dogmatically answered in the affirmative. And since this is perhaps one of the best attested instances of a Divine Voice speaking to man, we must set aside as "not proven" all such alleged instances. Then, as to the skeptic's first argument, viz., granting that a direct revelation to the human mind is possible, yet thoughts thus communicated would be so inextricably blended with one's own thoughts that he could not tell whence they came—this argument, Mr. Maitland frankly admits, is logically unanswerable. What, then, shall we think or say on this subject? Why, he answers: " Our whole mental constitution is not summed up in the *logical* understanding. We are endowed with a *conscience* that witnesses for the authority of a moral law; and a spiritual faculty which can think of God, can reverence and worship Him, and it is to this moral and spiritual faculty that God addresses himself." * Now, this is precisely my own view. We can not be sure that the Creator has ever literally " spoken " to man ; we can not prove that the great thoughts about God and religion which characterize the writings of the religious seers of all ages were *directly* infused into their minds in some mysterious way by the Creator, but we are sure that " the spirit of man is the candle of the Lord " (Proverbs, xx, 27): man's spiritual nature must have sprung from the Eternal Spirit, and hence it partakes of the nature of that Spirit; it is itself a partial revelation of God. " Every good gift, therefore, and every perfect gift is from above, and cometh down from the Father of lights " (James, i, 17).

Taking the view, then, that God sends men into the world endowed with special gifts of religious insight, the next question is, Are we to accept their " revelations " or deliveries as *absolutely infallible ?* Let us take an example—St. Paul. Are we to accept all his deliveries as absolutely infallible and binding on our-

---

* " Skepticism and Faith," pp. 104–127.

selves? That depends, of course, on what those deliveries are, and whether they are true. If, for instance, St. Paul teaches the Calvinistic doctrine of Adam's fall and man's total depravity, then his infallibility is disproved by science. Or, to take a more unquestionable instance, if he taught that Christ would return to earth within a few years after his death, then history proves him to have been mistaken. Let it be remembered that the question of a religious teacher's infallibility is simply a question of *fact* which must be settled by an appeal to his actual deliveries and not by any *a priori* considerations; and we have no other faculty than reason and conscience by which to judge of revelation itself. There are undoubtedly many statements in the Bible which we have ample reason to believe infallibly true, but whether *all* its statements are infallibly true is precisely the point to be proved, and we have already seen that this can not be done. However loathsome, therefore, may be the task, yet we *must* use our reason in the study of the Bible—we must discriminate. Even Prof. Huxley can tell us: " In the eighth century B. C., in the heart of a world of idolatrous polytheists, the Hebrew prophets put forth a conception of religion which appears to me to be as wonderful an inspiration of genius as the art of Phidias or the science of Aristotle. 'And what doth the Lord require of thee, but to do justly, and to love mercy, and to walk humbly with thy God?' (Micah, vi, 8). If any so-called religion takes away from this great saying of Micah, I think it wantonly mutilates; while if it adds thereto, I think it obscures the perfect ideal of religion. But what extent of knowledge, what acuteness of scientific criticism, can touch this, if any one possessed of knowledge or acuteness could be absurd enough to make the attempt? Will the progress of research prove that justice is worthless and mercy hateful? Will it ever soften the bitter contrast between our actions and our aspirations, or show us the bounds of the universe, and bid us say, ' Go to, now we comprehend the Infinite.' " *

In these words Prof. Huxley clearly states, first, the sort of religion, and, secondly, the sort of inspiration, which the truly scientific mind is disposed to accept—namely, a religion of justice, mercy, and humility, and an inspiration which consists in a functional endowment, *a native faculty*, by which the man so endowed is enabled to grasp more clearly than others the great truths of religion. But I quote him mainly to show that even an agnostic philosopher does not hesitate to attribute infallible truths to the holy men of the Bible. No extent of knowledge, no acuteness of criticism, can ever touch certain grand truths therein taught; and so the only question is, What *are* those unassailable truths? —a question which every one must settle for himself; and, with an open Bible, and an honest heart, and a level head, and an unbefogged mind, he will have comparatively little difficulty in finding those truths; or, rather, to quote Coleridge, they will "*find him.*" Even an Ingersoll finds unassailable (*alias* infallible) truths in the Bible. " Every good and noble sentiment," he says, " uttered in the Bible is still good and noble. Every fact remains. All that is good in the Sermon on the Mount is retained. The Lord's Prayer

---

* " Order of Creation." Controversy between Gladstone, Huxley, etc., p. 62. " Truth-Seeker Company," New York.

is not affected. The grandeur of self-denial, the nobility of forgiveness, and the ineffable splendor of mercy are still with us." *

Since, then, even the agnostic freethinkers admit that all truth is infallible, and that the Bible contains many truths, albeit the wheat is mingled with the chaff, the only remaining question is, *How much truth* is there in the Bible? If we find truths in the Pentateuch, *so far* its author was infallible. If we find truths in the Psalms, the Prophecies, the Gospels, the Epistles, *so far* their authors were infallible, and *no further*.

This, it seems to me, is the simplest and most rational way of dealing with the question of inspiration. We can never prove on *a priori* principles the inspiration or infallibility of a man. Let us, therefore, urge that God sends religious as well as philosophic and poetic geniuses into the world; and, although they are not absolutely infallible, yet so far as they discover and reveal truth they are infallible. But, of course, the thoughtful reader is asking himself, and doubtless would ask the author, Was *Christ* only partially infallible? No one can give a dogmatic answer to this question, for the simple reason that our Lord has not left us his teaching in his own name, and the accounts which his disciples have left us are *their* opinions and reminiscences of Him, not certainly and always his words. For my own part, I am content to know that He was decidedly the greatest religious teacher that ever lived, and, therefore, if He were not *absolutely* infallible, He was nearer so than any one else that ever lived on this earth.

---

* "North American Review," August, 1888, p. 160.

This conclusion is not in the least shaken by the difficulties of Biblical criticism. I dare say that there is not a single skeptic of any note—certainly not a Baur, a Renan, a Huxley—who will object to this conclusion. But if this conclusion is true, then Jesus of Nazareth—not a Zoroaster, a Confucius, a Buddha, a Socrates, a Mohammed, or a Paul—is our Master in religion. He is for us the divinest among men, and therefore we need not trouble ourselves with a question we can never solve. Let us suppose, for instance, that the Sermon on the Mount and the Lord's Prayer are at least substantially correct—that their *main* principles were enunciated by our Lord, and are true—then He was certainly so far infallible, and these contain the essentials to salvation from sin here and suffering hereafter. Why, then, trouble ourselves with (for instance) the question whether Christ believed and taught demoniacal possession as it appears in the Gospels?* We never can settle this question beyond doubt, and, since it is of no great practical importance, we may either ignore it or attribute the opinions about demons to the authors of the Gospels. At any rate, it should never be forgotten that none of the books in the New Testament were written by Jesus, and most of them were written many years after his death by more or less credulous and superstitious disciples, and hence no one should dogmatize on a point like that under consideration.

The view of inspiration, then, which I would maintain is, that God has sent men into the world at different times differently endowed with religious insight, and they have imparted truth as their fellow-men were able

---

* Keim, "Jesus of Nazara,'" iii, p. 236 *et seq.*

to receive it. The Bible "is a record of this progressive revelation divinely adapted to the hard heart, the dull understanding, and the slow development of mankind." I believe that "Holy Scripture *containeth* all things necessary to salvation" (Article VI, Episcopal Prayer-Book), and I am glad that I belong to a church which does not attempt to explain *how* those great truths were communicated "to the holy men of old." Nothing but failure and disaster can ever result from dogmatizing on such a subject. Give us the Scriptures of God in their broad outlines—the revelation of God in its glorious unity. "The last word of the sacred Book," says Dr. Farrar, "was a word of infinite significance. It was, 'Little children, keep yourselves from idols' (I John, v, 21). Idols are always a fatal hindrance to the attainment of the truth. Sooner or later they that make them become like unto them, and so do all who put their trust in them. Such idols—ignorant, well-meaning, credulous suspicions and fond conceits, those fleeting images born of confusions of language, false theories, and perverse demonstrations—only vanish when the light of God penetrates into the deep recesses of the shrine. History is a ray of that light of God. A great part of the Bible is History, and all History, rightly understood, is also a Bible. Its lessons are God's divine methods of slowly exposing error and of guiding into truth. *Facts* are God's words, and to be disloyal to God's facts is to dethrone Him from the world." * Let us then, go the Scriptures without *any* theory of inspiration, and study them in the light of History and Science, firmly believing that truth is eter-

---

* "History of Interpretation," preface, p. xii.

nal and can not be overthrown, while error must die even though it be bolstered up by authority for years.

Let no one imagine for a moment that, because the author has thus strongly denounced Bibliolatry and unauthorized dogma, and insisted on treating the Bible as only one of many pieces of religious literature, he either agrees with that flippant popular skepticism of our day that does little else than ridicule and tear to pieces, or would underrate that book of books. But I am thoroughly convinced that "the supremacy of the Scriptures is assured when, and only when, they are seen to be *human* as well as divine, and are not regarded as the sole source of revelation, but rather as the record of its progressive development." We then understand that the author of Genesis ought not to be expected to anticipate modern science. We then see why Abraham could have concubines and own slaves; how Joshua could slaughter the Canaanites and think he was doing God's will; how Deborah could bless Jael for her treachery, and how David could solemnly invoke God's wrath against his enemies. All these ancient saints were "enlightened with only a very small portion of that Divine Light which went on brightening ever more and more unto the perfect day" which dawned on the heights of Bethlehem and Nazareth. "In the name of the Son of God"—of a *Divine Life*, not a Book—'is the secret of our security, of our freedom, of our strength. If we build upon Him, we build on the one foundation. It is because they put themselves in place of Him, that hierarchies have fallen into corruption and ruin. It is because they failed to comprehend his nature that philosophies have passed away. It is because they thrust the dead letter in the place of his living Spirit, that religious movements have ended in hatred and obstructiveness. It is because they have mistaken the dawn for a conflagration that theologians have so often been the foes of light. It is because they have appealed to self-deceiving intentions as infallible proofs of their own human interpretations, that their cherished conclusions have so often been overthrown. But no church, and no system, and no man who has been rooted and grounded in Him in love has ever failed to increase with the increase of God. Amid the tyrannies of priestcraft, amid the aberrations of theology, amid the doubts and difficulties of criticism, the Bible has continued to be the inalienable possession of the Christian Church. No attempt to keep the sacred writings as a seven-sealed book in the hands of the clergy, no insuperable difficulties created by dogmas about inspiration, no false systems of interpretation built upon those dogmas, have been able to snatch the Bible wholly from the hands of that vast unknown multitude whom God has known for his and who have departed from iniquity. To them—the simple and the unselfish and the pure in heart—it has ever been as still it is a guide to the feet and a lamp to the path—'a granary of wholesome food against fenowed traditions.' Reading the Scripture not with eyes of partisanship, or suspicion, or of self-interest, but with the eyes of love, and into the soul's vernacular, they have found it rich in blessing and consolation. The secret of the Lord has been with them that fear Him, and He has shown them his covenant."

And so it ever will be. The Bible is by no means obsolete, a collection of "old wives' fables." "This collection of books," said that eminent freethinker,

Theodore Parker, " has taken such a hold on the world as no other. The literature of Greece, which goes up like incense from that land of temples and heroic deeds, has not half the influence of this book. It goes equally to the cottage of the plain man and the palace of the king. It is woven into the literature of the scholar and colors the talk of the streets." "How," asked Prof. Huxley, "is the religious feeling, which is the essential basis of conduct, to be kept up in the present utterly chaotic state of opinion, without the use of the Bible? By the study of what other book could children be so much humanized, and made to feel that each figure in the vast historical procession fills, like themselves, but a momentary space in the interval between two eternities, and earns the blessings or the curses of all time according to its efforts, to do good and hate evil?" * In another place he says: "Greatly to the surprise of many of my friends, I have always advocated the reading of the Bible, and the diffusion of the study of that most remarkable collection of books among the people. Its teachings are so infinitely superior to those of the sects, who are just as busy now as the Pharisees were eighteen hundred years ago, in smothering them under ' the precepts of men'; it is so certain to my mind that the Bible contains within itself the refutation of nine tenths of the mixture of sophistical metaphysics and old world superstition which has been piled around it by so-called Christians of later times; it is so clear that the only immediate and ready antidote to the poison which has been mixed with Christianity, to the intoxication

---

* Farrar's "History of Interpretation," preface, p. xxvii, and pp. 431–433.

and delusion of mankind, lies in copious draughts from the undefiled spring, that I exercise the right and duty of free judgment on the part of every man, mainly for the purpose of inducing other laymen to follow my example." *

Since, then, the Bible, *without the assistance of any theory of inspiration*, can exercise such an influence upon even the freest and most skeptical thinkers, since, taken in all its simplicity, as a book of books, as a record of religious experiences, it can do so much good, can draw so many to the throne of the Eternal, why should we obscure that simplicity and thwart that blessed work by insisting upon accepting our theories along with the Holy Scriptures? May God forbid!

Let us study and interpret those parts of the Bible which refer to natural phenomena by the light of modern science, making all due allowance for the times in which they were produced. Let us study the historical portions of Scripture in connection with the history of those nations with which the Israelites came in contact —Chaldea, Egypt, Babylonia, Persia, etc.

Let us study the Biblical philosophy and religion as a part of universal philosophy and religion. So shall we find our Bible a lamp unto our feet, and a light unto our path, as we journey through the wilderness of life to that city which hath foundations whose builder and maker is God.

---

* "Popular Science Monthly," June, 1889, p. 167.

CHAPTER III.

EVOLUTION AND THE TRINITY.

In the opinion of many good and learned people, all wisdom and knowledge on religious subjects was confined to the first three or four centuries of the Christian era. During that time the New Testament was originated and the popular doctrines concerning the Godhead and the Person and Mission of Christ were promulgated; and since then nothing has been added to the book of knowledge. These questions are forever "closed," and hence we frequently hear an "orthodox" clergyman denounce one—especially if he be a young man—who, he says, "preaches as if there were nothing settled in Christian theology."

Now it is true that there are some preachers who discuss the doctrines of the Godhead, Immortality, the Person and Mission of Jesus, etc., as if these questions were not "closed"; but they do so because these are precisely the questions which agitate thinking minds among all classes. While the various sects of Christendom are urging their "distinctive" claims to be *the* Church, such persons are asking, Is Christianity of divine origin? Wherein is it more divine than other religions—Buddhism, Mohammedanism, etc.? While theologians are wasting their mental energies discussing theories of the Sacraments, of the Atonement, and such like, other thinking men and women are asking, Is there a God? Is there a future life? Is there any *need* of an Atonement for sin? Rev. Frederick Robertson says somewhere, I think in a lecture to workingmen, that while the clergy, on a certain occasion, were in one hall discussing theories of the sacrament of the Lord's Supper, the workingmen were in a hall hard by discussing the question, Is there a God? I was once very much surprised by having the president of a Carpenters' Union —a Roman Catholic—tell me that he had written a paper on " Reason and Revelation," which he thought of having published, and it had taken him the whole of one winter to prepare this paper. These are the subjects which engage the attention of thinking minds even among " the masses," not the mint and anise and cummin of theology. How infinitely puerile must most of the questions discussed in the pulpit and ecclesiastical councils appear to one who is thinking about the great problems of God, the Soul, and Immortality! Say what we will and do what we will, there is *no* question absolutely "closed."

Every man born into this world, if he thinks at all, must sooner or later " open " the questions mentioned, and this is my apology to those who might demand an apology for " opening " a discussion about the Godhead. I find even among the so-called " weaker sex " (which, however, is very much stronger than is generally supposed) that it is the Trinity, the Divinity of Christ, the Origin and Destiny of Man, etc., which claim their attention, and they do not want to know what St. Athanasius taught or what any sect in Christendom teaches on these subjects; but they want to know whether the popular doctrines are *true* or *false;* and the latter alternative is being more widely and rapidly accepted than some people imagine. Hence I shall discuss these doctrines as if they were new problems, save only that I shall briefly trace the historical development of such doctrines, and then state the view which seems to be gaining ground and is destined to triumph.

We have already seen that man was probably *atheous* *—i. e., without any idea of God—in the beginning; but gradually he got, from the dream or otherwise, the idea of the Soul as distinct from the Body; and having thus got the notion of Power from his own *Ego* or *Self*, he attributed such power to every phenomenon, every moving thing; and hence he gradually came to think of spirits operating in all Nature around him. Thus arose Ancestor-worship, Fetichism, Nature-worship, Polytheism, and such like. It is not necessary to my purpose to trace the general development of ideas respecting the Deity, as this has been most ably done in the works of Mr. Spencer and others, and I am concerned mainly with the development of such ideas in the Israelitish nation. But this nation came out from another nation, viz., the Chaldean (Gen., xi, 27; xii, etc.), and came in contact with the Egyptians, the Babylonians, the Persians, the Greeks, and the Romans, and it is plain that its entire life was influenced more or less by these nations. Hence it is necessary to consider such influence in treating of Israel's religious life.

It is more particularly necessary to know what sort

---

* This word was happily coined by the Bishop of Carlisle, England. See his "Science and Faith," p. 46. John Murray, London, England, 1883.

of notions of Deity prevailed in that nation—the Chaldean—from which the Israelites sprang.

"The religion of the Chaldeans," says Canon Rawlinson, "from the very earliest times to which the monuments carry us back, was, in its outward aspect, a polytheism of a very elaborate character. It is quite possible that there may have been esoteric explanations, known to the priests and the more learned, which, resolving the personages of the Pantheon into the powers of Nature, reconciled the multiplicity of gods with monotheism, or even atheism. So far, however, as outward appearances were concerned, the worship was grossly polytheistic."* It was from this polytheistic nation that Israel sprang.

Abraham's father was an idolater (Josh., xxiv, 1–15), and the documents, on the Creation, the Deluge, etc. which Abraham probably took with him from "Ur of the Chaldees," and which now constitute the first chapters of our Genesis, were, no doubt, written by some of those "learned" men who, Canon Rawlinson says, gave "esoteric explanations" of the Chaldean doctrines concerning the gods. Perhaps we may see in the singular verb (*Bārā*—"created") of Genesis, i, 1, which follows the plural name Elohim (God), a trace of this esoteric explanation. The Chaldean *savants* may have been attempting to lead the popular mind to think of the Elohim as *one*, and among these *savants* we must class Abraham. This Patriarch's migration from Chaldea marks a stage in the development of religion. In Abraham we have the transition from Polytheism to

---

* Rawlinson, "Ancient Monarchies," vol. i, chap. vii, on "Religion of Chaldea."

anthropomorphic Henotheism—that is, an idealization and condensation of many deities into a single Deity with many human attributes. What is meant especially by " henotheism " is well expressed in the following passage from Prof. Max Müller's essay on " Semitic Monotheism ": "There are, in reality," he says, "two kinds of oneness, which, when we enter into metaphysical discussions, must be carefully distinguished, and which for practical purposes are well kept separate by the definite and indefinite articles. There is one kind of oneness which does not exclude the idea of plurality, there is another which does. When we say that Cromwell was a Protector of England, we do not assert that he was the *only* protector. But if we say that he was *the* Protector of England it is understood that he was the only man that enjoyed that title. If, therefore, an expression had been given to the primitive intuition of the Deity, which is the mainspring of all later religion, it would have been — ' There is *a* God,' but not yet, ' There is but *One* God.' The latter form of faith, the belief in One God is properly called monotheism, whereas the term henotheism would best express the faith in a single god." * Such was the faith of Abraham, but whether we accept this view or that of Mr. Herbert Spencer, who thinks that the story of Abraham's Call and Covenant with the Lord (Gen. xii, 15) implies nothing more than a transaction between " a terrestrial potentate "—a Chaldean king or ruler—and the Patriarch, yet, I think, we must admit that the story of Abraham's conversation with the three

---

* Max Müller's " Chips from a German Workshop," vol. i, pp. 349, 350.

men in "the plains of Mamre" (Gen., xviii), among other passages of Scripture, shows clearly that his idea of the Deity was decidedly anthropomorphic.

"The question is not that which theologians raise— "Who actually were these three men? Was the chief of them Jehovah? or his angel? or the Son? The question is, what Abraham thought, or is described as thinking, by those who preserved the tradition? Either alternative has the same ultimate implication."*

We seem, then, justified in holding this view of the origin of notions concerning the Deity in Israel: First, man in general and the Chaldeans in particular struggled upward from a lower state—probably an atheous condition—through Ancestor-worship, Nature-worship, Fetichism, etc., to the polytheistic state. Then, secondly, the Abrahamic movement occurred which marked the transition, in this nation, from polytheism to anthropomorphic henotheism. Third, this stage extended, in all its essentials, to the time of Moses, when Jehovah, the great "I Am" (Exodus, iii, 14), was set forth first as the national Deity, and the greatest among the gods, afterward as the "only God." "Hear, O Israel, the Lord our God is one Lord" (Deut., vi, 4, etc.). Of course, I do not mean to say that there were not lower forms of worship and lower notions of Deity coexisting with these higher views. No doubt, as Prof. Fiske says, fetichism, polytheism, ancestor-worship, and Nature-worship prevailed, to a greater or less extent, among the Israelites, especially among "the masses," while the nation as a whole was moving forward to a higher plane of religious thought—i. e., to pure monotheism—which was reached

---

* Spencer's "Sociology," i, p. 408, etc.

in the time of the prophets and apostles. "In order that the Jewish conception should come to be generally adopted, it was only necessary that it should be freed from its limitations of nationality, and that Jehovah should be set forth as Sustainer of the Universe and Father of all mankind. This was done by Jesus and Paul."*

From the foregoing brief sketch of the development of the idea of Deity it is evident, I hope, that such attempts as that of Canon Rawlinson to prove "the early prevalence of monotheistic beliefs" do not go to the root of this subject, and must be set aside in the light of evolution.†

After the lofty conception of God as the one Supreme Creator and Sustainer of the Universe had been reached, speculations as to the precise nature of the Deity came to the front, and of these speculations that known as "Trinitarianism" is the one which specially claims our attention in this chapter.

"The dogma of the Trinity," says an acute thinker, "existed long before Christianity. It is found among the ancient religions of antiquity. The wise men of Egypt fashioned this dogma, as a symbol—an imaginative expression—of the mystery in the Divine Being upon which they came through all their studies of Nature. The profound thinkers of India, musing over the same mystery of the Divine Being, as it presented itself to them, fashioned the very same conception.

"A doctrine of the Divine Trinity in Unity is the underlying idea of the venerable religion of the Brah-

---

* Fiske, "Idea of God," pp. 74–80.
† "Present-Day Tracts," No. xi.

mans. Christianity, in fact, probably owes this doctrine to the influence of Egyptian speculation, and possibly to the indirect influence of Hindoo speculation, in the early church.

"Our dogma was born in Alexandria (Egypt). It was nurtured at the hands of men who knew, in all probability, of this thought from the East; through whom the early Christians learned, unconsciously, the mystic lore of India." *

This notion that the Christian doctrine of the Trinity was borrowed from India is contradicted by many able writers. Thus, Dr. Hagenbach not only rejects this opinion, but quotes several other eminent German theologians who do the same. "Since, in the pagan systems of religion," says one of these, "the natural is most intimately blended with the divine, their triads are altogether different from the Christian doctrine of the Trinity: in the former, the triads only denote the elements (moments) of a *developing process*, and are therefore most fully found in those religions which occupy a very low position, but disappear when the identification of the divine with the natural is got rid of in the further development of the religious systems." † But while it is scarcely possible to trace any historical connection between the Indian Triad and the Christian Trinity, yet, Dr. Newton's assertion that "our dogma was born in Alexandria, Egypt," is quite true, and it is this fact which should be carefully considered.

The doctrine of the Divine Word or Logos (John, i, 1, *et seq.*) is an integral part of the doctrine of the

---

* Rev. Heber Newton, "Philistinism," pp. 59, 60.
† Hagenbach, "History of Doctrines," vol. i, pp. 113–115.

Trinity. Now, as Dr. Hagenbach truly observes, "we may find traces of this doctrine in the personification of the Divine Word and the Divine Wisdom found in the Old Testament, especially, however, in the doctrine of *Philo* concerning the Logos, and in some other ideas then current." In a note an eminent German theologian is quoted as saying, "Philo's doctrine of the Logos is the immediate prelude to the Christian idea of the Logos." The important question, therefore, is, Where did Philo get his theory of the Logos? From *heathen philosophy*, for it was by a combination of Plato's speculations with those of the Stoics that Philo formulated his doctrine of the Word.* This doctrine, somewhat modified and elevated, passed on into the Christian Church, through the medium of the "Gospel according to John," in which the term Logos is applied to Christ. Various of the early Fathers discuss and advocate the doctrine, while the "heretics" oppose it. Tertullian, in particular (second and third century), "strove to explain the mystery, wrestling hard with language; he employed the term Son in reference to the personality of the Logos more distinctly than had previously been done."

Origen, the great advocate of "universal restoration," who flourished and suffered in the third century, decisively adopted Tertullian's terminology, and was led to the idea of an *eternal* generation of the Son. But the early Fathers differed very widely in their opinions concerning the Logos, and it was not until the year 325 A. D., when the memorable Council of Nice was held, that the doctrine concerning the Word was

---

* "Encyclopædia Britannica," article "Philo."

fully developed and the dogma of the Trinity was formulated. This doctrine is forever associated with the name of Athanasius, Bishop of Alexandria in Egypt, who flourished during the fourth century, and in the Council of Nice enunciated this dogma.* The Creed, however, which is called after Athanasius was not framed by him, but, as Hagenbach says, "originated in the School of Augustine," and we may gladly relieve this great theologian of the heavy burden of incomprehensibility which this creed involves. Dr. Hagenbach truly observes, "By its repetition of positive and negative propositions, the perpetual assertion, and then again denial of its positions, the mystery of the doctrine is presented, as it were, in hieroglyphics, as if to confound the understanding." †

According to Athanasius, there are three Persons, viz., Father, Son, and Holy Ghost—in one Godhead, and these three are *coequal, coeternal, consubstantial* (i. e., of the same essence). Observe, it is not said that there are Three Persons in one *Person*, but three persons in one *God*—in one *Substance*. An illustration will make this idea clear. An English naturalist has shown that there are three fundamental colors in white light, namely, red, yellow, and blue. The red is the heat-giving ray, the yellow is the light-giving ray, and the blue is the life-giving ray; and these three rays unite and form white light, each ray at the same time maintaining its distinctive character and doing its particular work.‡ Here we have three powers uniting in one substance,

---

* "Encyclopædia Britannica," article "Athanasius"; Canon Robertson's "Church History," vol. i, pp. 284–303, etc.

† "History of Doctrines," i, p. 269.

‡ Christlieb, "Modern Doubt and Christian Belief," p. 277.

and yet maintaining their individuality. In some such manner, it is urged, the three persons of the Godhead are united in one substance. We must, of course, lay aside all thought of a material or physical union; we must remember that it is a spiritual union—a union of *thought, feeling, and will.*

But the Athanasian doctrine is only one of several theories of Divinity which have been held by pious and able theologians, and even by whole sections of Christendom. Indeed, it was a reaction against a view which was once almost universal in the Church, and is not by any means dead even now—the view, namely, which was set forth by *Arius*, a presbyter in the Church of Alexandria, who lived contemporaneously with Athanasius. He urged that "if the Son were begotten, the Father was *anterior* to him; therefore the Son had a beginning; once he was not. . . . The Word," he said, "was *created* by the Father, at his own will—before all time. He was the highest of creatures—a creature, yet not as one of the creatures—and therefore styled *only begotten.* He was framed after the pattern of the indwelling Divine Logos, or Wisdom, enlightened by it and called by its name."* This was the doctrine which raised such a furor in the early Church and was superseded in the Nicene Council by the Athanasian doctrine. It is still held in all essentials by the Unitarians; at least it was the view of the good Dr. Channing, who is acknowledged by the Unitarians as one of their leading theological authorities.†

---

* Robertson, "Church History," i, p. 281-289; "Encyclopædia Britannica," article "Arius."

† "Encyclopædia Britannica," article "Channing," and his "Works."

A third view of the Godhead is that formulated and advocated by *Sabellius*, a presbyter of Ptolemais, who lived about the middle of the third century. He maintained that "the appellations, Father, Son, and Holy Spirit, were only so many different manifestations and names of one and the same Divine Being.

"He ackowledged three persons, but he used the word in a sense which may be termed merely *dramatic* —as meaning characters assumed or represented. He illustrated his idea by comparison with the three elements of man—body, soul, and spirit; and with the threefold combination in the sun, of shape or substance, light, and heat." *

These, then, are the three great doctrines of the Godhead, the Athanasian, the Arian, and the Sabellian, which have at different times been held in the Church. The Athanasian, as is well known, is considered the "orthodox" view, and is the popular doctrine. The Arian theory, as already stated, is held at least by many of the Unitarians; and the Sabellian view is held by some profound philosophers of our day, especially among the Naturalists.†

Now, my object in thus tracing, first, the idea of God as the Supreme Creator and Governor of the Universe, and, secondly, the speculations concerning his specific nature, to their historical fountain-head, has

---

* Hagenbach, "History of Doctrines," i, p. 246; Robertson, "Church History," i, pp. 119–122; "Encyclopædia Britannica," article "Sabellius."

† See Le Conte's "Religion and Science," pp. 196–211, etc., where the author expresses and adopts essential Sabellianism. Swedenborg also seems to have held the Sabellian doctrine—"The True Christian Religion," p. 280, *et seq.*

been to show their *natural* and *human* origin. Undoubtedly, we may study the writings of Philo, Athanasius, and others like them, with much profit, but we should never exalt them into oracles, or accept their opinions as absolutely infallible. We should be at perfect liberty to accept *any* theory of the Godhead which may commend itself to our enlightened conscience and reason, and reject any which may not so commend itself. Does, then, the Athanasian dogma seem Scriptural and rational? It is not necessary to discuss the other two views, since they are considered " heresies," and so whoever rejects the Athanasian may accept either the Arian or the Sabellian view with impunity. What does Athanasianism attempt? It attempts to explain the exact *relationship* which exists between Father, Son, and Holy Ghost. Does the New Testament do this? I answer unhesitatingly, no; and since Athanasius attempts to do that which the writers of the New Testament did not, we may decline to accept him as authority, unless, indeed, he can prove himself superior to them in wisdom, which is hardly possible. But, of course, it would be urged that, " although the Athanasian dogma is not *expressly and verbally* enunciated in the New Testament, it is *impliedly* taught; it is necessarily *involved* in its teaching." To which it may be replied: First, on so important a subject as that under discussion we can not accept alleged implications, which may be nothing more than the reading into the Scriptures the preconceived opinions of the theologian. Secondly, it is simply a matter of individual opinion as to whether or not the Athanasian theory is necessarily involved in the teachings of the New Testament. To one who accepts the verbal inspiration of all its books it may be possible to string together a few disjointed texts so as to make out a *prima facie* case for St. Athanasius; but it is not so easy for one who does not accept verbal inspiration to do this. It is doubly hard for him to do so if he considers the Fourth Gospel the work of a Philonic dogmatist rather than that of the "Beloved Disciple." And if Holy Scripture does not justify such transcendent speculation as that implied in the Athanasian doctrine of the Godhead, certainly *reason* does not. According to Athanasius, there are three persons in one Godhead; but *what constitutes Personality? Self-consciousness*—i. e., the recognition of Self as a thinking and willing being. "Each of us has his own distinct circle of consciousness, and they do not and can not touch each other. Hence, we can not believe that a separate consciousness is the nature of the distinction between the different modes of Divine existence, for this is inconsistent with unity. And yet this separate consciousness is what we mean by personality, when applied to man." * In short, Personality, as we understand it, consists of something (viz., self-consciousness) which can not be shared with more than one being. If, therefore, there be three self-consciousnesses or three persons in the Godhead, there must be three Gods. But perhaps the short and easy way of proving, if not the irrationality of the Athanasian doctrine, at least its absolute *super*-rationality, is to refer the reader to Mr. Herbert Spencer's "First Principles," and Dean Mansel's "Bampton Lectures" there quoted. Whatever may be the defects of Agnosticism, whatever objec-

---

* Le Conte, "Science and Religion," p. 200.

tions may be urged against the Spencerian exposition of its principles in particular (and let it be remembered I do not accept Agnosticism), yet all, I think, who have studied it must admit that it has demonstrated, if not the absurdity, at least the *inutility*, of all such attempts as that of St. Athanasius to "fly up into secrets of the Deity on the waxen wings of the human understanding."

Why not, then, content ourselves with the simple teachings of Jesus as laid down in the Sermon on the Mount, the Parables, etc.? Why not believe that when the Master speaks of the Father, Son, and Holy Ghost, He expresses the different relations of God to man— his different *attitudes*, so to speak? As the Father, He created and sustains us; as the Son, He has revealed to us "the Way, the Truth, and the Life"—the way of salvation from sin and suffering; as the Holy Ghost, He enables us to walk in that Way, to find that Truth, to inherit that Life.

Do you say this savors of Sabellianism? I reply, Yes, but no more than popular Trinitarianism savors of *Tritheism*. "There are," says Frederick Robertson, "in almost every congregation, themselves not knowing it, Trinitarians who are practically Tri-theists, worshiping three Gods." Nay, I may add, much of "orthodox theology," itself, *when sharply analyzed*, is Tritheistic on this subject, and why? Why, because human thought and human language can not conceive and express the Infinite. Why, then, attempt it? Why not say to our fellow-men, "My brothers, use your God-given conscience and reason to the best of your ability, and accept whatever view of Deity satisfies your mind, and leave the rest in God's hands"? At any rate, this is my own view, and as a Protestant I claim the right of refusing to accept any man-made theory which I believe to be either positively erroneous or so transcendental that the theorist himself does not know what he means by it. I for one am content to rest in the thought *that* God is, without attempting to define exactly *what* He is. But lest some one be unable to rest here with me, and demand that I say at least what truth lay at the root of the doctrine of the Trinity, and gave birth to it, I shall quote the following profound words of Dr. Heber Newton which will answer this question: "All Nature" (he says) "suggests an ultimate unity. The spectroscope reveals the same elements of matter in Mars and Jupiter as those out of which our earth is builded. All forms of force are forever slipping and sliding, in a baffling way, into one another, and light, and heat, and electricity prove but one and the same energy. The stars of heaven sweep through their majestic orbits, under the leash of the law which draws the curve of the apple as it falls from the tree. One type of structure runs through all the varied organisms of earth. Man's body is that of the dog, set upon its hind-legs and with its fore-paws turned into hands, and the dog is a tree moving about. The oyster on your table presents you with Nature's rough draft of the internal organs which you carry within you. This is the fascinating mystery of unity which all Nature discloses. This unity is an expression of the Divine Being. God is one. But in this unity what a bewildering manifoldness!

"How infinite the changes of form which the Divine Being takes! No fixed or changeless unity is this of the Divine Being, but a unity which comprehends all multiplicity, and subsists under all variety. God is not a unit—He is unity. He is not a melody, He is the harmony of all things. . . .

"Now, the number which first finds expression for this unity in variety is the number three. 'One' is the mere unit. 'Two' represents mere variety without a bond of unity. It is the number which denotes the analysis—the severing and differentiating of primal unity.

"'*Three*' *expresses a return to a higher unity—harmony.* It makes a new synthesis. It is unity in trinity. The child saw this of old, and the philosopher simply saw that this mystery ran through all Nature, up into the mystery of the human being. He saw that life arranges itself in triads and combinations of triads. He saw that the possibilities of space are exhausted in a 'here,' 'there,' and 'everywhere'; that the possibilities of time are exhausted in a 'past,' 'present,' and 'future'; that the possibilities of individuality are exhausted in an 'I,' 'thou,' and 'he'; that the possibilities of personality are explained in a 'body,' 'mind,' and 'soul'; and so, fascinated by this secret of the inner rhythm of Creation, he expressed it in a dogma of the Divine Trinity. He *meant by it that the Divine Being is one substance in many persons—personæ or masks;* or, as we should say now, in many forms." *

To the same effect writes Frederick Robertson. "It is the law of being" (he says) "that, in proportion as you rise from lower to higher life, the parts are more distinctly developed, while yet the unity becomes more entire.

"You find, for example, in the lower forms of ani-

---

* Dr. Newton's "Philistinism," pp. 61–63. Cf. James Freeman Clarke's "Ten Great Religions," p. 124.

mal life one organ performs several functions, one organ being at the same time heart and brain and blood-vessels. But, when you come to man, you find all these various functions existing in various organs, and every organ more distinctly developed; and yet the unity of man is a higher unity than that of a limpet. . . . Now, the Trinitarian maintains, against the Unitarian and the Sabellian, that, *the higher you ascend in the scale of being, the more distinct are the consciousnesses, and that the law of unity implies and demands a manifold unity.* . . . The Sabellian and the Unitarian maintain that the unity of God consists simply in a unity of persons, and in opposition to this does the Trinitarian maintain that grandness, either in Man or in God, must be a *unity of manifoldness.*"*

"I am sure," says Dr. Phillips Brooks, "that the divine nature is three persons, but one God; but how much more than that I can not know. That deep law that runs through all life, by which the higher any nature is, the more manifold and simple at once, the more full of complexity and unity at once, it grows, is easily accepted as applicable to the highest of all natures—God. In the manifoldness of his being these three personal existences, Creator, Redeemer, and Sanctifier, easily make themselves known to human life."† Now I think very few people would hesitate to accept the doctrine of the Trinity as thus stated, for, according to these theologians, it is merely a symbolic expression of the manifoldness of God.‡ But when it is urged that

---

* Robertson's sermon on "The Trinity."—"Sermons," pp. 471, 472.

† Dr. Brooks's "Sermons," first series, sermon xiii, p. 230.

‡ The eminent Unitarian, James Freeman Clarke, accepts this view. See his "Ten Great Religions" p. 500.

God's nature is not *manifold*, but only *threefold*—that "the Father is Eternal, the Son is Eternal, and the Holy Spirit is Eternal, and yet there are not three Eternals, but one Eternal; that the Father is Omnipotent, the Son is Omnipotent, and the Holy Spirit is Omnipotent, and yet there are not three Omnipotents, but one Omnipotent; and the Father is God, the Son is God, and the Holy Spirit is God, and yet there are not three Gods but one God" (Athanasian Creed)—when all this self-contradictory theology is urged upon us, we beg leave to decline its acceptance, on the ground that it is "confusion worse confounded"—that neither the creed-maker nor the creed-accepter, in this case, knows whether his formula is true or false. I have quoted the three theologians just mentioned—first, because some one may find relief in their statements of the dogma of the Trinity; and, secondly, because it is interesting to note the change which is slowly coming over theology. There is no such dogmatism evident in these writers—indeed, there is no such dogmatism visible in any of the leading theologians of our day—as that which we find in the older theologies, whether patristic, mediæval, or post-Reformation. Dr. Brooks tells us: "It is not for us to catalogue and inventory Deity. The doctrine of the Trinity is the description of what we know of God. We have no right to say that it is the description of God; for what there may be in Deity of which we have no knowledge, how can we tell? We are only sure that the divine life is infinitely greater than our humanity can comprehend; and we are sure, too, that not even a revelation in the most perfect form, through the most perfect medium conceivable, could make known to the human intelligence anything in God save that which has relationship to human life." * In another place he says, "He (God) not merely does not, he can not, make to us a revelation of Himself which shall uncover all the secrets of His life and leave us nothing for our wonder, nothing to elude or bewilder us." † Likewise, Robertson tells us that "the doctrine of the Trinity is the sum of all that knowledge which has as yet been gained by man. I say gained *as yet*. For we presume not to maintain that, in the ages that are to come hereafter, our knowledge shall not be superseded by a higher knowledge." Any one familiar with Sir William Hamilton's "Philosophy of the Unconditioned," as expounded by Dean Mansel in his "Bampton Lectures," and later by Mr. Herbert Spencer, in the second chapter of his "First Principles," must be struck with the essential sameness of all these philosophies and theologies. We read, are entertained, instructed, and bewildered by turns, and we finally settle back on the simple teaching of Jesus of Nazareth about the Universal Father who loves and saves us, and we allow the theological and philosophic gladiators to cut and slash one another to their hearts' content, smiling all the while at such logomachy. This, then, is about what Evolution has to say on the subject of the Trinity: First, it traces the general ideas of Deity to their fountain-head, showing how the rills of ancestor-worship, fetichism, Nature-worship, idol-worship, anthropomorphism, etc., finally converged and blended into one stream—monotheism. Secondly, it traces the speculations concerning the specific nature of One Supreme God to their human ori-

---

* "Sermons," *ut supra*, p. 229.
† "Sermons," second series, p. 306.

gin, and shows, in particular, that the Trinitarian theory originated by a combination of heathen philosophy with Semitic theology, and hence we are at liberty to accept or reject such speculations according to their rationality or irrationality.

Finally, it reveals a God who is immanent in Nature, whose nature seems to be psychical or spiritual, and certainly is *manifold;* and it bids us accept, if we choose, the Trinitarian dogma as merely a symbolic description of this manifold Infinite Spirit.

CHAPTER IV.

EVOLUTION AND THE DIVINITY OF CHRIST.

Thus far in this treatise I have spoken of Jesus merely as a man, and perhaps I would better explain, at the beginning of this chapter, why I have done this. I have done it simply because history and science concern themselves with *human* beings and things, if not exclusively, at least primarily; and so far I have been considering Jesus from the historical and scientific point of view. No one, not even the most rigidly "orthodox" theologian, can object to this mode of treatment, for, even according to the traditional dogma concerning Christ's nature, he was man as well as God, and the title "Son of Man" was a favorite name which our Lord used of Himself. Now, the *relation* of the Son of Man, the Human Jesus, to the Son of God, the Divine Christ, is the subject of this chapter, and this is a question primarily of Philosophy and Theology, and only secondarily of History and Science. The latter must always consider the Human rather than the Divine side of Jesus Christ.

Even in our theologizing and philosophizing on the question of the relation of Jesus to the Divine Spirit it is best to begin with the human element, for this is, so to speak, more palpable—more indubitably a historical fact—than the divine element in this great Character, and from this basis we may be able to climb to the pinnacle of divinity.

The exact way in which Science—Evolution in particular—affects the doctrine of the Incarnation, or the Divinity of Christ, is not by denying the possibility of such an event, but by *explaining how the idea of divine incarnations in general and of this incarnation in particular may have naturally arisen.* The ideas of supernatural agents are traced to their origin in the primitive man's notion of a *ghost-world*, and from this primitive philosophy, it is claimed, sprang all those notions, so prevalent in ancient times and among modern savages, about spirits possessing men and producing various good and evil effects—insanity, epilepsy, etc., and marvelous feats of military prowess, legal, philosophic, and religious insight. Thus men learned to think of *all* great men as divinely inspired or god-descended.

"That the story of a god-descended person," says Mr. Spencer, "should be habitually spoken of by Christians as though it were special to their religion, is strange, considering their familiarity with stories of god-descended persons among the Greeks—Æsculapius, Pythagoras, Plato.*

"But it is not the Greek religion only which furnished such parallels. The Assyrian king Nebuchadnezzar asserted that he had been god-begotten. It is a tradition among the Mongols that Alung Goa, who herself had a spirit for her father, bore three sons by a

---

* " Encyclopædia Britannica," articles " Æsculapius," " Pythagoras," and " Plato."

spirit. In ancient Peru if any of the virgins of the Sun appeared to be pregnant, she said it was by the Sun, and this was believed, unless there was some evidence to the contrary. And among the existing inhabitants of Mangaia it is the tradition that the lovely Ina-ani-vai had two sons by the great god Tangara." * Strauss, long before Spencer, as is well known, urged this same idea even more ably than the great Agnostic does. "No proof," he says, "is wanted to show that in the province of the Græco-Roman religion the idea of Sons of God was currently in vogue. It referred not merely to the demigods of the mythical period, but was also applied to historical personages of the later times. In many cases it may have been the vanity of rulers or the flattery of subjects; in others it was undeniably a real faith of a narrower or wider circle, and this faith sometimes appears very early, almost before personages so worshiped have departed this life. To say nothing of Pythagoras, whom, at a later period, his enthusiastic adherents represented as a son of (the god) Apollo, there was a legend current about Plato in Athens, even in the lifetime of his nephew Speusippus that Apollo had had intercourse with his mother Perictione. Alexander the Great may, indeed, have himself originated the report that he was begotten of Zeus with Olympias. Livy, also, insinuates that the elder Scipio favored the rise of a similar legend that was current about him among the Roman people. But, however they may have arisen, histories of this kind were believed under many forms at a time, with the impulse of which toward contact with the supernatural world they

---

* Spencer's "Ecclesiastical Institutions," p. 702.

correspond, and thus we can not be surprised if the Christians sought to give to their Messiah a birth of equal rank with these teachers of philosophy and rulers of divine origin." He further urged that those passages in the Old Testament in which the Messiah is called the Son of God (Psalms, ii, 7), and the virgin-born Immanuel—i. e., *God with us* (Isaiah, vii, 14), etc., formed the basis of the legends about Jesus being the Son of God, born of a virgin. The early disciples, especially in Greece and Rome, lived in an atmosphere permeated by such heathenish ideas as those just stated, and when they found, in the Old Testament, instances (such as that of Sarah, Abraham's wife) of God's opening the barren womb—of virgin-birth, of a Son of God and an Immanuel, they would soon forget the figurative meaning of these terms, and begin to apply them to the Christ in the heathen sense of the words.*

Dr. Keim takes essentially the same view. "The entrance of great men into the world's history," he says, "is wont to gather round it clouds of mystery. As manifestations of towering grandeur which mock at all endeavors to explain them by the cognizable forces and self-repeating cycles of their age and their surroundings, they do constitute a real mystery, which verges in its turn into the unsolved riddle of universal being and growth. But to the mystery of the reality is added the mystery of the imagination," and so he thinks that the Old Testament, and the peculiar intellectual atmosphere which surrounded the early disciples, afforded sufficient materials for the legend of the virgin-birth by the Holy

---

* Strauss, "Life of Jesus," vol. ii, English translation, pp. 39–46.

Ghost.* And it is much easier to sneer at such notions than it is to refute them. The "Gospel according to John," in which the divinity of Christ is most clearly enunciated, was evidently written by a Philonic philosopher, and so Philo's peculiar views about the "Logos" or "Word" helped to mold the dogma of Christ's divinity. The stories in "Matthew" and "Luke" are late productions by unknown authors; and when we reflect that the birth of Jesus was precisely the fact which legend seized upon, and, in the apocryphal writings, such as the "Gospel of James," gave us the most absurdly incredible accounts of this event, we find it rather hard to draw the line between the stories in "Luke" and "Matthew" and the confessedly mythical accounts.

Sure I am that if we found such stories about any *other* person than our Saviour, we should not hesitate to class them all in the category of legend. But not only does Evolution affect the Christian doctrine of the Incarnation by showing the natural genesis of such notions, it affects it more seriously and fundamentally by setting forth an idea of God which absolutely precludes the traditional and popular view of the Incarnation, though, as we shall soon see, it does not necessarily affect the more modern and philosophic view. As long as the notion that God was a sort of *man* prevailed, it was comparatively easy to think of "God manifest in the flesh," but Evolution holds that God is the Infinite Spirit or Energy that permeates and sustains all things, and hence the doctrine that this Energy should be *gathered up*, so to speak, in

---

* Keim, "Jesus of Nazara," ii, pp. 38–101.

a finite being—man—seems highly doubtful. We are not surprised, therefore, to hear Mr. Spencer say that the doctrine of the Incarnation involves several incredible propositions.

"One is," he says, "that the Cause to which we can put no limits in Space or Time, and of which our entire Solar System is a relatively infinitesimal product, took the disguise of a man for the purpose of covenanting with a shepherd-chief in Syria. Another is that this Energy, unceasingly manifested everywhere, throughout past, present, and future, ascribed to himself under this human form, not only the limited knowledge and limited powers which various passages show Jahveh (Jehovah) to have had, but also moral attributes which we should now think discreditable to a human being." *

This passage carries us to the root of our subject. But is the idea of the Incarnation here set forth the true philosophic doctrine as held by the best theologians? I think not. It undoubtedly expresses the popular notion of the Incarnation; it is the idea which crude minds generally set forth from the pulpit; it even receives some countenance from otherwise philosophic theology, which too frequently dwells too exclusively and emphatically on the *divine* element in Christ's character. But, as stated at the beginning of this chapter, Jesus, according to orthodox theology, was a *Man*—was human *and* divine—human on the one side, and divine on the other. Hence the question is not that raised by Mr. Spencer, viz., Did the Cause to which we can put no limits in Space or Time, and of

---

* Spencer, "Ecclesiastical Institutions," p. 704.

which our entire Solar System is a relatively infinitesimal product, take the disguise of man? but it is rather, *What is the relation of the Man Jesus to the Divine Spirit?*

Now, philosophic theology claims that the union of the human spirit of Jesus with the Divine is essentially *perfect*—i. e., it is a complete union of *thought, feeling,* and *will:* we have in this case, in the most profound sense, "two souls with but a single thought — two hearts that beat as one." And this perfect union in thought, feeling, and will of the human Jesus with the Divine Spirit constitutes him the Only Begotten Son of God—the God-Man. And I believe with another, that this doctrine is not only "consistent with the doctrine of evolution," but, "without such a conception as that of God manifest in the flesh, the real grandeur and vastness of the process of evolution is not recognized."* According to Evolution the universe, especially our earth, in the beginning of its development, was "without form and void," was simply a cloud of atoms, and the form of force then operating was what we call "gravity"—i. e., the force which moves a stone and holds the stars in their courses. Soon, however, a higher form of force manifested itself, namely, that which we call "chemical affinity"—i. e., the force by which gases are compounded to produce, for instance, water. Later on a still higher form of force appeared, viz., life, first in plants, and next in animals. Then came mind in a very low form which gradually and slowly developed into the mind of man, and Prof.

---

* Symposium on "Christianity and Evolution," by Dr. Matheson, etc., p. 75. (Whittaker.)

Fiske has explained to us, in a most striking manner, how, when physical evolution had completed its course, mental evolution took up the work and carried it forward to its present high level, which is by no means its ultimate goal. "In its rude beginnings," he says, "the psychical life was but an appendage to the body; in fully developed humanity the body is the vehicle for the soul."* Very well: if the whole physical and spiritual creation has been moving forward and upward from lower planes; if the immaterial part in particular has developed as just stated, why is it not probable, nay, almost *necessary*, that it should reach *perfection*?

Such a thing is quite probable and thoroughly rational and credible from the evolutionist's standpoint.

The general law of evolution, then, suggests such a manifestation of the Divine in human form—such an Incarnation as that claimed above. Taking our stand on this basis, let us glance over the history of the world and ask, Is there a man, and, if so, *who* is he, that seems to be such an embodiment of the Divine Spirit? Is it an Abraham, a Moses, an Isaiah, a Paul, a Buddha, a Confucius, a Zoroaster, a Socrates? Surely not! We gladly acknowledge the merits of these noble men of God—we believe them to have been the prophets of the living and true God—but will any one, be he the freest of the freethinkers and skeptics, say that any one of these good men equals Jesus of Nazareth in godliness of character and divineness of teaching?

Were they not mere preludes to the angel song which burst on the heights of Bethlehem?—the first streaks of the rise of that Sun of Righteousness whose beams

---

* Fiske, "Destiny of Man," p. 65.

have illumined the Western world — the most highly civilized portion of the globe? Perhaps some hyper-skeptic would urge just here that " we don't know *what* Jesus was and what he taught, his life and teachings have been so obscured by legend." To which I reply, Notwithstanding all legendary accretions, we can clearly make out the *essential* features of Christ's character and teaching.

That he was a wonderful Character is clearly proved by the marvelous stories about him found in the New Testament, for, even if these be pure myths, yet myths do not grow up around an ordinary life. But eliminating all these legendary (i. e., the miraculous) features from the narratives of Christ's life, we certainly have left enough reliable evidence to prove that the moral character of Jesus was, if not absolutely perfect, at least transcendently unique. The man who could deliver the Sermon on the Mount (Matthew, v–vii), the Lord's Prayer, and the various Parables in the Gospels—the man who could inspire even a Saul of Tarsus with veneration, and could exert the wonderful influence in the moral and religious spheres, among the most enlightened people on earth, which Jesus has done, is certainly a peer in the spiritual realm. Of course, I know that there are some skeptics radical enough to deny that the wonderful teaching ascribed to Jesus is his; but I pass by such irrational skepticism as unworthy of serious attention, for, if Jesus were not the author of such teaching, then the *unknown authors of our Gospels* were, and so we are forced to believe the utterly absurd proposition that obscure Jewish or Gentile peasants originated the most wonderful system of moral and spiritual truth ever originated and ascribed it to the

Nazarene Peasant, who knew nothing about it. Truly such a notion refutes itself.

That the foregoing view is rational and credible even so radical a skeptic as M. Renan admits. "Jesus," he says, "is that individual who has caused his species to make the greatest advance toward the divine. Humanity, as a whole, presents an assemblage of beings, low, selfish, superior to the animal only in this, that their selfishness is more premeditated. But, in the midst of this uniform vulgarity, pillars rise toward heaven and attest a noble destiny. Jesus is the highest of these pillars which show to man whence he came and whither he should tend. In him is condensed all that was good and lofty in our nature." * This is sufficient for my purpose, for, although Renan adds that "Jesus was not sinless," yet in the words quoted he admits enough to prove that Jesus, if any one, was the man in whom the process of spiritual evolution reached perfection.

Defining, then, the divinity of Jesus Christ to consist in a perfect union of his human spirit with the Divine, we undertake to prove that this union existed from these three great facts, viz.: First. The spirit of *every* man is ultimately derived from God—is an effluence from the Father of Spirits—and so the spirit of Jesus, of course, came from God, and differs from the ordinary human spirit only in the degree of perfection. Secondly. The doctrine of evolution would lead us to believe that the process of spiritual development, which began many ages ago, would *culminate*, first, in some individual, and then in all other individuals. Third.

---

* Renan's "Life of Jesus," p. 375.

We find ample reliable evidence to prove that in Jesus this goal of the evolutionary movement was realized, and therefore we conclude that he was the "Son of God" in a special sense—the Divine Man—who came to lead his fellow-men to that high state of spiritual perfection to which he has attained. Of course, this is the barest skeleton of the view of the Incarnation which we (evolutionists) hold, and it is earnestly hoped that the reader will accept it as such and try to clothe it with flesh and blood. To this end he should, first of all, master the theory of evolution as advocated by such philosophers as Profs. Fiske and Le Conte.* I have aimed to give their central idea only, and so a perusal of their works is necessary to a full realization of the force of this argument for Christ's spiritual perfection. After having mastered the evolutionary argument, the student should then read such books as Dr. Ullmann's "Sinlessness of Jesus," Dr. Young's "Christ of History," Canon Row's lecture on "The Superhuman Action of Jesus Christ in History" ("Bampton Lectures," No. II), and he will need no further proof of the view of the Incarnation just enunciated.

Even a historian so unbiased as Mr. Lecky says: "It was reserved for Christianity to present to the world an ideal character which through all the changes of eighteen centuries has filled the hearts of men with an impassioned love, and has shown itself capable of acting on all ages, nations, temperaments, and conditions;

---

* Fiske, "Destiny of Man"; Le Conte, "Evolution and Religious Thought," Part III, chap. iv; "Religion and Science," chap. xvi; "Man's Place in Nature," "Princeton Review," November, 1878.

has not only been the highest pattern of virtue, but the highest incentive to its practice ; and has exerted so deep an influence that it may be truly said that the simple record of three short years of active life has done more to regenerate and soften mankind than all the disquisitions of philosophers and than all the exhortations of moralists. This has indeed been the well-spring of whatever has been best and purest in the Christian life. Amid all the sins and failings, amid all the priestcraft, the persecution, and fanaticism which have defaced the Church, it has preserved in the character and example of its Founder an enduring principle of regeneration." "This passage," as Canon Row truly observes, "will be admitted even by unbelievers to be a correct statement of the facts as they are presented to us by history," and he then proceeds to draw out and emphasize the full meaning of Lecky's weighty words, which can not be too profoundly pondered by all.*

Said the acute skeptic, W. R. Greg, in his powerful little book, "The Creed of Christendom" (pages 306, 307):

"Jesus of Nazareth was the most exalted religious genius whom God ever sent upon the earth ; in himself an embodied revelation ; humanity in its divinest phase, 'God manifest in the flesh,' according to Eastern hyperbole ; an examplar vouchsafed, in an early age of the world, of what man may and should become, in the course of ages, in his progress toward the realization of his destiny ; an individual gifted with a grand, clear intellect, a noble soul, a fine organization, marvelous moral intuitions, and a perfectly balanced moral be-

---

* Row's "Bampton Lectures" (1877), p. 96.

ing; and who, by virtue of these endowments, saw further than all other men—

> 'Beyond the verge of that blue sky
> Where God's sublimest secrets lie.'"

"Call him (Jesus) what you please," says another freethinker, " he was an avatar (i. e., an incarnation) of the God of justice, love, and order; and as such I worship him. I look in vain to Benares, to Pekin, to Mecca, to Athens, or to any other nucleus of mental or moral activity, in past or present times, for such an original and complete guide, through the labyrinth of practice and opinion." *

And so I might quote skeptic after skeptic, who vie with one another in eulogizing the wonderful moral and religious character of Jesus; but these quotations are sufficient to show that the most unbiased minds agree with the author in placing Jesus at the head of the human race, and especially at the head of religious teachers. True, these authors do not think that the moral and spiritual transcendency of Jesus proves his divinity, and it does not prove such a doctrine as that set forth in crude popular theology and embodied in Mr. Spencer's "Ecclesiastical Institutions," but it *does* prove that the process of spiritual evolution, which from general considerations we believe must reach perfection, has, in this case, been perfectly realized, and we claim that this implies the closest and most vital union of the spirit of Jesus with the Divine Spirit from whom it sprang, which union constitutes what I at least understand by the divinity of Jesus Christ. The per-

---

* Prof. J. P. Leslie, "The Forum," January, 1888, p. 495, etc.

fect Jesus was the human side of the Divine Christ—
the "second person of the Trinity." He was "the
Divine under *the limitations of humanity*." We, then,
freely grant that the popular doctrine of the incarnation
which teaches, in the first place, that God is a sort of
man, and, in the second place, that this Man-God was
manifested *bodily* in Jesus of Nazareth, has been exploded by evolution, which shows us the natural genesis of such ideas of God and His manifestations to man,
and also exalts our notion of the Deity so as to preclude
His *focalization*, so to speak, in a finite being, like
man. We further grant that miracles can not prove
the divinity of our Master, first, because the occurrence
of few, if any, miracles can be demonstrated; and, secondly, even if this could be done, it would merely prove
that Jesus was an extraordinarily endowed man, like
the Prophets and Apostles. More particularly, we grant
that the stories of the virgin-birth of Jesus and his generation by the Holy Ghost may be poetical, hyperbolical
representations of a great fact; but we urge that there
was a great fact back of these legends, for "the absurdest report," you remember Mr. Spencer says, "may in
nearly every instance be traced to an actual occurrence."
The "actual occurrence," in this case, was the birth of
a Being who was the Ideal of Humanity, and who, as
such, sustained the most perfect relation to the Divine
Spirit which it is possible for a finite spirit to have
with the Infinite, and hence He deserves to be called
the "Only Begotten of the Father."

I would therefore ask, on the one hand, serious
skeptics, and, on the other, independent theologians of
all schools, to consider the definition of the Incarnation
given above, and to say whether it is not rational and

credible in the light of the facts of science and history, and whether it does not remove most if not all of the difficulties attaching to the old dogma, while at the same time it maintains the *kernel* of this the fundamental article of our faith?

It is evident to almost all scientific minds that the doctrine of the Incarnation must be, if not reconstructed, at least purged of the unphilosophical and even heathenish elements it contains. The low anthropomorphism of the popular dogma is unworthy of the theology of the nineteenth century, and so it is earnestly hoped that the foregoing suggestions may stir up discussion of this subject from the evolution point of view. Whether evolution be true or false, many eminent and learned men *believe* it to be true, and they are unable to reconcile their science with the theology they have been taught. These men are by no means hostile to religion. They feel the need of religion. They would gladly be reckoned among the followers of Jesus; but, as the late Dr. Carpenter—one of the profoundest thinkers and most reverential writers of our century—says, "There is so much in what claims to be the 'orthodox' systems of Theology that runs counter to the strongest and best instincts of Humanity, that those who have been led by scientific study to build up their fabric of thought on the basis of their own Intellectual and Moral Intuitions, find it impossible to fit into this a set of doctrines which are altogether conformable to it."

Surely the Church owes something to such men. Surely she ought, as Dr. Carpenter further insists, " to admit into Christian communion every one who desires to be accounted a disciple of Christ, and humbly en-

deavors to follow in the steps of his Divine Master." *
But so long as Theology opposes Science as it has done
during the last half-century, and offers these men the
time-worn scholasticism—the *haven of intellectual stagnation*—as the place of spiritual rest, so long will the
great mass of them avoid it altogether, and unless they
can find anchorage elsewhere, will drift away into either
vague *un*belief or absolute *dis*belief. The author
humbly hopes that this book, and this chapter in particular, may help these troubled minds to find such spiritual anchorage as they desire.

Of course, I do not expect to affect the confirmed
skeptic or the omniscient Traditionalist, for it may be
doubted whether Divine Power and Wisdom itself can
overcome prejudice; but there are many that are not
so rooted and grounded in the dogmas of disbelief or
of theology as to be absolutely unimpressible by arguments on "the other side." There are many who can
look at a question from more than one point of view,
and who, while they may not accept their opponent's
view, may yet admit that it is at least tenable, and so
may give him the right hand of fellowship agreeing
to disagree on the point at issue. To such the above
suggestions may appeal with some force. As for the
confirmed disbeliever, he can not be converted to faith
in the Divine Master until he is made, by some means
or other, to feel the need of a spiritual guide—until
Divine aspirations are stirred within him. It is one of
Frederick Robertson's finest thoughts that "only to
him in whom infinite aspirations stir can an Infinite

---

* Carpenter's "Mental Physiology," pp. 698-708; read the whole of this instructive passage.

One be proved." And so we must be made to realize the awful mystery of Life and Death; we must be made to confess that we are

> "Infants crying in the night,
> Infants crying for the light,
> And with no language but a cry."

We must begin to long for Eternal Goodness; for Godlike Character; and then, and not till then, will we try in earnest to discover such character, and so trying we shall finally conclude that the Nazarene Peasant was such a one; "an avatar of the God of justice, love, and order," and we shall worship Him. On any hypothesis, indeed, even on the supposition that Jesus was only an extraordinary man not related in a specially unique manner to the Father of Spirits, we should be safe in worshiping His *spirit*. "The whole life of a man of science," says Prof. Leslie, in the article quoted, "disciplines him into a positive and habitual worship of genius; makes him an enthusiastic admirer and imitator of the *spirit* of every master in science. Why not in morals? Why not far more, infinitely more, in morals? As the conduct of life is every way grander than any scientific work can possibly be, so the Sun of Righteousness must outshine the lesser luminaries of physical knowledge.

"Therefore I recognize no inconsistency when Keplers and Newtons, a Linnæus, a Davy, a Joseph Henry, or a Cuvier worship Jesus of Nazareth; or when a Washington or a Lincoln confesses to the self-molding of his whole life on the well-known, perfectly comprehensible and comprehended Christian model." True, this is hero-worship, but Carlyle's remark that "all religion hitherto known" rests on hero-worship deserves earnest consideration. "Hero-worship," he adds, more plainly, "heart-felt, prostrate admiration, submission, burning, boundless, for a noble, Godlike form of man —is not that the germ of Christianity itself?

"The greatest of all heroes is One—whom we do not name here! Let sacred silence meditate that sacred matter; you will find it *the ultimate perfection of a principle extant throughout man's whole history on earth.*"[*] If we remember, then, that the spirit of Jesus, in its essence, must have been divine; must have been an effluence from God; we are perfectly safe in worshiping *it:* we are doubly safe if we believe, as above, that this divine effluence is most intimately united with its Eternal source. "It is then" (to quote Leslie again) "with a sense of buoyant exultation that I say I worship Jesus of Nazareth as the Ideal Man and King of men; the man of all ages and races; the image of the realized perfection in human being, the risen Sun of Righteousness; the Son of God—meaning by God all that is best, and by Son the best personified in man. Nor is the word 'worship' a whit too strong."

---

[*] Carlyle's "Heroes and Hero-Worship," Lecture I.

CHAPTER V.

EVOLUTION AND THE ATONEMENT.

The popular notion of religion is that it is a profound and incomprehensible mystery, which only a blind faith or credulity can accept, and this idea is sanctioned and strengthened in various ways by the clergy, who, many of them, are always asserting and emphasizing the mysterious character of this or that article of faith.

The doctrine of the Trinity is a mystery, say they, the Fall of Man is a mystery, the doctrine of the Atonement is a mystery, the future life, and, in short, all the articles of the Christian Creed, are incomprehensible mysteries which we must *believe* but can not *prove* —or, at least, the only proof we can give of the truth of these mysteries is (in Butler-fashion) to cite analogous mysteries in physical Nature.

Now, I verily believe that this sort of preaching is largely responsible for the spread and popularity of Agnosticism; for what is more natural and rational, supposing these views to be true, than to conclude that we can know *nothing* about God and Nature, the origin of Sin, the work of Christ, etc.? Let us, then, reject this silly and dangerous notion that our religion consists of a blind belief in inexplicable and incredible mysteries. Undoubtedly there are mysteries in Nature. Man himself is the greatest mystery of all, while we need no Herbert Spencer to assure us that the finite can not comprehend the Infinite. The fall of a stone, the formation of a dew-drop, the growth of a plant, the instinct of animals, are all mysteries; but to these natural mysteries are added artificial, man-made mysteries, or rather intellectual puzzles which can not be too quickly or too strongly rejected. Undoubtedly it is a mystery, even on the evolutionary theory, that man should

"see the right and approve it too,
Abhor the wrong and yet the wrong pursue."

But to this natural mystery is added the artificial mystery of Adam's fall from a state of perfect innocence. Our theological puzzle-makers are not content with the mysterious *fact* of sin, but they must conjure up a being who is perfect in every part and faculty of soul and body, who is a little god, and place him in a beautiful paradise where all his surroundings are equally as perfect as himself, save only one tree; and, further, they must put him on the most intimate terms of communion with the Deity; and yet this perfect being, in a perfect environment, with all his inclinations *toward* the good and *away from* the evil, deliberately chooses the latter, and is thereby totally depraved in every part and faculty of soul and body. We reject such a notion as not only absurd and incredible, but as a needless stumbling-block to faith.

Again: Our theological riddle-makers are not content with the awful fact of pain and suffering in the world, but they must add to this mystery the more horrible dogma that a good God can only be "satisfied" by the suffering of His *innocent Son*. Away with such diabolical ideas! If we can not explain the facts of which these expressions are caricatures; if we can not tell why men prefer to sin rather than to do the right, or why pain and suffering exist, yet we can explain the origin of the *dogmas* of Adam's Fall and Christ's Atonement: we can show that the popular notions on these subjects are relics of barbarism. As might have been expected, there are all sorts of theories of Christ's Atonement for sin, but the traditional and popular theory is very well expressed by Dr. Charles Hodge. The various modifications of the doctrine he formulates are confined principally to certain "schools" of theological thought which have comparatively little effect upon the great mass of men. The hair-splitting distinctions which professional theologians draw are too subtle ever to affect the popular mind, and hence we must simply aim to get at the kernel which all accept, and pass over their modifications of the husk, for, after all, these modifications of the Calvinistic views scarcely affect anything more than the husk of this dogma.

"The word Atonement," says Dr. Hodge, "is often used, especially in this country, to designate the priestly work of Christ." But he objects to the use of this word, because it is ambiguous, and not sufficiently comprehensive, and prefers the term "satisfaction," which "is the word which for ages has been generally used to designate the special work of Christ in the salvation of men.

"By the satisfaction of Christ," he continues, "is meant *all* he has done to satisfy the demands of the law and justice of God, *in the place* and in behalf of sinners." The first part of this clause defines atonement, the second defines *vicarious* atonement.

"There are two kinds of satisfaction, which, as they differ essentially in their nature and effects, should not be confounded. The one is *pecuniary* or commercial, the other *penal* or forensic. When a debtor pays the demands of his creditor in full, he satisfies his claims, and is entirely free from any further demands. In this case the thing paid is the precise sum due; it is a simple matter of commutative justice; it matters not to the creditor by whom the debt is paid, whether by the debtor himself, or by some one in his stead, because the claim of the creditor is simply upon the amount due and not upon the person of the debtor. In the case of *crimes* the matter is different. The demand is then upon the offender. He himself is amenable to justice. Substitution in human courts is out of the question. The soul that sins, *it* shall die. And the penalty need not be, and rarely is, of the nature of the injury inflicted. All that is required is that it should be a just equivalent. . . . The satisfaction of Christ was not pecuniary, but penal—a satisfaction for *sinners*, and not for those who owed a certain amount of money."

Our author then defines the two important words, "penalty" and "vicarious," as follows:

"The words penal and penalty do not designate any particular kind or degree of suffering, but any kind or degree which is judicially inflicted in satisfaction of justice. . . . By vicarious suffering or punishment is not meant merely suffering endured for the benefit of others, for in this sense the sufferings of martyrs, patriots, and philanthropists would be vicarious. But this word includes the idea of *substitution*. Vicarious suffering is suffering endured by one person in the *stead of* another—i. e., in his place. It necessarily supposes the exemption of the party in whose place the suffering is endured. A vicar is a substitute, one who takes the place of another, and acts in his stead, as the Pope is said to do when he assumes to be the vicar of Christ on earth." * According to this elaborate definition, then, the atonement of Christ consisted in his satisfying the demands of God's violated law by suffering the penalty of such violation in the stead or in the place of man. Dr. Hodge claims, and that truly, that " the symbols of the Lutheran and Reformed Churches agree entirely in their statement of this doctrine." But, as already stated, there are modifications of this doctrine prevalent in the theological schools, the most important of which, perhaps, being that affecting the notion that Christ bore the *penalty* of sin. The idea that an innocent being should bear the punishment due to the guilty is so contrary to all reason that many eminent theologians hold that Christ did not bear the penalty but only the *burden* of sin. They seem to mean this: He, the Holy One, came into this world to do God's will—to do what man had failed to do—i. e., fulfill the Divine Law. He, perceiving as no man ever did the awful heinousness of his brethren's sin, suffered in spirit on their account, somewhat as a good man is (as we say) bowed down beneath the burden of an erring brother's sin, and in his attempts to rescue man from sin and its punishment he laid down his life. His suffering and death therefore were not, strictly speaking, the penalty but merely the *consequence* of sin. There is a great difference between bearing the penalty and bearing the consequence of sin. Penalty or pun-

---

* Hodge's "Systematic Theology," vol. ii, pp. 464–591.

ishment is suffering inflicted upon an offender for his crime; but as Christ was not an offender—was an innocent Person—He could not be justly punished. If a brave man attempts to rescue another from drowning and dies in the attempt, we do not say his death was a punishment, but rather that it was the consequence of his act. So Christ came into collision with the world's evil in attempting to save his brethren in the flesh from sin, and he suffered the consequence—persecution and death. "He approached the whirling wheel and was torn in pieces." It will be perceived at once that this is a great advance on the dogma advocated by Dr. Hodge. It not only gets rid of the horribly irrational idea that God inflicted suffering upon an innocent being for the sins of others, but it also disposes of the equally incredible notion that the all-good and all merciful God could be satisfied with *suffering* as such. We can never believe that pain of any kind which any being endures can give any satisfaction to a good God. Even the sufferings of the vilest wretch on earth afford no satisfaction to God; they are not what He desires. He wants man to *do his will—to obey*, rather than to suffer. This and this alone can satisfy Divine Justice and Love; and since the Calvinistic dogma furnishes as an equivalent for the violation of God's law what He does not want, viz., suffering, while, at the same time, it teaches that this suffering was inflicted on the wrong man—the Holy One—it must be rejected.

Evolution so exalts our idea of Deity as to preclude such a doctrine as that enunciated by Calvinism and held by the great mass of Christians. It reveals a God of infinite wisdom, power, justice, and love, who resides in and presides over all Nature, and such a being can not either inflict punishment upon an innocent person for the sins of others, or accept the self-inflicted suffering of such an one as a satisfaction for the violation of his law.

But not only does Evolution explode the Calvinistic dogma of the Atonement by showing its inconsistency with any true idea of God; it disposes of it more effectually perhaps by showing that it is a relic of barbarism.

Mr. Spencer argues that "propitiations of deities were developed from propitiations of the dead." The idea that death was merely a long-suspended animation led to the deposition with the corpse of food, drink, and other things, and these offerings to the dead gradually "grew into sacrifices and libations to the gods; while immolations of victims, blood-offerings, mutilations, cuttings off of hair, originally occurring at the grave, occur afterward before idols and as marks of fealty to a deity." *

It is most probable that we have the origin of sacrifices here truly indicated; but, however this may be, we know that the idea that "without the shedding of blood there is no remission of sins" prevailed throughout the ancient world and prevails among modern savages as well as among Christians. "Alike in sunny Greece, and stately Rome, and apostatizing Israel, and scorching Africa, and in the far sweet islands of the sea, to hideous emblems of some savage deity—a Moloch, an Odin and Atua, a Sheeva; in the rushing stream, or the molten furnace, or on the blade of the consecrated sword, has the blood of man been

---

* Spencer's "Sociology," i, chap. xix.

shed in abominable sacrifices, or his life robbed of all health and joy in horrible self-torture." *

There were two kinds of sacrifices generally prevalent in the ancient world, viz., *honorific* and *piacular* sacrifices.

The first consisted of *gifts*—fruits, grain, wine, oil, the flesh of animals, etc.—which were offered to the deity. We have a striking instance of such an offering in Exodus, xxiii, 15, where the rule is laid down that no one is to appear before Jehovah empty-handed. But we are more especially concerned with the piacular sacrifices. "Among all primitive people there are certain offenses against piety, especially bloodshed within the kin, which are regarded as properly inexpiable: the offender must die or become an outlaw. Where the god of the kin appears as vindicator of this law, he demands the life of the culprit. If the kinsmen refuse this, they share the guilt. Thus the execution of a criminal assumes the character of a religious action. If, now, it appears in any way that the god is offended and refuses to help his people, it is concluded that a crime has been committed, and not expiated. This neglect must be repaired, and, if the true culprit can not be found or can not be spared, the worshipers as a whole bear the guilt until they or the guilty man himself finds a substitute. The idea of substitution is wide-spread through all early religions, and is found in honorific as well as piacular sacrifices; the Romans, for example, substituted models in wax or dough for victims that could not be procured according to the ritual, or feigned that a sheep was a stag, and the like." †

---

* Farrar's "Silence and Voices of God," pp. 99, 100.
† "Encyclopædia Britannica," article "Sacrifices."

Such notions were imbibed, first by the Israelites and then by the Christians, and so we are to-day drinking from a stream whose fountain-head lies far away among the mountains of the East. Abraham came from " Ur of the Chaldees," the capital of a large empire wholly given to idolatry. In his native land he was accustomed to see the smoke of even human sacrifices ascend to the gods; " households, in times of special trouble, presenting their eldest son as a burnt-offering for the sins of the family." * And although Abraham when tempted to do the same thing (Gen., xxii), did not yield to the temptation; although, in this case, we have an advance in the spiritual evolution of this people, yet sacrifices continued to be offered in Israel, and the practice was strengthened by the nation's experience and contact with other nations—especially Egypt. As a result of the Egyptian bondage, the sacrificial system was fully developed, embodying among other striking rites that of the Passover, which offered an admirable framework for the subsequent Christian doctrine of the atonement.

" The preaching of the prophets was a constant protest against the grosser forms of sacrifices, and there are indications that, when Christianity arose, bloody sacrifices were already beginning to fall into disuse. A saying that was attributed to our Lord repeats this protest in a strong form: 'I have come to abolish the sacrifices, and, if ye do not cease from sacrificing, the wrath of God will not cease from you.' Among the Greeks the philosophers had come to use both argument and ridicule against the idea that the offering of

---

* Geikie's " Hours with the Bible," i, chap. xviii.

natural things could be needed by or acceptable to the Maker of them all. Among both Jews and Greeks the earlier forms of the idea had been rationalized into the belief that the most appropriate offering to God is that of a pure and penitent heart, and among them both was the idea that the vocal expression of contrition in prayer or of gratitude in praise is also acceptable. The best instances of these ideas in the Old Testament are in Psalms l and li, and in Greek literature the striking words which Porphyry quotes from an earlier writer: 'We ought, then, having been united and made like to God, to offer our own *conduct* as a holy sacrifice to Him, the same being also a hymn and our salvation in passionless *excellence of soul.*' The ideas are also found both in the New Testament and in the early Christian literature : 'Let us offer up a sacrifice of praise to God continually, that is, the fruit of the lips which make confession to His name' (Heb., xiii, 15). 'That prayers and thanksgivings, made by worthy persons, are the only perfect and acceptable sacrifices, I also admit' (Justin Martyr, *Trypho*, chap. cxvii). "We honor God in prayer, and offer this as the best and holiest sacrifice with righteousness to the righteous Word" (Clement of Alexandria, Strom. vii, 6).*

This, then, is about what Evolution has to say on the subject of the Atonement: It first shows how the doctrine of sacrifice originated from the low idea that God was a sort of man, who must be pacified as an offended earthly ruler is, either by gifts or the suffering of the offender. The idea of substitution also originated from the fact that in barbarous societies the offender was

---

* "Encylopædia Britannica," article "Sacrifices."

allowed to furnish a substitute. Hence the notion of "vicarious atonement."

Secondly. Evolution so exalts our idea of Deity as to preclude such a dogma. It purges this idea of its low anthropomorphism and reveals a God of Infinite Wisdom, the Creator and Governor of all things, "who dwelleth not in temples made with hands; neither is worshiped with men's hands, as though He needed anything, seeing He giveth to all life, and breath, and all things" (Acts, xvii, 24, 25). It tells us that the ancient law of sacrifices was a mere "shadow of good things to come, and not the very image of things, and those sacrifices, which were offered year by year continually could never make the comers thereunto perfect. . . . For it is not possible that the blood of bulls and of goats (or even of man) could take away sins. Wherefore when He (Jesus) cometh into the world, he saith, Sacrifice an offering thou wouldst not, but a body hast thou prepared me: in burnt offerings and sacrifices for sin thou hast had no pleasure. Then said I, Lo, I come to do thy *will*, O God. . . . He taketh away the first, that he may establish the second (Hebrews, x, 1–9, etc.). Observe, a second sort of atonement is established. Evolution does not simply tear down, "take away," the old view; it gives us a higher and better doctrine in its place. That doctrine, as gathered from Reason and Revelation, seems to be this: Man is a sinner—i. e., a being endowed with the power to obey or disobey Divine Law; who *does* disobey that law. He therefore suffers, as a natural, necessary consequence, certain ill effects which we call punishment. How shall he escape from such punishment? By *escaping from sin, and by no other means*. God, his Father, therefore sends

Jesus to save His people from their *sins* (Matthew, i, 21) first by setting them an example of perfect obedience to God's will, and then by assigning a *motive* to virtue strong enough to enable men to live soberly, righteously, and godly.

That motive is *the fatherly love of God toward man;* which love was manifested in the mission and person of Jesus.

Does this view satisfy all the demands of the case? First, it gets rid of the low idea that God is a Being who can be "satisfied" with suffering—who will accept, as an equivalent for the violation of His moral law, pain, physical and mental; and it teaches instead that "to obey is better than sacrifice" (1 Samuel, xv, 22)—that God wants justice, mercy, and humility (Micah, vi, 8) rather than suffering. It holds that the full and perfect operation of God's laws—i. e., absolute obedience to them—must redound to the welfare of the universe, especially of man.

Secondly. It gets rid of the heathenish idea that an innocent being may be substituted in place of the guilty, and emphasizes the grand and just truth that "whatsoever a man soweth that shall *he*," and not another, "reap"; "the soul that sinneth, *it*," and not another, must suffer the penalty, and the only satisfacton which it can make to God is to quit sinning and keep His commandments. The sufferings of Christ, and especially his death, it holds, was not a punishment for others' sin, but merely the consequence of his undertaking to do God's will in the midst of a wicked world. We should, therefore, speak of his blood not as *itself* the atoning element in his work, but as the *symbol* of that *love of Divine Justice and Humanity* which led him to lay down his life in attempting to obey the will of his Father and to save his brethren in the flesh from sin.

Third. It freely satisfies the demand that *past* violations of the Divine Law, whether racial or individual, be atoned for, by citing the perfect obedience to that law of One individual which is the earnest of the perfect obedience of all his disciples.

Fourth. It fully recognizes the difficulties in the way of ordinary human beings fulfilling the Divine Law, and provides the only motive power which has ever enabled *any* one to keep that law, viz., Divine Love. Of course, any one is at liberty to deny the sufficiency of this motive power, but he will be unable to find a more effective incentive.

Finally. It gives due weight to *fear* as a motive to right conduct by insisting that, if a man sow the wind, he must reap the whirlwind (Hosea, viii, 7; Galatians, vi, 7).

This view of the Atonement will doubtless be branded as Socinianism or something worse; but I am not concerned with such charges, for it is high time to have done with the despicable mode of refuting certain theories by pointing out their connection with some supposed "heresy." Only weak minds are excusable for resorting to this method of answering an opponent; for it is obvious that the question in every case is not, Who is the author of such and such a view? but simply and only, *Is it true?* And in attempting to answer this question, in the present case, let no one appeal to the mere letter of Holy Scripture, and, by stringing together a few disjointed texts, try to refute the above theory of the Atonement. This is the popular method of arguing on this and other subjects. Their profoundly mysterious character—their utter incomprehensibility—is first asserted, and then it is urged that we must "bow to the authority of Scripture," which generally means nothing more than the authority of the particular *interpreter* of Scripture who happens to be arguing on the given subject. But this sort of argumentation will not satisfy an intelligent, independent thinker, especially of the Evolutionist school.

He will urge that, while there are great mysteries in life yet we quite understand the origin of certain dogmas; we can explain the naturalness of their rise, and thus show that they are man-made riddles rather than real mysteries. He will urge that the Bible is merely the record—the paper equivalent—of certain *thoughts* to which holy men of old gave expression; and so he will go *back* of the record to the original—to the human mind who conceived the thoughts it contains, and he will compare these thoughts with the thoughts of other ancient and modern religious minds and judge of their rationality. If they prove to be rational and credible, he will accept them; if not, he will not accept them, even though they be venerable with age and authority.

This is the issue which the Evolutionist presents to the dogmatic Traditionalist, and hence I have not attempted to prove any doctrine of the Atonement by an appeal to the letter of Holy Scripture. I have merely defined the popular dogma, traced its historical development, shown its irrationality in the light of evolution, and attempted to formulate a theory, which seems to meet the demands of a philosophical theology or rather soteriology.

No one realizes more fully than I do that the ground whereon I stand is holy—that the subject in hand is one of supreme practical importance to the human race; and so I have tried to discuss it candidly and reverently. No one realizes more fully than I do how deep and terrible is the pain of a thoroughly aroused sinful conscience, how earnestly the awakened sinner longs for a Saviour; and since this, the practical side of the Atonement, is so important, I may be pardoned for giving my own experience in this matter, in the hope that others may be helped to a right apprehension of their relation to God through Jesus Christ.

I became a Christian when sixteen years of age, being aroused from a youthful indifference to religion by reading Baxter's "Call to the Unconverted." Of course, from such a beginning I very naturally passed on to an acceptance of the whole of traditional theology, especially the dogmas of endless punishment, justification by faith, and the atonement by substitution. Still I continued to sin after my "conversion," and consequently suffered much pain and anxiety about my condition. This anxiety was completely removed, however, by reading a sermon on "Justification by Faith" from the words, "Therefore, we conclude that a man is justified by faith, without the deeds of the law" (Romans, iii, 28). The word "law" was defined to mean natural as well as revealed (Biblical) law, and it was argued that a man is justified by faith in Christ, "without regard to *any* law, whether natural or revealed." In short, this sermon, though preached by an Episcopalian divine, was a thorough exposition of the Lutheran doctrine of justification by faith alone. This sermon set my conscience at rest as nothing else had done, and I concluded that all I had to do was to believe in Jesus as the Son of God and the Saviour of men, and do the best I could (whatever *that* might be), and I would be saved. I began my ministry with this idea, and many a restless soul has been quieted by this theology; but it is needless to say that my views on this subject have undergone a change. I no longer believe that Jesus bore the penalty due my sins, but I know that I must suffer the consequences—the penalty—of my own sin; that whatsoever I sow, that I shall also reap. I no longer believe that the *sort* of faith which popular orthodoxy advocates can justify a man. I *do* believe that a man is justified by faith in Christ, but it is a faith that has less regard to Christ's *nature and work* than to his *holiness*. The faith that will justify and save us is the faith by *which Christ's holy character is formed within us*—a faith which produces repentance of sin, love of God, and love of man. This and this alone can save us, and if we have such faith we shall be happy forever, whether we believe the traditional view of Christ's nature and work or not.

In looking back over my experience I ask, Why was it that I suffered so before reading the sermon referred to, and why has not that suffering returned since I have rejected the views it advocated? The simple answer is, I *got the wrong idea of God in the first place*. I was taught at my mother's knee to pray, "Our *Father*, who art in heaven," but that blessed truth—the Fatherhood of God—was obscured by the fire and brimstone gospel which I heard proclaimed from the pulpit. God was held up, not as one who pitieth us more than an earthly father pitieth his children, but He was set forth as a stern judge who was ready to cast us into a lake of fire that burneth forever for the slightest offense. "He that offendeth in one point is guilty of the whole," it was urged, and so I became deeply alarmed at the prospect before me—an implacable Judge and an endless hell. Just here the sermon came, assuring me that "Jesus paid it *all*, all the debt I owe," and hence I had nothing to do but to believe and I should be saved, and so I found rest for my soul. But I now see that that rest would have been mine *all along* if the heavenly Father had been held up before my eyes in all his glorious attractiveness.

Hence I urge all those who may fancy that any other theory of the Atonement than that which substitutes Jesus in our place, and makes him bear the punishment due our sins, can not afford us comfort and peace of soul to consider this experience, which is given, not because I would obtrude my inner experience upon their attention (for this is far from pleasant), but because it is one of many experiences which prove to demonstration that Traditionalism is *not* the only anchorage for the sin-tossed soul. Let us believe firmly in the God of Love, let us accept Jesus of Nazareth as the finite manifestation, the positive, objective, historical proof of Divine Love; let us repent of our sins as they are committed, and strive to overcome them by prayer and effort, until Christ shall be formed into us (Galatians iv, 19), and we need fear nothing here or hereafter.*

---

* Consult on the subject of this chapter McLeod Campbell on "The Nature of the Atonement"; "A Symposium on the Atonement," by Farrar, etc. (Whittaker, New York); Canon Medd's "One Mediator," "Bampton Lectures" for 1882; Van Oosterzee's "Christian Dogmatics"; Martensen's "Christian Dogmatics," and other systems of theology. Compare Maurice's "Theological Essays," No. VII; Robertson's "Sermons," No. IX (1st series) No. VII (3d series) and No. XX (4th series), Liddon, "University Sermons," 1st series, No. IX, etc., etc.

CHAPTER VI.

EVOLUTION: HEAVEN AND HELL.

NOTHING more decisively indicates the intellectual progress of this century than the change which has come over the popular views of heaven and hell. In the days of the fathers the imagination reveled in the most excruciating and irrational pictures of hell. Listen to this horrible caricature of a great truth: "God's heavy hand shall press the *sanies* and the intolerableness, the obliquity and the unreasonableness, the amazement and the disorder, the smart and the sorrow, the guilt and the punishment out from all our sins and pour them into one chalice, and mingle them with an infinite wrath, and make the wicked drink off all the vengeance, and force it down their unwilling throats, with the violence of devils and accursed spirits."* Again, we are assured that "when Iniquity hath played her part, all the Furies of Hell leap upon the man's heart, like a stage. Thought calleth to Fear; Fear whistleth to Horror; Horror beckoneth to Despair, and saith, Come and help me torment this sinner. Irons are laid upon his body, like a prisoner. All his lights are put out at once. 'Give us a millstone,' say the damned, 'as large as the

---

* Bishop Jeremy Taylor, quoted in Farrar's "Eternal Hope," p. 61.

whole earth, and so wide in circumference as to touch the sky all around, and let a little bird come once in a hundred thousand years and pick off a small particle of the stone not larger than the tenth part of a grain of millet, and after another hundred thousand years let him come again, so that in ten hundred thousand years he would pick off as much as a grain of millet: we wretched sinners would desire nothing but that thus the stone might have an end, and thus our pains also.'"*
To these and similar passages quoted in his eloquent and popular little book of sermons on the future life, Archdeacon Farrar adds, in his able work, "Mercy and Judgment," many other quotations from eminent divines of all ages, beginning with St. Cyprian (A. D. 258) and ending with John Forster (1843), all of whom speak to the same effect, and teach that "souls are to be plunged into a material hell-fire, miraculously created or kept aflame, and to be tormented with excruciating physical pangs during billions of ages for every second of sin, while saints and angels rejoice at their sufferings. . . . These views," our author adds, "are at present half asserted and half believed by some; and multitudes, especially of the poor and ignorant, who neither assert nor believe them, yet suppose that they are a part of the doctrines of the Church." On another page he quotes this dreadful passage from Jonathan Edwards: "The pit is prepared, the fire is made ready, the furnace is now hot, ready to receive the wicked; the flames do now rage and glow. The God that holds you over the pit of hell, much in the same way as one holds a spider or some loathsome insect, abhors you and

---

* "Eternal Hope," pp. 62, 67.

is dreadfully provoked. He will trample them beneath His feet with inexpressible fierceness; He will crush their blood out and will make it fly, so that it will sprinkle his garments and stain all his raiment" (Edwards's "Works," vii, p. 499). "You can not stand before an infuriated tiger even; what, then, will you do when God rushes against you in all His wrath?" ("Sinners in the Hands of an Angry God"). "Let it not be said," Dr. Farrar adds, "that religious teachers have long repented of unconscious blasphemies like these, for this very sermon has been lately printed and circulated as a tract, to the delight of all who love to watch the spread of infidelity." *

Of course, it has been said (and doubtless will be said again) that "these pictures and descriptions come only from a few writers of past generations, and those only the most passionate and the most vulgar." While it is true that but few intelligent and learned preachers of the present merciful and philanthropic age boldly declare their belief in a material hell and endless punishment; while they for the most part keep this dogma in the background and assert it with many qualifications and explanations, yet the endlessness of punishment is still considered by the vast majority of Christians, the " orthodox view;" while occasionally we find a theologian bold enough not only to assert this "orthodox"(?) dogma, but even to accept, or at least incline to accept, the idea of a material hell. Thus, so late as 1887 Messrs. Funk and Wagnalls published a book by the Rev. J. B. Reimensnyder, a Lutheran clergyman, entitled "Doom Eternal," in which the doctrine of end-

---

* " Mercy and Judgment," chap. iv.

less punishment was not only maintained, but in answer to the question, "Is hell-fire a material one?" the author says: "The Bible describes it as such, ... and yet that these descriptions *may be figurative* (italics his) we are not prepared positively to deny, although the probabilities favor their literalness. . . . Whether literal or figurative," he adds, " whether material or spiritual, they are *none the less real.*" He then quotes and emphasizes Dr. Van Oosterzee's question, " Who shall say that the reality will not infinitely surpass in awfulness the boldest pictures of it?" * Both of these theologians say that " Holy Scripture requires us to believe in a properly so-called *place* of punishment"; and when we thus find professional and acknowledged leaders in the theological world maintaining such low, heathenish views of hell, it is surely unnecessary to apologize for exposing and refuting those views. Whatever refinements of this crude dogma may prevail in the theological shcools, yet its central contention, viz., that the wicked shall be punished forever with spiritual if not material sufferings, is, as already stated, generally considered the "orthodox view," and there is no surer way of gaining the desirable label of "heretic" than by opposing this dogma. On this subject, however, as well as on some other so-called "orthodox" doctrines, we are glad to be considered heretical. Evolution refutes this tenet of popular theology, not merely by exalting our ideas of Deity and tracing the doctrine to heathenism, but its fundamental postulate seems utterly inconsistent with the notion of the eternity of evil.

---

* "Doom Eternal," pp. 191–194; cf. Van Oosterzee's "Christian Dogmatics," vol. ii, p. 790.

It teaches that the whole creation is moving forward and upward from a state of imperfection to perfection, and hence the conclusion seems inevitable that the day is coming when there shall be " new heavens and a new earth wherein dwelleth righteousness," and righteousness alone, when " *God* shall be *all and in all.*" In the fourteenth and fifteenth chapters of his " Principles of Sociology " Mr. Spencer sketches the evolution of the idea of another life and another world. From him we learn that the belief in another life is originally qualified and partial:

" The second life may (it is believed) be brought to a violent end; the dead man's double may be killed afresh in battle; or may be destroyed on its way to the land of the dead; or may be devoured by the gods. Further, there is in some cases a caste-limitation; in Tonga it is supposed that only the chiefs have souls." The after-life "is suppos'd to differ from nothing in this life." The dead require provisions, food, clothes, arms, companions, etc. Hence these things are deposited with the corpse, and wives, slaves, and friends are slain at the pyre or grave to bear company to the departed. In social arrangements, also, the future life is like this. " Subordination, both domestic and public, is expected to be the same hereafter as here." Not only do such ideas prevail among modern savages, many instances of which Mr. Spencer cites, but the conceptions of higher races are essentially the same. " The legend of the descent of Ishtar, the Assyrian Venus, shows us that the residence of the Assyrian dead had, like Assyria, its despotic ruler, with officers levying tribute. So, too, in the under-world of the Greeks, we have the dread Aïdes, with his wife Persephone, as rulers; we have

Minos 'giving sentence from his throne to the dead, while they sat and stood around the prince, asking his doom'; and Achilles is thus addressed by Ulysses: 'For of old, in the days of thy life, we Argives gave thee one honor with the gods, and now thou art a great prince, here among the dead.' And while men are thus under political and social relations like those of living men, so are the celestials. Zeus stands to the rest exactly in the same relation that an absolute monarch does to the aristocracy of which he is the head.

"Nor did Hebrew ideas of another life, when they arose, fail to yield like analogies. Originally meaning simply the grave, or, in a vague way, the place or state of the dead, *Sheol*, when acquiring the more definite meaning of a miserable place for the dead, a Hebrew Hades, and afterward developing into a place of torture, Gehenna, introduces us to a form of diabolical government having gradations. And though, as the conception of life in the Hebrew heaven elaborated, the ascribed arrangements did not, like those of the Greeks, parallel terrestrial arrangements domestically, they did politically. As some commentators express it, there is implied a 'court' of celestial beings. Sometimes, as in the case of Ahab, God is represented as taking counsel with his attendants and accepting a suggestion. There is a heavenly army, spoken of as divided into legions. There are archangels set over different elements and over different peoples; these deputy-gods being, in so far, analogous to the minor gods of the Greek Pantheon. The chief difference is that their powers are more distinctly deputed, and their subordination greater. Though here, too, the subordination is incomplete; we read of wars in heaven and of rebellious angels cast down to Tartarus. That this parallelism continued down to late Christian times is abundantly shown. In 1407 Petit, Professor of Theology in the University of Paris, represented God as a feudal sovereign, heaven as a feudal kingdom, and Lucifer as a rebellious vassal. . . . That a kindred view was held by our Protestant Milton is obvious." * "A kindred view" is stated in the "Collect for St. Michael and all Angels' Day" (Episcopal Prayer-Book), which says God has "ordained and constituted the services of angels and men in a wonderful order."

And Dean Goulburn, commenting upon this collect, says, "Scripture gives us to know for certain that there is a distinction of ranks and degrees among the angels, a constituted order among them, even as there is in human society." † A writer in the "Encyclopædia Britannica" (article "Eschatology") gives, perhaps, a more satisfactory sketch of the notions that have prevailed concerning the future state than Mr. Spencer does. "Eternity of punishment," he says, "is often assumed to be a truth of natural religion—an intuitive human belief. It would be truer to say that in all races the first vague guesses at immortality include no thought of retribution at all." He then cites proofs of his assertion from the Greek and Hebrew writers.

"Homer speaks of life and form in Hades, but says there is no *mind* there at all. The movement, freedom, joy of existence, ended for the Greek at death. . . . The primitive Hebrew conception was even less tolerable than the Greek. Sheol—translated in the Septua-

---

* "Spencer's "Sociology," i, pp. 190, 191.
† Goulburn on the "Collects," vol. i, p. 340.

gint 'Hades,' and by our Authorized Version, with curious impartiality, thirty-one times 'grave,' and thirty-one times 'hell'—was, as originally conceived, a vast subterranean tomb, with the barred and bolted gates common to Hebrew tombs, in which the ghosts (Rephaim) did not even flit about, but lay like corpses in a sepulchre. No thought of retribution was connected with this deep and gloomy under-world. It was the common receptacle of all. The distinctions there were social and national, not moral.

"This primitive idea had, by the time of Christ, developed under influences of a very different kind. In the first place, the horror with which the ancient Hebrew had contemplated death, because in Sheol he would be cut off from all communication with the covenant God, was dissipated under the truer religious feeling struggling into life in the later Psalms and the book of Job. At first it had been believed that Jehovah's control did not reach to the under-world. The King of Terrors was its only king. They who had been God's sheep when alive, in Sheol had a new shepherd, Death (Psalms, ix, 14).

"But truer views of God's nature dissipated this horror, and pious souls who despaired of redress in this life began to look even in Sheol for a manifestation of divine justice and a proof of divine love. At length was grasped the hope of a deliverance from the prison-house of the dead, and the doctrine of the resurrection crowned this hope and gave a definite shape to the eschatology of the Jews.

"Analogies have been found between the Greek 'Tartarus' and the Hebrew hell, and the influence of the Western mythology traced in the latter; but in order to supply symbolism of torment of surpassing horror, no foreign influence was necessary. Gehenna (i. e., the valley of Hinnom, or the sons of Hinnom, southeast of Jerusalem, in which children were burned to the idol Moloch and the fires were kept up perpetually) and its ghastly associations were ready to supply images terrible beyond any the mind of heathen poet or philosopher had conceived. Already known as the perpetual abode of corruption and fire—the place where lay the corpses of those who have transgressed against Jehovah, and 'their worm shall not die, neither shall their fire be quenched'—it had become the apt symbol of utter moral depravity and ruin. But it was the unknown author of the book of Enoch * who first saw it as the accursed of the accursed forever, who first placed in the dark ravine one of the mouths of hell, and thus from an emblem of the moral ruin attending sin, made it the actual place of punishment for sinners. Henceforth, Gehenna (hell) becomes known as a part of Hades or Sheol." Paradise, Elysium, the abode of the blessed, was on the other side of Hades.†

"The popular views of a future state regard the use Jesus made of current terms as a sanction of their literal meaning.

"But from the very earliest Christian times another interpretation has been given them. It has been understood that Christ treated popular religious terms as only the symbols of a false creed can be effectually treated.

---

* See "Encyclopædia Britannica," article "Apocalyptic Literature"—Enoch.

† See parable of "rich man and Lazarus," Luke xv, and compare Bishop Harold Brown's "Exposition of the Thirty-nine Articles," Episcopal Prayer-Book, Article III.

He rescued them for the service of the new and true. He took from their future and remote, in order to give them a present and immediate force and aspect. He employed the familiar images of heaven and hell to impress on men's consciences the supreme bliss of righteousness and the awful misery of sin." *

This, then, seems to be the line of historical development of the ideas of heaven and hell: First, men, when they got the idea of the soul as distinct from the body, thought of the ghost-self as close at hand, haunting the old home; but gradually "the regions said to be haunted by the souls of the dead become wider. Though they revisit their old homes, yet commonly they keep at some distance." What changes the idea of another world close at hand, to the idea of another world comparatively remote? The answer is simple—migration. The dreams of those who have lately migrated, initiate beliefs in future abodes which the dead reach by long journeys.

"Having attachments to relatives left behind, and being subject to home-sickness (sometimes in extreme degrees) uncivilized men, driven by war or famine to other habitats, must often dream of the places and persons they have left. Their dreams, narrated and accepted in the original way as actual experiences, make it appear that during sleep they have been to their old abodes. First one then another dreams thus, rendering familiar the notion of visiting the fatherland during sleep. What naturally happens at death, interpreted as it is by the primitive man" as merely a long-suspended animation? "The other self is long absent—

---

* "Encyclopædia Britannica," article "Eschatology."

where has he gone? Obviously to the place which he often went to, and from which at other times he returned. Now he has not returned. He longed to go back, and frequently said he would go back. Now he has done as he said he would."

The notion that the place of the departed was underground is thus accounted for by Mr. Spencer: "Where caves are used for interments they become the supposed places of abode for the dead; and hence develops the notion of a subterranean world." The Greeks, Romans, and Jews especially believed in such a subterranean abode of departed spirits, in which were placed, on the one hand the happy fields of Elysium or Paradise, and on the other the gloomy realms of Tartarus, a huge fortress, surrounded by a fiery river and echoing sounds of torture.*

The conception of another world as *above* or outside of this world, Mr. Spencer ingeniously urges, arose from the fact of burial on hills and mountains. "The transition from a mountain abode to an abode in the sky, conceived as the sky was by primitive man, presents no difficulties. Burial on hills is practiced by many peoples; and there are places, as Borneo, where, along with the custom of depositing chiefs' remains on some peak difficult of access, there goes the belief that the spirits of the departed inhabit the mountain-tops. The highest mountain in sight is regarded as a world peopled by the departed; and in the undeveloped speech of savages, living on a peak up in the heavens is readily confounded with living in the heavens."†

---

* Homer's "Odyssey," Book XI; Virgil's "Æneid," Book VI; cf. Bishop Browne on "The Thirty-nine Articles"—Article III.

† Spencer's "Sociology," i, chap. xv.

Since, then, we can thus trace the historical development of the notions concerning heaven and hell—can show their natural genesis from primitive man's idea of a ghost-self, another self, who could leave and dwell apart from his body, what shall we think of the huge mass of inferences which have been drawn from these facts as stated in the Bible? Shall we set the whole aside as "old wives' fables"—baseless, useless human speculation and fancy?

Surely not. Surely "there is a soul of truth in things erroneous" in this case also. Surely the universal belief in the existence and immortality of the soul, together with the belief in a heaven and hell, is at least a *presumption* in favor of immortality and future retribution! It is not reasonable to suppose that all men have been deceived on this subject—have reasoned falsely—have believed a lie; and therefore it is our duty to search for the kernel of truth in the husk of error.

Assuming, then, the existence and immortality of the soul, which will be more fully considered in another chapter, and confining our attention strictly to the subject in hand, let it be observed:

First, that we must give up the crude idea of heaven and hell as *places*, and think of them as *states*, or spiritual conditions. "Hell," says Archdeacon Farrar, "is a temper, not a place. So long as we are evil, and impure, and unloving, so long where we are is hell, and where hell is there we must ever be. The true Gehenna is not a burning prison but a polluted heart—alienation from God; hatred of truth; hatred of purity; a hard, bitter, railing, loveless spirit; mean, base, selfish, sensual desires; these are the elements of hell—and as long as any man—be he Pharisee or be he a publican—is given to these, so long will he be made to feel with the evil spirit:

> 'Which way I fly is hell, *myself am hell*,
> And in the lowest deep a lower deep,
> Still gaping to devour me, opens wide,
> To which the hell I suffer seems a heaven.'

"On the other hand, we must think of heaven not as of 'some meadow of asphodel' beside the crystal waters, or golden city in the far-off blue, but as an extension, as a development, as an undisturbed continuance of righteousness and peace and joy in believing; whatever else it be, or mean, heaven means *holiness;* heaven means *principle;* heaven means to be *one with God*." *

To the same effect speaks Dr. Martensen. "If it be asked," he writes, "*where* those who are fallen asleep find themselves after death, nothing certainly is more preposterous than the idea that they are separated from us by an outward infinity—that they find themselves in some other material world—and so forth. By such notions we retain the departed within those limits and conditions of sense beyond which they certainly are. No barrier of sense separates them from us, for the sphere in which they find themselves differs, *toto genere*, from this material sphere of time and space. . . . *The tendency or direction of the soul in death is not outward but inward, a going into itself, a going back, not a going forth*"; and instead of the modern notion that the soul wings its way to the stars, which is sometimes understood literally, the idea is far more cor-

---

* Farrar's "Eternal Hope," pp. 25 and 125.

rect that *it " draws itself back to the innermost and mystical chambers of existence which underlie the outward.*

"The realm of the dead must be described, in relation to this world of sense, as an *inward realm.*"* This gives a profoundly philosophical meaning to the article of the Apostles' Creed which speaks of Christ's descent into hell. This was no material descent into the bowels of the earth, but a withdrawal of his spirit from the outward and visible sphere of matter into the unseen spiritual universe; and, on the other hand, his ascension into heaven must not be thought of as a literal ascent from the hills of Palestine into the skies, but rather a withdrawal into the immediate and glorious presence of his Father—the Infinite Spirit "in whom we live and move and have our being."

The whole doctrine of evolution as it is expounded, not simply in the writings of modern philosophers, but as it appears in the fifteenth chapter of First Corinthians, teaches this view—that the future life is to be a higher and more spiritual state than this earthly state is.

Secondly, the idea of an *endless* hell must be given up for it contradicts both the statements of Scripture and the facts of evolution-philosophy. Such eminent theologians as Archdeacon Farrar, Canon Row,† Rev. John Page Hopps,‡ and others have conclusively shown that neither the special nor general teachings of Scripture nor the dictates of conscience and reason prove the popular doctrine of hell. The main *word* in this great

---

* Martensen, "Christian Dogmatics," pp. 459, 460; cf. Stewart and Tait's "Unseen Universe," *passim.*

† Row's "Future Retribution."

‡ "Future Probation; a Symposium," by Rev. J. P. Hopps, Dr. Leathes, etc. (Whittaker).

discussion is the word "eternal" (Greek αἰώνιος = *aionios;* Hebrew עלם *olam*), and this has been shown to have at least *four* meanings in Scripture:

First, it unquestionably means "everlasting," in some cases, as when it is applied to *God* (Deuteronomy, xxxiii, 27). But—

Secondly, it is no less certain that it means *limited duration*, as, for instance, when it is applied to a landmark, "Remove not the *ancient* landmark" (Proverbs, xxii, 28). The original of the word "ancient" is (Hebrew) "olam," which certainly must have the meaning of limited duration in this case, for the landmark has long since passed away, as all landmarks must in course of time. Then—

Thirdly, the word "eternal" means *indefinite duration*, as when it is applied to the hills (Genesis, xlix, 26); and—

Finally, in the "Gospel according to John" this word loses the element of duration altogether and expresses a *spiritual condition.* "Eternal life" here means *happiness in the unseen world,* eternal punishment or death means misery in the spirit-world.* The only remaining question, then, is this; when the word "eternal" (*olam* or *aionios*) is applied in Scripture to the state of the wicked after death, does it *necessarily* mean endless duration? In answer the advocates of everlasting punishment cite Matthew, xxv, 46, in which it is said: "These (the wicked) shall go away into everlasting (i. e., aionian) punishment; but the righteous into eternal (aionian) life, " where, it will be observed,

---

* Maurice's "Theological Essays," pp. 377-416, Farrar's "Eternal Hope," excursus iii, etc., "Mercy and Judgment," pp. 378-405.

the same word is used to describe the condition of the righteous and the wicked after death. Hence, from the days of St. Augustine (fourth century) to the present it has been urged that "if the misery of the wicked in hell be temporary, so must the blessedness of the righteous in heaven be temporary"—to which sophistry the following crushing reply has been given: We find no intimation in the New Testament that the happiness of the righteous will ever end; on the contrary, it is over and over again said to be endless. On the other hand, we have not only special passages of Scripture which seem to teach clearly that the wicked will have an opportunity of salvation in the spiritual world, but the *general* teaching of the New Testament would lead us to believe in the ultimate total extinction of all evil and suffering.

The special passages referred to are, of course, the following: In Matthew, v, 26, it is distinctly said that one may pay the *last* farthing and *come out* of the prison of punishment. In Matthew, xii, 31, 32, it is said that blasphemy against the Holy Ghost shall not be forgiven, "neither in this world, neither in the world to come." And if this passage be applied, as it generally is, to the state of the wicked after death, it certainly implies that some sins *will* be forgiven in the world to come, but blasphemy against the Holy Ghost is not one of these. The most conclusive special passage, however, in favor of a possible salvation after death is I Peter, iii, 18-20, and iv, 6. Here it is distinctly said that Christ, after he was put to death in the flesh, during the three days between his crucifixion and resurrection, went and preached the *gospel* to the dead in prison—i. e., Hades, the unseen world—that they might be judged according to men in the flesh, but live according to God in the spirit. Of course, various theological subterfuges have been invented to explain away the obvious meaning of this passage. But such attempts are unworthy of their source, and any unbiased mind must see in this passage a clear expression of belief in salvation after death. However, the opponents of endless punishment not only urge special passages of Scripture against the traditional and popular doctrine of future punishment; they argue much more strongly that the New Testament clearly teaches that all evil and suffering are to be ultimately extinguished from God's universe. Thus we read of "new heavens and a new earth wherein dwelleth righteousness" (II Peter, iii, 13). We are told that the day is coming when "in the name of Jesus every knee shall bow, of things in heaven and things in earth, and things under the earth, and every tongue shall confess that Jesus Christ is Lord, to the glory of God the Father" (Philippians, ii, 10, 11). We read of a "restoration of all things" to a state of perfect purity (Acts, ii, 21), and, more conclusively, we are told that a day is coming when "all things shall be subdued unto God, and he shall be *all in all*" (I Corinthians, xv, 28). It is rather hard to believe that God will be "all in all" if evil is to be endless.*

For a moment I have taken the Traditionalist on his own ground—"the Bible and the Bible only"—and have very briefly indicated the answers which the New Theology gives to his time-worn, threadbare arguments,

---

* See, for further passages of Scripture and crushing arguments, Farrar's "Eternal Hope," pp. 219-225, and the other able works referred to.

or rather crude inferences; but, of course, the evolutionist must go back of the letter of any book to the spirit of the man who wrote it and ask, Why should we accept his utterances as authoritative and infallible instead of the opinions of others? Of course, if he be infallibly inspired of God, then his utterances are law to us, but we have seen that the Bible writers, although the greatest religious geniuses whom God ever sent upon earth, have by no means left us absolutely infallible productions. It is simply amazing that intelligent theologians, who know how uncertain are the authorship and the authenticity of the "Gospels," should yet insist that their literal meaning is binding upon us; that in them we have a perfect transcript of Divine Wisdom. It is plain to all unprejudiced minds that they, and indeed all the books of the New Testament, contain much, especially on the subject in hand, that is directly traceable, not to Divine Wisdom, not to Jesus of Nazareth, but to the *Jewish schools of theology*, and hence we unhesitatingly set it aside—unless, indeed, it be confirmed by other and more rational teachings.

In short, it must be evident to all that, notwithstanding the Traditionalist's claim that Reason has no voice on this question of a future state; that the Bible is the only authority which can be recognized—we are compelled to appeal to Reason at every point to say whether such things are true or false. Canon Row, in his powerful work on "Future Retribution" (chapter ii), has annihilated the popular fallacies about our Reason being an untrustworthy witness on the subject under consideration. He shows that the legitimate conclusion of the popular teaching is *blank Agnosticism*.

It is commonly urged that we have no right to infer

from our conception of Justice, Love, and Mercy anything as to God's dealings with the wicked, because our ideas on these subjects may be false; we can form no true notion of Infinite Justice, Love, and Mercy; they may be different attributes from what we think them to be. In other words, it is meant that injustice on earth may be justice in heaven; love on earth may be hatred in heaven; mercy in this world may be cruelty in the next; and, *vice versa*, injustice, hatred, and cruelty, as we understand them, may be the very essence of justice, love, and mercy in the spiritual world!

Could any theory be more subversive of all religion and philosophy than this? Is it not the most dangerous sort of Agnosticism? I hold, then, with Canon Row and others, that what is unjust, unmerciful, and unloving in our estimation, is *infinitely more so in God's estimation*, and from this we may argue forcibly against the popular dogma of future punishment. First, given a God of infinite power, wisdom, and love, such as Jesus revealed, and given infinite time and means for the accomplishment of His purposes, it is simply absurd to say that He *can not* accomplish those purposes. What those purposes are we may not know absolutely, but we may rationally urge that a God of Love must desire the *happiness of all* His creatures; and, if so, He will bring it about, if not in one way then in another. In short, the endless existence of evil in the universe is utterly inconsistent with the infinite power, wisdom, and goodness of God; although its temporary existence may serve a good purpose.

Secondly, say what we may, we can not believe that a God of Love will either damn one of His children, or *allow him to damn himself*, everlastingly, for any sin however heinous. God can not be more cruel than man, and no earthly father would condemn his child, or, if he could help it, allow his child to be condemned, to endless punishment.

Thirdly, the whole law of evolution, as already stated, is opposed to the doctrine of endless evil and suffering. It teaches that the whole creation is moving forward and upward to a state of *perfection* in every respect.

It, no less than the Seer on Patmos, beholds afar off "the New Jerusalem descending out of heaven from God, having the glory of God; and her light like unto a stone most precious, even unto a jasper stone; and the gates of pearl, and the foundations of precious stones, and the pure river of the water of life clear as crystal, and the Tree of Life with its leaves for the healing of the nations" (Rev., xxi, xxii).

When that beatific vision shall be realized, "they shall hunger no more; neither shall the sun light on them, nor any heat. For the Lamb that is in the midst of the throne shall feed them, and shall lead them unto living fountains of waters; and God shall wipe away all tears from their eyes" (Rev., vii, 16, 17). "And there shall be no more curse, but the throne of God and of the Lamb shall be in it; and his servants shall serve Him; and they shall see His face; and His name shall be in their foreheads" (Rev., xxii, 3, 4). Symbols these—only symbols, but as Dr. Farrar truly says: "If we need any symbols to help us, they are symbols of transparent meaning; green meadows, where men may breathe God's fresh air, and see His golden light; glorified cities, with none of the filth and repulsiveness of these, but where no foul step intrudes ; white robes, pure emblems of stainless innocence; the crown, and the palm-branch, and the throne of supreme self-mastery over our spiritual enemies ; and the golden harp and the endless song, which do but speak of abounding happiness, in that form of it which is of all others the most innocent, the most thrilling, the most intense."

Now, of course, there are many, myriads indeed, who will raise the familiar war-cry of Traditionalism: "This is a *dangerous* doctrine; this teaching will make men careless and more indifferent to religion than they are now." To which it may be replied : First, it is not a question of *consequences* but a question of *truth*. If the foregoing doctrine is true, we must preach it, regardless of consequences.

Secondly, the dogma of an endless hell is by no means so potent a factor in the conversion of the world as many fancy. For hundreds and thousands of years it has been preached most vigorously ; and yet, according to its own showing, the vast majority of men, even in Christian lands, are forever lost. It is about time that we try the Gospel of Love in place of the gospel of fire-and-brimstone. But, alas! not only has preaching endless punishment failed to convert the majority of those who have listened to it; it has made *infidels* by the score and by the thousand. An advocate of this cruel and irrational dogma has no show whatever in an argument with a profound and brilliant skeptic.

Thirdly, if preaching the Gospel of Love make men indifferent; if they are so beastly as to put off coming to God till after death just because He is a merciful God, then *not only will they be punished most severely for this negligence,* but, according to our view, our depleted ranks may be filled up in the unseen sphere from those unnumbered millions whom traditional "orthodoxy," or rather heterodoxy, consigns to an endless hell. We are certain that these died in a state of sin and are suffering the consequences, and we might prefer a doctrine which holds out hope to that vast unknown multitude to a dogma which condemns them, under the delusion that its proclamation is necessary to the salvation of unborn generations. I say "delusion," for, after all, how does the Traditionalist know so much about the "consequences" of preaching the "Larger Hope"? By what power of foresight has he been able to peer down the vistas of the future and behold unborn myriads marching to hell because of the proclamation of the Gospel of Love? Judging from the past, we should infer that the very opposite would be the result.

Finally, let it be distinctly understood that, while we disbelieve in the eternity of evil—in *endless* punishment—we by no means disbelieve in *future* punishment. Nay, "Whatsoever a man soweth that shall he also reap," and more—"sow the wind, reap the *whirlwind.*"

"Sow an act, reap a habit; sow a habit, reap a character; sow a character, reap a destiny." It is this awful fact—the *hardening* effect of sin—that led Archdeacon Farrar to believe in the possibility of endless punishment; but it is apparent from the foregoing that the author, among others, believes even a character so stereotyped in sin may ultimately be recovered by Infinite Power, Wisdom, and Love. But while believing this, I no less firmly assert the terrible depth of sin and of punishment to which a human soul may sink, *and God only knows how long it may take Infinite Power, Love, and Wisdom itself to rescue such a soul.* Is there any sane man in existence who wishes to take such a risk? We do not believe it; but if there be such a fool, such a wretch on God's green earth, we say to him in the words of the olden preachers: "Walk in the ways of thine heart and in the sight of thine eyes; but know thou that for all these things God will bring thee into judgment" (Ecclesiastics, xi, 9). "Woe unto them that call evil good and good evil; that put darkness for light and light for darkness; that put bitter for sweet and sweet for bitter. Therefore, as the fire devoureth the stubble and the flame consumeth the chaff, so their root shall be as rottenness, and their blossom shall go up as dust: because they have cast away the law of the Lord of hosts, and despised the word of the Holy One of Israel" (Isaiah, v, 24).

"There is a dreadful coercion," says Dr. Farrar, "in our iniquities, an inevitable congruity between the deed and its consequences; an awful germ of identity in the seed and in the fruit. We recognize the sown wind in the harvest whirlwind. We feel that it is *we* who have winged the very arrows that eat into our heart like fire. It needs no gathered lightning, no miraculous message to avenge in us God's violated laws. *They avenge themselves.* You may laugh at Bibles, sneer at clergymen, keep away from churches, and yet your sin coming after you with leaden footstep, and gathering form and towering over you, smites you at last with the iron hand of its own revenge.

"You may be saved, indeed, at last, if God will; saved not from Him and His wrath, but from yourself and your self-destruction; but even then there may be a sense in which it may be awfully true that our millenniums depend upon our moments; the path of repentance may never be closed to us; but oh, how *hard* may that path of repentance be—over what bleeding flints; through what a scorch of fiery swords; through what deep shame, what dread corruption, what pain of body, what misery of remorse, what agony of soul! Oh, were it not better to cut off the right hand and pluck out the right eye, than go of our own choice into the Gehenna of aionian fire, here and hereafter!"

That fire "is the glare of illumination which *Conscience* flings over the soul after a deed of darkness. It is the revulsion of feeling on which we did not calculate when we have done with the sin, but the sin has not done with us. It is the little grain of conscience within the very worst of us which makes forbidden pleasures sour. It is the fact that none of us can be quite wicked enough to *enjoy* wickedness. It is the aching crave after the brief intoxication. It is the Dead Sea apple shriveling into hideousness the moment it has been tasted. It is the horror of the murderer when his passion of vengeance is spent, and the cold gray dawn reveals the face of his murdered victim." It is the vision of the young man suffering from *delirium tremens;* "the blood-red suffusion before the eyes quenched suddenly in darknesss—the myriads of burning, whirling rings of concentric fire—millions of foul insects seeming to weave their damp, soft, webs about the face, the bloated, hideous, ever-changing faces of their visions—the eyes that glare from wall to roof—the feeling as if a man were falling, falling, falling, falling, endlessly into a fathomless abyss!"

This is hell, and such a hell begins *below* and extends into the dark and hidden depths of eternity; and if any one be foolhardy enough to cast himself headlong into this lake of fire because God's mercy endureth forever, he must suffer the consequences, knowing all the while that he was fully warned of his fate.*

---

* See Archdeacon Farrar's most eloquent and powerful sermon on "The Consequences of Sin," "Eternal Hope," sermon v.

CHAPTER VII.

EVOLUTION AND THE PROBLEM OF EVIL.

Mr. Maurice begins the third of his "Theological Essays" with these profound words: "I suppose if any of us met with a treatise which professed to discuss the origin of evil, our first and most natural impulse would be to throw it aside.... The man must have great leisure," we should say "or be very youthful who could occupy himself with such a subject as this. After six thousand years of experience of evil, and almost as many of hopeless controversy about its source, we may as well reckon that among the riddles which men are not to solve, and pass to something else.

"The resolution may be a wise one as far as it relates to discussions, philosophical or theological, on this topic. Possibly the chief good they have done is, that they have shown how little they can do; that they have proved how inadequate school logic is for the necessities of human life. But if we suppose when we closed the book, that we had done with the question it raised and which it tried to settle; if we thought that it would not meet us again in the law court and the market-place, and mix itself most inconveniently in all the common business of the world, a little experience will have shown us that we are mistaken. We *must* consider the origin of evil, whether we like it or not. We are debating it with ourselves; we are conversing about it with others; we are acting on some conclusions we have formed about it every day of our lives."

Now, this is my reason and apology for undertaking to discuss this sorely vexed and most difficult problem in this work. It is *not* purely a theoretical question; it is an intensely practical question; it forms, if not the *sine qua non* of the Church, at least one of its chief corner-stones, and so we must consider the *fact* of evil, and this consideration will lead us directly to a discussion of its origin. Let me add that on this, as on most of the subjects treated in this book, I have no original contribution to make. My aim is simply to bring together and condense and popularize, if possible, what I consider the best thoughts that have been expressed on the subjects in hand. Adhering to this plan, I shall freely quote from the most modern and, in my opinion, the ablest writers on the problem of evil, merely throwing in explanatory notes which may seem necessary.

The question at issue naturally divides itself into two parts, viz., the origin of *physical* evil and the origin of *sin;* and we must keep them separate. For a long time it was supposed that the earth was cursed on account of Adam's sin (Genesis, iii, 17, 18), that death itself is the wages of sin (Romans, vi, 23), and by this was understood not spiritual but physical death.* But geological and biological science has clearly disproved this notion by showing, first, that death, among plants and the lower animals, wrought its dreadful work on this planet millions of ages before man appeared; and, secondly,

---

* Hodge's "Theology," ii, p. 92.

that whatever man may be spiritually—however widely separated from the lower animals in soul—he at least belongs physically to the animal kingdom. "From the natural or *animal* point of view," says Prof. Le Conte, "man belongs to the animal kingdom. In that kingdom he has no department of his own; he belongs to the department of Vertebrata, along with birds, reptiles, amphibians, and fishes. In that department he has no privileged *class* of his own; he belongs to the class Mammalia, along with all four-footed beasts. In that class he has no titled *order* of his own; he belongs to the order of Primates, along with apes, baboons, lemurs, etc. Even the privacy of a *family* of his own, the *Hominidæ*, is grudgingly accorded to him by some." * Dr. Hodge admits the truth of this.† Since, then, the lower animals which existed before man was originated died, and since he, at least as regards his body, "belongs to the animal kingdom," the conclusion is inevitable that bodily death is not the wages of sin, except, of course, in those cases where a man kills himself by drink or some other sinful means. But not only does science prove that death is not the wages of sin; it further proves that the supposed "curse" on the ground in Genesis, iii, 17, 18, is groundless.

The earth brought forth "thorns and thistles" long before the advent of man: essentially the same physical phenomena everywhere existed in all lower creation in pre-human times that exist nowadays. Hence the cause of all evil and suffering is not sin. What, then, is the cause of physical evil? The answer is—

---

* "Princeton Review," November, 1878.
† "What is Darwinism?" p. 5.

GOD. And if any one be shocked by this bald way of stating the truth, his pain will vanish when he considers the subject more profoundly. Even supposing that human sin—i. e., the act of man, or of some other personal wicked spirit (the devil)—were the cause of evil, the question at once arises, What is the cause of that cause—who created man or the devil?—for surely neither is self-originated or self-existent; and the answer to this question must be—God. It is, therefore, apparent that, by calling in some finite cause to account for the existence of evil, we merely stop at a half-way house—we do not go to the root of the matter. Science, recognizing the truth of all this, posits One Supreme Cause of all things, and holds that "not a sparrow falleth" without Divine permission; that everything happens according to Divine Law. It thus boldly declares that God is the author of what we call evil, and then seeks to explain the why and the wherefore of His permitting the existence of what we call evil. Observe, I say, "what we call evil," because evolution holds that evil is merely *good in disguise*—a necessary condition of higher development—of greater happiness. And this idea has been so clearly expounded by Prof. Le Conte, that I borrow his exposition in full.

"The necessary condition of evolution of the organic kingdom," he says, "is a *struggle* for life—a conflict on every side, with a seemingly inimical environment, and a survival of only the strongest, the swiftest, or the most cunning—in a word, the fittest. Now, suppose the course of organic evolution finished in the introduction of man, and from this vantage-ground we look back over the course and consider its *results*. Shall we call that evil which was the necessary condition of the progressive elevation which culminated so gloriously? Evil doubtless, it seemed to the individual struggling animal, but is this worthy to be weighed in comparison with the evolution of the *whole* organic kingdom until it culminated in man? Is it not rather a *good* in disguise?

"But organic evolution completed in man was immediately transferred to a higher plane, and continued as social evolution; material evolution is transformed into psychical evolution; unconscious evolution, according to *necessary* law, to conscious voluntary progress toward a recognized goal, and according to a *freer* law. But in this transformation the fundamental conditions of evolution do not change. Man is also surrounded on every side with what at first seems to him an evil environment, against which he must struggle or perish— heat and cold, tempest and flood, volcanoes and earthquakes, savage beasts and still more savage men. What is the remedy, the only conceivable remedy? *Knowledge of the laws of Nature*, and thereby acquisition of *power* over Nature. But increasing knowledge and power are equivalent to progressive elevation in the scale of psychical being. This conflict with what seems an evil environment is, therefore, the necessary condition of such elevation. It is not too much to say that without this condition, except for this necessity for struggle, man could never have emerged out of animality into humanity, or, having thus emerged, would never have risen above the lowest possible stage. Now suppose, again, this ideal to have been attained—suppose knowledge of physical laws and power over physical forces to be complete—suppose physical Nature completely subdued, put beneath our feet, and subject to our will, and, from the high intellectual position thus attained, we look back over the whole ground and consider the result. Shall that be called evil which was obviously the necessary condition for attaining our then elevated position? Evil it doubtless seemed to the individual who fell, and still seems to us who now suffer, by the way in the conflict; but is physical discomfort or even physical death of the individual to be weighed in comparison with the psychical elevation of the individual, and especially of the race?

"Evidently, then, physical evil, even in the case of man, is only *seeming* evil, but *real* good. But there is a more dreadful form of evil than that which results from *external* physical nature—an evil far more subtle and difficult to understand and conquer. I mean *internal* organic evil—disease in its diversified forms and with its attendant weakness and suffering, inscrutable often in its causes, insidious in its approaches, contagious, infectious, spreading from house to house, carrying suffering and death in its course, and leaving sorrow and desolation behind. Is there any remedy which can transmute this evil into good? There is. It is again *knowledge*—knowledge of the laws, and power over the forces, of *organic nature*. Is it not evident that complete knowledge of the laws of health and the causes of disease would put this evil also under our feet?

"Is it not evident that a perfect knowledge of the laws of health, and a perfect living according to these laws, would so entirely subdue this evil that men would no longer die except by natural decay or by accident?*

---

* See Spencer's enunciation of the conditions of *physical immor-*

Is it not evident, also, that the race will not attain this knowledge unless it is forced upon us by the necessity of avoiding the dread evil of disease? Now suppose, again, this ideal attained, suppose this dread evil subdued by complete knowledge, and again from our elevated intellectual position we look back over the ground. Shall we call that evil which was the necessary condition of our intellectual elevation? Evil, doubtless, it seems to us individuals who have suffered and are still suffering through our ignorance; but is such individual suffering or individual death to be weighed against the psychical elevation of the race? Ought not the individual to be willing to suffer thus much vicariously for the race? Is not this seeming evil also a real good?

"May we not, then, confidently generalize? May we not say that *all* physical evil is good in its general operation, and, if sometimes evil in its specific operation, is so only through our ignorance?" * The Law of Being thus fully elaborated was more simply stated by the late F. W. Robertson. "The mountain rock," he says, "must have its surface rusted into putrescence and become dead soil before the herb can grow. The destruction of the mineral is the life of the vegetable. Again the same process begins. The 'corn of wheat dies,' and out of death more abundant life is born. Out of the soil in which deciduous leaves are buried, the young tree shoots vigorously, and strikes its roots deep down into the realm of decay and death. Upon the life of the vegetable world the myriad forms of higher life

---

tality and Drummond's comments upon it, "Natural Law in the Spiritual World," chapter on "Eternal Life."

* "Evolution and Religious Thought," pp. 328-332.

sustain themselves—still the same law: the sacrifice of life to give life.

"Further still: have we never pondered that mystery of nature—the dove struck down by the hawk—the deer trembling beneath the stroke of the lion—the winged fish falling into the jaws of the dolphin? It is the solemn law of vicarious sacrifice again. And as often as man sees his table covered with flesh of animals slain, does he behold, whether he thinks of it or not, the deep mystery law of being. They have surrendered their innocent lives that he may live." *

There are two obvious though somewhat superficial objections to this teaching—that physical suffering is a law of being whose operation, on the whole, benefits creation.

The first is clearly stated by Prof. Huxley in these words: "We are told," he says, "to take comfort from the reflection that the terrible struggle for existence tends to final good, and that the suffering of the ancestor is paid for by the increased perfection of the progeny. There would be something in this argument," he adds, "if, in Chinese fashion, the present generation could pay its debts to its ancestors; otherwise it is not clear what compensation the *Eohippus* (*First Horse*) gets for his sorrows in the fact that, some millions of years afterward, one of his descendants wins the Derby." †

The answer to this is simply that the life of every *individual*, although it suffers much, is, on the whole, a happy one; its joys far outweigh its sorrows, and

---

* Robertson's "Sermons," first series, No. IX.
† "Popular Science Monthly," April, 1888, pp. 733, 734.

hence life is worth living in every case. Could each animal accept Byron's advice—

> "Count o'er the joys thine hours have seen,
> Count o'er thy days from anguish free,"

he would by no means agree with the pessimistic poet that

> "Whatever he has been, 'tis something better not to be."

On the contrary, he would confess that life was the greatest of blessings. Life, with all its trials and sufferings, is not only worth living, but it is far better than non-existence.

Indeed, all this talk about the *rights* of creatures is nonsense. We are utterly bankrupt in relation to God. "In Him we live and move and have our being"; all that we are or have are gifts to us, and hence it is absurd to talk about God's *owing* us anything. Once show that a thing happens to us according to a law of Nature—i. e., a law of God—and that must stop all complaints against One to whom *we* owe everything. Prof. Huxley's remark that the present generation owes something to its ancestors is only another way of saying that the *Creator* owes certain things to the creature, which we may safely deny *in toto*.

But, secondly, it is urged: "Given an almighty, all-wise, and all-good God, and it necessarily follows that any production of His should be perfect. Hence there ought to be no *necessity* for such a law of suffering as Le Conte and Robertson assert. Everything should be *created* perfect."

We answer this objection with a single question: *How could the universe be created by different laws from those we observe in operation?* Those who think the Creator could produce a world by different laws from those adopted make several absurd assumptions: First, they assume that Infinite Wisdom deliberately chose a method of operation which even a finite mind would not have adopted. Is not this necessarily implied in Prof. Huxley's remark that to say that "this is the best of all possible worlds seems little better than a libel on possibility"? Our author, had he existed in the beginning, would evidently have made some highly important suggestions to the Creator as to the proper method of His procedure! Let us, then, cease making such absurd charges against Infinite Wisdom.

Second, those who make the objection under consideration not only accuse the Creator of deliberate folly, but they also forget *what is involved* in the creation of a finite order of things.

If a finite universe exist at all, must not the Infinite Creator make a *condescension*—must He not limit Himself in producing it?

The truth is, "a certain crude-minded class of theologians are accustomed to draw the most sweeping inferences from the omnipotence of God. They take the word omnipotence in an undiscerning and coarse way; as if it followed indubitably that a being omnipotent can do everything he really wishes to have done. But force has no relation to the doing of many things." * It can not, for instance, impel a free agent without destroying his freedom to the doing of a given act; and I incline to think that it could not have created the world by different methods from those adopted. At

---

* Horace Bushnell, "Nature and the Supernatural," p. 93.

any rate, if we find reason to believe in Infinite *Wisdom* as well as Infinite Power as the prime Cause of all things, we argue most rationally in urging that the best laws of operation have been adopted in the production of the universe; and those who doubt this must not indulge in brilliant generalities about what Omnipotence might have done or ought to do, but must instruct Omniscience in detail; must say exactly how a world of minerals, plants, and animals might be produced absolutely perfect without any sacrifice on the part of individuals. And even if they can, by some unimaginable flight of the imagination, imagine the production of such a world, let them ask themselves this question: " Is not the gradual evolution of a perfect world from chaos a greater display of wisdom and power than the spasmodic momentary exertion of omnipotence which they probably have in mind would be?"

So, then, we conclude that physical suffering is a great and necessary law of evolution, whose operation will ultimately redound to the glory of the Creator and the welfare of His creatures.*

---

* It may have weight with some to remark that Mr. Spencer holds essentially the view expressed above. "Slowly but surely," he says, "Evolution brings about an increasing amount of happiness; all evils being but incidental. By its essential nature, the processes must everywhere produce greater fitness to the conditions of existence, be they what they may. Applying alike to the lowest and the highest forms of organization, there is in all cases a progressive adaptation, and a survival of the most adapted. If, in the uniform working out of the process, there are evolved organisms of low types, which prey on those of higher types, the evils inflicted form but a deduction from the average benefits. The universal and necessary tendency toward supremacy and multiplication of the best, applying to organic creation as a whole as well as to each species, is ever diminishing the damage done; tends ever to main-

This seems to be the place to make a few remarks on the directly practical side of the problem we are considering:

Many years ago the cholera broke out in England, and the English Church bade the nation to *prayer* against the dread disease. Among the sensible Christians who raised their voices against this plague was good Charles Kingsley. He said his prayers against cholera, and then rose from his knees, and, in his memorable sermons on the cholera, gave utterance to the following sentiments: "We have just been praying to God to remove from us the cholera," he said, "which we call a judgment of God, a chastisement. But we can hardly expect God to withdraw His chastisement unless we correct the sins for which He has chastised us; and therefore, unless we find out what particular sins have brought this evil on us. We can not flatter and persuade the great God of heaven and earth into taking away the cholera from us, unless we find out and confess what *we* have done to bring on this cholera, and unless we repent and bring forth fruits worthy of repentance, by amending our habits on that point, and doing everything for the future which shall not bring on the cholera, but keep it off. Do not let us believe this time, my friends," continued the earnest preacher,

---

tain those most superior organisms which, in one way or other, escape the invasions of the inferior and so tends to produce a type less liable to the invasions of the inferior. Thus the evils accompanying Evolution are ever self-eliminated. Though there may arise the question, Why could they not have been avoided? there does not arise the question, Why were they *deliberately* inflicted?" Whatever may be thought of them, it is clear they do not imply gratuitous malevolence," which *is* involved in the old view, according to our author ("Principles of Biology," vol. i, p. 354, etc.).

EVOLUTION AND THE PROBLEM OF EVIL. 349

"in the pitiable insincere way in which all England believed when the cholera was here sixteen years ago. When they saw human beings dying by thousands, they all got frightened, and proclaimed a fast and confessed their sins, and promised repentance in a general way. But did they repent of and confess those sins which had *caused* the cholera? Did they repent of and confess the *covetousness, the tyranny, the carelessness, which in most great towns, and in too many villages also, forced the poor to lodge in undrained, stifling hovels, unfit for hogs, amid vapors and smells which send forth on every breath the seeds of rickets and consumption, typhus and scarlet fever, and worst and last of all the cholera?* Did they repent of their sins in that? Not they. Did they repent of the carelessness and laziness and covetousness which sends meat and fish up to all our large towns in a half-putrid state; which fills every corner of London and the great cities with slaughter-houses, overcrowded graveyards, undrained sewers? Not they. And when those great and good men, the Sanitary Commissioners proved to all England fifteen years ago (1834) that cholera always appeared where fever had appeared; and that both fever and cholera always cling exclusively to those places where there were bad food, bad air, crowded bedrooms, bad drainage and filth; that such were the laws of God and Nature, and always had been—they took no notice of it, because it was the poor rather than the rich who suffered from such causes." *

These are very instructive words in every respect, but I shall merely emphasize two important thoughts

---

* Kingsley's "National Sermons," sermon xiii, pp. 134-136.

expressed by Kingsley: First, he speaks of the cholera as a "chastisement" sent by God on account of the sins of men, and he shows how this was profoundly true in the case of the cholera plague, albeit in a different and more rational sense than is popularly understood. We often hear people speak of this or that calamity as "a Divine visitation." When Johnstown, Pennsylvania, was destroyed (1889) by a flood, which resulted from the breakage of an imperfectly built dam, it was seriously asked, "Were the Johnstown people sinners above all other men that they should be thus afflicted by the Almighty?" Such a notion is heathenish! This was the idea which the ancient Israelites entertained concerning Noah's flood and the destruction of Sodom and Gomorrah. But those who hold such views would do well to remember our Lord's remarks to those who told him on one occasion that Pilate had mingled the blood of certain Galileans with the sacrifices. "Suppose ye," he said, "that these Galileans were sinners above all the Galileans, because they suffered such things? I tell you nay! Or those eighteen upon whom the tower in Siloam fell, and slew them, think ye that they were sinners above all men that dwelt in Jerusalem? I tell you Nay; but, except ye repent, ye shall all likewise perish" (Luke, xiii, 1, 5).

This is a distinct condemnation of the popular idea of "Divine visitations," and a clear enunciation of the grand fact that God is not a Being, like man, who gets angry with his children because they do not act to suit him and by a special effort of his will destroys them. He has indeed established certain laws the violation of which brings certain evil consequences, and He has endowed man with power to violate these laws, and if he abuses this power he suffers in consequence. It is a law of God that fire burns and water flows; and so, if a man put his finger in the fire, or undertake to stop the flow of water by building a weak dam, he must suffer the consequences. It is a law of Nature that certain conditions will produce disease: bad food, bad water, bad air, bad drainage, etc., will produce fever and the like, and the only escape from these evils is, as Prof. Le Conte says, knowledge—knowledge of the laws of Nature, of the laws of health, and conformity to these laws. Hence—and this is the main fact suggested by Kingsley's remarks—when a man violates God's laws, he must not blame God for the suffering he receives in consequence. God has given him a mind by which he may learn to avoid these evils, and if he fails to use it *he*, not God, is to blame. Let me not be misunderstood: I do not say that man is omniscient or omnipotent, and hence can by wise conduct avoid *all* the " ills that flesh is heir to," but I do say that many of those ills are due to man's own foolish or careless or sinful action and *not* to any special " Divine visitation," and in such cases the blame should be laid at the right door —man's door. "The Popular Science Monthly" for February, 1888 (page 555, etc.), had an admirable editorial on "The Act of God and Human Responsibility," which is very suggestive on this subject. It seems that an eminent attorney of a certain railroad had written an article "to prove that some railway accidents proceed from causes so far beyond human control that we might properly apply to them the old expression 'act of God.' The suggestion is that in such cases the railroad companies should hardly be held responsible." The editor of the "Monthly," seeing clearly the terrible results which might flow from such teaching, very properly joined issue with the lawyer, and urged " human responsibility " in essentially the same manner as has been urged above in other instances. It can not be too earnestly insisted upon that man, whether he be absolutely free or not, has power to do certain things, and so far he is responsible for the results of his actions. Hence such awful events as the Johnstown flood, railroad accidents from weak bridges, disease from improper ventilation, and the like, are attributable to man, not to God.

And when this fact is fully and practically recognized, the problem of evil will become less difficult of solution.

We pass now to the *moral* aspect of this problem—to a consideration of *sin*. And the first question to be asked and answered here is, What *is* sin? Probably no one will object to this definition: Sin is the deliberate refusal to act according to the knowledge and power which the Creator has given us. When we perceive that the laws of Nature (i. e., the laws of God) dictate a certain course, and we refuse to pursue that course, we are guilty of sin. For instance, when we clearly understand that theft, murder, adultery, and the like, are contrary to the laws of Nature (of God), and yet we steal, murder, and commit adultery, we are guilty of sin. Of course, if man was originally a savage animal, devoid of the power of knowing that such acts were contrary to Divine law, and if his will-power were then so weak that, even if he had known this, he could not have acted according to such knowledge, he was not *then* guilty of sin—i. e., willful violation of what was known to be Divine law. But, whatever he may have been originally, man has for many ages been able to discern between good and evil, and to choose the one or the other; hence he has *so long* been guilty of sin and is responsible for his conduct. But the question is, Why did and does man deliberately, willfully, consciously choose to violate Divine law? Is he incited thereto by an external spirit—the Devil? It is well known that this is the popular idea, but, as already stated, this theory simply carries us one step further back, and does not solve the difficulty. For the question inevitably arises, What is the cause of the Devil? And if we say that God is the author of the Devil, we might as well say at once that God is the author of sin, or that He causes man to sin, and have done with it. Here is the place to trace the evolution of the idea of a personal Evil Spirit or Devil which is characteristic of at least a portion of the Scriptures.

"Devil is a name," says a writer on this subject, "which has been given in the New Testament and in Christian theology to a supreme evil personality supposed to rule over a kingdom of evil spirits, of whom he is the chief, and to be the restless and unfailing adversary of God. The Hebrew term denoting 'adversary,' or 'Satan,' is also applied to this supreme Evil Spirit, or prince of the kingdom of evil. There can be no question that such an Evil Spirit is frequently spoken of in the New Testament. He is designated by various names, such as 'the Tempter,' 'Beelzebub,' 'the Prince of Devils,' 'the Strong One,' 'the Wicked One,' 'the Enemy,' or 'the Hostile One.' Throughout the Gospels these terms are used interchangeably, and in all cases seem to denote the same active power or personality of evil outside man and exercising influence over him. It may be a question how far Jesus Christ himself acknowledges the existence of such an evil power, but there can not be any question that such a being was recognized in the current belief of the Jews in his time. But it is also certain that this belief among the Jews was one of gradual growth, and is not to be traced in the Old Testament in any such definite form as we meet with in the New.

"The expression 'Satan' is indeed found in the Old Testament, but only five times, if so frequently, as a proper name—thrice in the book of Job (i, 6, 12; ii, 1), once in the opening of the twenty-first chapter of I Chronicles (although here the allusion to a distinct personality may be held doubtful), and in Zechariah (iii, 1). In all other places where the word occurs, 'Satan' is used in its common sense of 'adversary,' a sense in which it also occurs in the Gospels in the well-known passage (Matthew, xvi, 23) where our Lord addresses St. Peter, 'Get thee behind me, Satan,' or 'adversary.' The books of Chronicles and Zechariah are indisputably among the last writings of the Old Testament; and, although the date of Job is unsettled, it may also be presumed to belong to a late period in the history of Revelation.

"In the earlier prophetic literature of the Hebrews, there is no recognition of any spirit of evil at war with Jehovah. All power and dominion are, on the contrary, clearly ascribed to Jehovah himself, who is supreme in heaven, on earth, and under the earth.

"The connection of Satan with the serpent in the garden of Eden in Genesis (iii, 1–7) is an inference of later dogmatic opinion, arising probably out of the use of the expression 'old Serpent' applied to Satan in Revelation (xx, 2), but receives no countenance from the Scriptural narrative itself, which speaks of the serpent purely as an animal, and pronounces a curse against him with reference to his animal nature solely.*

"The idea of a distinct personality of evil, therefore, is not to be found in the earlier Hebrew Scriptures, and is in fact inconsistent with the principle of the older Hebrew theology that Jehovah was the sole source of all power, the author both of good and evil, who hardened Pharaoh's heart (Exodus, x, 27, cf. Amos, iii, 6) and sent a lying spirit among the prophets of Ahab (Kings, xxii, 20-23). Even in the later Scriptures in which 'Satan,' is spoken of as a distinct person, there is little or no analogy between what is said of such a person in these Scriptures and what is said of him in the New Testament. The 'Satan' of the book of Job is described as coming among 'the sons of God,' to present himself before the Lord. He is the image of malice, restlessness, and envy—the willing messenger of evil to Job; but he is not represented as the impersonation of evil, or as a spiritual assailant of the patriarch. He is really a delegated agent in the hands of Jehovah to execute His will, and the evils with which he assails Job are outward evils. The picture is quite different from that of the 'archangel ruined,' or the Devil, or Satan, of later theology.

"The question then arises as to the special source of the conception of the Devil as a fallen and evil spirit. The explanation commonly given by our modern critical schools is that it sprang out of the intercourse of the Jews with the Persians during their period of exile.

---

* Cf. Canon Row's "Future Retribution," chap. vii, pp. 157, 158, and Dr. W. H. Thompson's "Great Argument," chap. iii, pp. 81-83, etc.

"In the Persian, or Iranian, mythology it is well known that a personal power of evil was conspicuously recognized. The Iranian religion divided the world betwixt two opposing, self-existent deities, the one good and the other evil, but both alike having a share in creation and man. Ormuzd, or Ahuramazda, was holy and true, and to be honored and worshiped. But Ahriman, or Anramainyu, the evil-minded, the spirit of darkness, was no less powerful, and claimed an equal share of man's homage. These were the good and the evil in thought, word, and deed. Man was to choose betwixt the two. He can not serve both. With this dualistic system the Jews came in contact during their captivity at Babylon, and are supposed to have retained permanent traces of it in their subsequent theology. . . . The process by which the Jewish mind worked out the conception and the whole scheme of demonology found in the New Testament was of course gradual. The Book of Wisdom, a product of Alexandrian-Jewish thought, in the second century before Christ, which speaks of the Devil having 'through envy introduced evil into the world' (chapter ii, 24) is supposed to represent a stage in the development; and the apocryphal books of Enoch and Esdras (iv), the former of which is pre-Christian (in part at least) indicate further stages. Another stage is supposed to be marked by the recognition of the 'devil' or evil spirit, under the name of Asmodeus, in the book of Tobit (chapter iii, 8, etc.— written about 150 B. C.).

"There is certainly a remarkable analogy betwixt parts of the eschatological teaching of the book of Enoch and other apocryphal books and that of the Gospels. But the development of Jewish theology as a whole, in the ages immediately antecedent to Christianity, is still involved in considerable obscurity, and it is not necessary, in this connection, to enter into details."* Suffice it to know the origin of the conception of an Evil Power antagonistic to the Good; and that it *was a gradually developed human speculation on the problem of evil.* What shall we think of this speculation?

First, let it be remembered, as already more than once stated, that the idea of a devil as the author of temptation and sin does not solve this difficult problem, but rather embarrasses us; for if such a spirit were created, then God—the Supreme Spirit—was his Creator, and we thus make God the author of sin; while, on the other hand, if the devil be uncreated and eternal, God is no longer the *Supreme* Being. In the next place, let it be observed that we freely grant the *possibility* of the existence of a prince of the devils or evil spirits. Believing as we do in the immortality of the soul, and that death does not in any way affect the soul, we believe that there is in the unseen world, as there is in this, a large number of evil spirits, and as in this world such spirits are frequently if not always marshaled under a *leader*, so it may be in the spirit-world. It is one of Frederick Robertson's most profound thoughts that, in the spirit-sphere, spiritual likenesses will draw together. The spiritual and intellectual affinities will determine the relationships of that state. "I shall know," he said, "and converse with men whom I have never seen, yet for whom my spirit has the profoundest reverence, while many with whom

---

* "Encyclopædia Britannica," article "Devil."

I have been in constant communication on earth I shall never see in that other world." * If so—if " spiritual likenesses draw together," and we know they do on earth—then it is quite reasonable to suppose that the evil spirits in the unseen sphere will be drawn together under one leader. But—

Thirdly, as to whether these spirits or their leader *can and do influence men in this life, we can never know.* The influence of an embodied spirit over another in the flesh is an insoluble mystery. We know the *fact,* and this fact is sufficient to prevent our dogmatically asserting that a disemboded evil spirit can not affect an embodied spirit, but the whole question is incapable of solution; unless, indeed, we are prepared to accept Spiritualism pure and simple, but we are not quite ready for this now. The main point to be remembered is that even if we accept either the popular doctrine of the devil or the Spiritualist's notion, we are as far to seek as ever for the prime origin of temptation and sin.

The result, then, of our inquiry thus far is that we are driven from the external to the internal; we can not find in the environment of either the devil or man a sufficient explanation of the origin of sin; it, at most, merely furnishes the occasion, the *sine qua non*, of sin, but does not give the *impelling motive* to sin; and hence we must look *within the finite spirit itself* for the cause of sin.

But how shall we do this with any degree of satisfaction? Are not these eloquent words of a brilliant Agnostic perfectly true? " The dark continent of *mo-*

---

* Robertson's " Life and Letters," appendix i, p. 385.

tive and *desire* has never been explored. In the brain, that wondrous world with one inhabitant, there are recesses dim and dark, treacherous shores, where seeming sirens tempt and fade; streams that rise in unknown lands from hidden springs, strange seas with ebb and flow of tides, resistless billows urged by storms of flame, profound and awful depths hidden by mists of dreams, obscure and phantom realms where vague and fearful things are half revealed, jungles where passion's tigers crouch, and skies of cloud and blue where fancies fly with painted wings that dazzle and mislead ; and the poor sovereign of this pictured world is led by old desires and ancient hates, and stained by crimes of many vanished years, and pushed by hands that long ago were dust, until he feels like some bewildered slave that mockery has throned and crowned." * *Why*, therefore, a man should

> " see the right, and approve it too;
> Abhor the wrong, and yet the wrong pursue,"

we can not tell. We know the fact; we are conscious of the power to choose good or evil, and all the metaphysical gymnastics ever invented can never disprove this direct dictum of consciousness ; we know that we are influenced by some power called "motive," or rather by various motives, and we know that we can act *in spite* of certain motives; but, when we attempt to explain the *origin of motive*, we are lost in the mysterious and the insoluble. We can only be sure that the Good Spirit (God) tempteth no man, for such an idea

---

* Colonel Ingersoll, in "North American Review," June, 1888, p. 636.

is not only blasphemous, it is absurd; for God would not ordain laws for His creatures and then impel them to violate those laws; but why man should be drawn away of his own lusts (James, i, 13–17), especially when he sees the right, and approves it too, and is conscious of power to do it, is an inexplicable mystery. If any one can solve it, he is the man we are looking for. Let him tell us why a man should murder another for money, when he not only knows that it is wrong, but also that he will surely suffer in consequence? Why such *greed?* Or why should one who has a loving wife and family ruin a young girl by seduction, when he knows it is wrong and that he will be punished for his crime? I, for one, can not answer these and many other closely allied questions. I accept the facts, and I assert the man's *responsibility* for such acts, and wait for more light on the theoretical aspect of this transcendental problem. Now, I fancy I hear some lover of dogmatics exclaim in disappointment: "So, then, this is the upshot of your long disquisition on the origin of sin—that we know and can know nothing about it! I knew that before," he would doubtless add; and I would reply: "Pardon me, my friend, you were ignorant before, but you did not know *why* you were ignorant. If this disquisition has done nothing but show you why we are ignorant on this subject; if it has exploded any of the popular fallacies of theology and clearly stated the exact point at issue; and, finally, if it has aroused thought on that issue—surely it is worthy of attention, and this is all its author claims for it."

We turn now to the hardly less difficult question, Why should the Creator originate such a being as man —a being endowed with power to disobey Divine law, when He knew the terrible results which would flow from such a creation? The answer which Evolution gives is an old answer in a new light, and may be unsatisfactory to some, but it is quite satisfactory to many others. It is that the temporary existence of sin and suffering will ultimately redound to the welfare of God's creatures. It was impossible for even Omnipotence to create a being with the *power of choice* between two given courses without *thereby* allowing the possibility of sin, and we know from experience that this being has abused this power for some reason (self-pride, a desire to show his independence, or for some other reason), and yet the creation of such a being was not only the crowning glory of the evolutionary movement, but, *without the endowment of him with the aforesaid power (choice), moral character—the grandest thing in God's universe—could never have been a fact.* * Evolution, therefore, urges that the ultimate result of the creation of such a being as man, notwithstanding all his evil conduct, will redound to the glory and welfare of God's universe. But, as already fully stated, the dogma that evil is to be everlasting, hopelessly complicates this problem—renders even the approximate solution given invalid; but, thank God! neither our own conscience and reason nor the utterances of the holy men whom He has sent into this world to be our religious guides, compel us to believe this irrational dogma.†

If Evolution did not commend itself to our minds on any other ground, it ought to commend itself by the

---

* See Horace Bushnell's "Nature of the Supernatural," chapters iv-vii.

† See "Death of Death," by John M. Patton, Randolph & Co., Richmond, Va.; a most powerful work.

rainbow of hope which it flings across the dark clouds of sin and suffering which lower in our moral skies. It does this not by urging "dithyrambic hypotheses and evasive tropes," not by basing its claim on "the halting reconciliation of ambiguous and opposing texts of Scripture," but by pointing to the Revelation of God in its glorious unity as it appears in Nature and in Man. It shows us the onward and upward march of Being—and, pointing to Perfection and Happiness, it says, "There is the one far-off divine event to which the whole creation moves," and thus it removes the terrible incubus of sorrow and doubt that has weighed down the spirits of so many of God's saints, and which gave birth to these melancholy lines:

"Fix me on some bleak precipice,
 Where I ten thousand years may stand,
Made now a statua of ice,
 Then by the summer scorched and tanned.

"Place me alone in some frail boat
 'Mid the horrors of an angry sea;
Where I, while time shall move, may float,
 Despairing either land or day;

"Or, under earth my youth confine
 To th' night and silence of a cell,
Where scorpions may my limbs entwine,
 O God! so Thou forgive me hell!"

WILLIAM HABINGTON.

CHAPTER VIII.

EVOLUTION AND BODILY RESURRECTION.

ONE of the most impressive scenes in Shakespeare is the first scene of the fifth act of Hamlet. Hamlet and Horatio, it will be remembered, enter a church-yard where a "clown" is digging a grave, and, after a short conversation with the grave-digger about the different skulls which are exhumed, Hamlet takes one of the skulls, and, turning to Horatio, remarks: "To what base uses we may return, Horatio! Why may not imagination trace the noble dust of Alexander, till he find it stopping a bung-hole?" "'Twere to consider too curiously to consider so," replies Horatio. "No, faith, not a jot," answers Hamlet; "but to follow him thither with modesty enough, and likelihood to lead it; as thus: Alexander died, Alexander was buried, Alexander returneth into dust; the dust is earth; of earth we make loam; and why of that loam, whereto he was converted, might they not stop a beer-barrel?

> "Imperial Cæsar dead and turned to clay,
> Might stop a hole to keep the wind away;
> O, that that earth which kept the world in awe,
> Should patch a wall to expel the winter's flaw!"

To one who held the view of the good old Bishop Pearson, that the very particles of which our bodies are composed at death will, on the resurrection morning, be gathered together from the four corners of the globe, to which they may have been borne, such a train of thought was anything but pleasant, and might raise many doubts.* Pearson's view has been variously modified by modern theologians. It is now generally admitted, among educated minds, that the fifteenth chapter of First Corinthians not only negatives the idea of the re-collection of the precise atoms which are dissolved in and by death, but it further teaches that the celestial body will be very different in every respect from the terrestrial body. "Flesh and blood can not inherit the kingdom of God," and so our celestial bodies will be of a spiritual and immortal nature. It is well known that all physicists, of any eminence at least, believe in the existence of *ether*—i. e., a very thin, attenuated substance not even discernible by the microscope, whose vibrations produce light. Suppose, then, this ether formed into a bodily shape as the basis of thought, feeling, and action, and we have an illustration of what St. Paul is supposed to mean by a spiritual body; it is a body *etherealized*, composed of refined, endurable matter; incapable, therefore, of destruction by dissolution.† This is merely an illustration. But this highly spiritual doctrine is by no means universally prevalent, even among professed religious teachers and theologians. One of the most remarkable expositions of the old crude and irrational dogma of a gross mate-

---

* Pearson's "Exposition of the Creed," articles "Christ's and Man's Resurrection."

† See a recent work, "The Foundations of the Creed," by the Bishop of Carlisle (Dr. Goodwin). John Murray, London, England, article "Resurrection of the Body."

rial resurrection was given some time ago by that popular though erratic preacher, the Rev. T. De Witt Talmage:

"You have noticed," he said, "in reading the story of the resurrection, that almost every account of the Bible gives the idea that the characteristic of that day will be a great sound. I do not know that it will be very loud, but I know it will be very penetrating. In the mausoleum where silence has reigned a thousand years that voice must penetrate. In the coral cave of the deep that voice must penetrate. Millions of spirits will come through the gates of eternity and they will come to the earth, and they will cry: 'Give us back our bodies; we gave them to you in corruption, surrender them now in incorruption.' Hundreds of spirits hovering about the crags of Gettysburg, for there the bodies are buried. A hundred thousand spirits coming to Greenwood, for there the bodies are buried, waiting for the reunion of body and soul.

"All along the sea route from New York to Liverpool, at every few miles where a steamer went down, departed spirits coming back hovering over the wave. There is where the City of Boston perished. Found at last. There is where the President perished. Steamer found at last. There is where the Central America went down. Spirits hovering, waiting for the reunion of body and soul. Out on the prairie a spirit alights. There is where a traveler died in the snow. Crash goes Westminster Abbey, and the poets and orators come forth. Wonderful mingling of good and bad—Wilberforce the good, Queen Elizabeth the bad. Crash go the pyramids of Egypt, and the monarchs come forth. Who can sketch the scene? I suppose, one moment before that general rising, there will be a universal silence, save as you hear the grinding of the wheels or the clatter of the hoofs of a procession passing unto the cemetery. Silence in all the caves of the earth, silence on the side of the mountain, silence down in the valleys and far out into the sea. Silence! But in a moment, in the twinkling of an eye, as the archangel's trumpet comes pealing, rolling, crashing across the mountain and the sea, the earth will give one terrific shudder, and the graves of the dead will heave like the waves of the sea, and Ostend and Sebastopol and Chalons will stalk forth in the lurid air, and the drowned will come up and wring out their wet locks above the billows; and all the land and all the sea become one moving mass of life—all conditions gazing in one direction and upon one throne, the throne of the resurrection. 'All who are in their graves shall come forth.'"

It is not necessary to point out the absurdity of this crude, grossly materialistic view of the resurrection; but I cite it merely to call attention to the fact that one of the most popular preachers in the land, by clinging to the mere letter of a few disjointed texts of Scripture, can declare to a large and applauding audience of New-Yorkers such utter nonsense. Surely a chapter on "bodily resurrection," therefore, is not unnecessary. And first we will trace, as clearly as possible, the historical development of this doctrine. Mr. Spencer thinks it originated from the primitive idea that death was "a long-suspended animation. Savages attempt to revive the corpse by ill-usage; they call it by names, and address to it reproaches or inquiries; they endeavor to feed it, and leave food and drink with it; they supply fire to cook by or to keep off cold; they take care to prevent injury by wild beasts and arrest decay (hence the mummies of Egypt); and they inflict injuries upon themselves to signify their subordination to the departed in the hope of recalling to its 'tenement of clay,' the 'other-self' which, they fancy, has merely gone away for a longer time than he usually did during sleep, swoon etc." *

The doctrine of the resurrection was a part of the old *Persian* (Zoroastrian) Creed. "We find it plainly stated in portions of the Zendavesta (Persian Bible), which, if not among the earliest, are at any rate of very considerable antiquity." † "The doctrine of the resurrection of the body," says Dr. Charles Hodge, "is not exclusively a doctrine of the Bible. It is found, in different forms, in many of the ancient religions of the world. The rationalists," he adds, "assume that the Hebrews borrowed this doctrine from their heathen neighbors, in proof of which they urge that the doctrine does not appear in those portions of the Scriptures which were written before the Babylonish captivity." ‡ But, of course, our author aims by various unsatisfactory arguments to disprove "the rationalist's" conclusion.

All such attempts, however, fail in the presence of these three facts:

First, that the Persians held the doctrine of the resurrection.

Secondly, that this doctrine does not appear in the earliest portions of the Hebrew Scriptures; and—

Thirdly, after the Babylonish captivity, during

---

* Spencer's "Sociology," i. pp. 157-168.

† Rawlinson's "Ancient Monarchies," "Third Monarchy," chapter iv.

‡ Hodge's "Theology," iii, pp. 771-789.

which the Jews came in contact with the Persians, this dogma assumes a prominent place in their religious system.

Even Dean Milman says that in II Maccabees, xii, 44 ("for if he had not hoped that they who were slain should have *risen again*," etc.), we have the " earliest *distinct* assertion of the Jewish belief in the resurrection." * The Samaritans and the Sadducees, who originated about the time of the Babylonish captivity, rejected the dogma of the resurrection; † while the Pharisees, who also originated about the same time, adopted and strenuously advocated this doctrine; and thus it passed on into the Christian creed. As already intimated, this doctrine has been a great stone of stumbling and rock of offense to many pious and thoughtful minds, and especially in our day, when our conceptions of the future life are being elevated, purified, and spiritualized, the notion of a material resurrection is becoming peculiarly offensive.

Relief has been sought, first, by taking the word resurrection in a *figurative* sense, and understanding it to mean "the rising of the *soul* from spiritual death to spiritual life." This seems to have been the view of the ancient heretics, Hymenæus and Philetus, who said of Christians that their "resurrection was past already" (II Timothy, ii, 17, 18). Again: "The Swedenborgians hold that man has *two bodies*, an external and an internal, a material and a psychical. The former dies and is deposited in the grave, and there remains, never to

---

* Dr. William Smith's "New Testament History," student's series, p. 39, note.

† Ewald, "History of Israel" (English translation), vol. iv, p. 215 *et seq.*, and v, p. 275 *et seq.*, and viii, 83 *et seq.*, Matthew xxii, 23.

rise again. The other does not die, but in union with the soul passes into another state of existence. The only resurrection, therefore, which is ever to occur, takes place at the moment of death."

Thirdly, others seek relief from the absurdities of the old dogma in St. Paul's exposition of it in I Corinthians xv. The Apostle there states that "flesh and blood can not inherit the kingdom of God," and hence the body "sown in corruption is raised in incorruption; it is sown a natural body, it is raised a spiritual body; this corruptible must put on incorruption." In short, the Apostle seems to mean that the body which is buried perishes utterly and "God giveth us bodies as it hath pleased him" (v, 38).* This is certainly a great advance on the old Jewish view, but there are many good and learned people nowadays who do not believe even this theory of the resurrection.

In the first place, they see no *necessity* for any resurrection of bodies. The spirit, as all admit, will exist for ages, between death and the resurrection morning, without any body, and it certainly seems wholly unnecessary that then it should be given a body.

Secondly, it is urged by scientific minds that the material universe is *wearing out*, and it will finally be utterly dissolved, will vanish "into thin air" or rather something infinitely thinner, and this dissolution, of course, involves the destruction of human as well as cosmical bodies. Thus Profs. Stewart and Tait, in their most remarkable little book, "The Unseen Universe," tell us: "The visible universe may with per-

---

* See the Bishop of Carlisle's (Dr. Goodwin's) recent work on "The Foundations of the Creed," chapter xii.

fect truth be compared to a vast heat-engine. . . . The sun is the furnace or source of high-temperature-heat of our system, just as the stars are for other systems, and the energy which is essential to our existence is derived from the heat which the sun radiates, and represents only an excessively minute portion of that heat. But, while the sun thus supplies us with energy, he is himself getting colder, and must ultimately, by radiation into space, part with the life-sustaining power which he at present possesses. Besides the inevitable cooling of the sun, we must also suppose that, owing to something analogous to ethereal friction, the earth and the other planets of our system will be drawn spirally nearer and nearer to the sun, and will be at length ingulfed in his mass. In each case there will be, as the result of the collision, the conversion of visible energy into heat, and a partial and temporary restoration of the power of the sun. At length, however, this process will have come to an end, and he will be extinguished until, after long but not immeasurable ages, by means of the same ethereal friction his black mass is brought into contact with that of one or more of his neighbors. . . . Thus the tendency is that the sun shall ultimately absorb the various planets of the system, his heat and energy being recruited by the process. Now, let us imagine that the same processes are simultaneously going on in one of the nearer fixed stars, say for instance in *Sirius*. After unimaginable ages these two stars, the sun and Sirius, having each long since swallowed up his attendants, but being nevertheless exhausted in heat-energy on account of radiation into space, may be imagined to be traveling toward one another, slowly at first, but afterward with an accelerated motion. They will at last approach each other with a great velocity, and finally form one system. Ultimately the two will rush together and form one mass, the orbital energy of each (or rather that portion of this energy which remains after ethereal friction) being converted into heat, and the matter being in consequence probably partly smashed into mere dust, and partly enveloped and transformed into a gaseous, nebulous condition. Ages pass away and the large mass ultimately shares the same fate that long since overtook the single masses which composed it; that is to say, it shrinks and throws off planets, but gives out the greater part of its light and heat into space and gradually becomes cold and dark, until at length it comes to form one of the constituents of a still more stupendous collision and has its temperature raised once again by the conversion of visible energy into heat." This process of killing off worlds, our authors argue, will go on until "the very *material of the visible universe will ultimately vanish into the invisible.*" *

The grand and fundamental idea of this remarkable little book is, as its name implies, that the visible and material universe has been developed out of the invisible, spiritual universe and will return into it. The spiritual has, so to speak, assumed a material, mortal coil which, given time enough, it (he) will " shuffle off " and return to its originally purely spiritual condition. It is obvious, therefore, that the doctrine which holds that we shall possess material bodies " in the unseen universe " is inconsistent and irreconcilable with such

---

* "The Unseen Universe," pp. 126, 127, and 165–167, Macmillan & Co., 1886.

teaching. "Under these circumstances," our authors truly say, "we have three honest alternatives. In the first place, we may acknowledge the truth of their position and change our views; or, secondly, we may combat their argument regarding the alleged incompatibility of the Traditionalists' position with the *Principle of Continuity*, advocated by the scientists; or, lastly, we may decline to accept this scientific principle in matters which concern our faith."

But, as the authors also remark, "the members of the religious school who believe in a material resurrection do not choose either of these alternatives, but rather attempt to brand them" (Stewart and Tait) "as infidels and materialists, apparently forgetting (as usual) that such a method of conducting a discussion is neither Christ-like nor convincing." * Not only, it may be added, do the Traditionalists attempt to refute such arguments by branding their authors as infidels and materialists (although they believe the *Spiritual* to be the only real substance!), but their favorite method of disposing of such arguments is to exclaim: "All speculation! all theory! unprovable hypothesis!" It is necessary, therefore, to remark here, once for all, that while hypothesis plays an important part in physical science (although to no greater extent surely than in *Theology!*), yet there are certain great facts which Science is as sure of as it is possible to be sure of anything. No intelligent person would be so silly as to deny the rotation of the earth on its axis and around the sun because the physicists can not explain the nature of that force ("gravity") which produces this effect. The *ultimate*

---

* Preface to third edition of "The Unseen Universe," pp. 20, 21.

destruction of the material world is as certain as the revolution of the earth, and hence no one should demur to conclusions drawn from this "coming event," which is casting more than a "shadow" before, because of its supposed speculative or hypothetical character. It is certain to come, no matter how long its advent may be postponed, and it is not rational that those who believe in *eternity*, and the *eternal* life of soul and body, should hesitate to glance down the vistas of the future to the time of that awful catastrophe. It is the height of folly to teach a doctrine about eternity which we know eternity will explode. Under such circumstances, it seems rational to adopt Profs. Stewart and Tait's view that we are to exist as pure spirits in "the unseen universe."

Of course, there is manifestly one great difficulty, perhaps more, in holding this view: we can not conceive or think of pure spirits existing and operating without some sort of form—i. e., body. But our inability to conceive such action by no means proves its impossibility. It is more than probable that, if we now existed as disembodied spirits, we should be unable to conceive of a spirit's acting with, on, in, or through a body. The inconceivability of a thing by a finite mind is by no means a proof of its impossibility. From all this it appears that the real question is, *Shall we believe in the eternity of matter?* Few Christians believe that "matter" has always existed, but, on the contrary, they think it was created: *once it was not.* If so, is it not unreasonable to suppose that, once in existence, it will last forever? Of course, if it should exist forever, then we might more reasonably believe in the immortality of physical bodies, but sound philosophy as well as sound science negatives this idea.

Now, the Traditionalist will doubtless fall back on the mere letter of St. Paul's teaching, and urge that he has settled this question for us. No one has a profounder reverence for St. Paul than I have. His theory of the resurrection was certainly a great advance on the older Pharisaic doctrine, yet its infallibility may be questioned for two reasons: First, while it is an advance on the older Pharisaic dogma, we have no reason to believe that it is anything more than another stage in the evolution of that doctrine. If St. Paul erred in his idea of Christ's *second advent* (and it must be admitted that he expected the speedy return of the Master), it is not unreasonable to suppose that he was fallible on the subject of the resurrection, which was so closely connected in the mind of the primitive Christian with the second advent. But, secondly—*and this I would urge strongly*—are we not told in another part of the New Testament that "the day will come in the which the heavens shall pass away with a great noise and the elements shall melt with fervent heat, the earth also and the works that are therein shall be burned up"? (II Peter, iii, 10). Should we not "interpret Scripture by Scripture," and is not this teaching of Second Peter exactly the same as that of "The Unseen Universe"? (this verse heads chapter iii of that work). Are we not then justified in concluding that, while St. Paul knew much, was profoundly inspired, there was one even among the early disciples who looked further than he—

"Beyond the verge of that blue sky
Where God's sublimest secrets lie"?

Second Peter is being confirmed by later investigations, while First Corinthians is not; and therefore we must make a choice. As a Protestant I claim the right of private judgment in the interpretation of Scripture, and I hold that the Bible and Science lead us to believe that the future state is to be a higher and more spiritual state in every respect than this, and hence we must give up, among other things, the Talmagean conception of the final judgment, and of heaven and hell, which shall consist of a grand assize in which bodies shall be seen rising out of the ocean, scrambling down from the mountain-top, treading with weary feet over vast prairies or perhaps borne by some invisible hand through mid-air to the Great White Throne, there to be judged and sent away, some to the Celestial City with golden streets and silver palaces; others to the lower regions "where their worm dieth not and the fire is not quenched"; and we must rather believe that the present material universe shall gradually pass into a spiritual cosmos or order, from which all sin and sorrow and suffering and ignorance shall be banished, and God shall be *all and in all*—the center of the Spiritual System around which shall revolve all finite spirits, or rather in whom we shall, in a far deeper sense than now, "live and move and have our being." All, therefore, that we can rationally mean when we say, in the Apostles' Creed, "I believe in the resurrection of the body," is that we believe in *individual* immortality or the immortality of *individual self-conscious spirit*. This is the great truth which lies at the root of this article of the Christian creed. Many believe in the immortality or eternity of the universal *Being*, but not in the eternity of individual souls. These, it is claimed, are like bubbles on the ocean—they arise for a short time and then sink back into the sea of Being. The Christian creed protests against this error, and asserts the immortality of individuals.

CHAPTER IX.

EVOLUTION AND IMMORTALITY.

WHAT am I? Whence came I? Whither am I going? These are the great questions that agitate all thinking minds, even among the masses. While theologians are wasting their energies discussing questions of Church polity or theories whose foundations are of sand, men and women everywhere are crying out for some assurance that Death does not end all; that when Life's fitful dream is ended they shall forever rest their weary heads upon the bosom of a loving Father. The Christian and the Spiritualist, of course, believe in immortality, on the ground of (alleged) positive evidence, viz., the manifestation of Jesus and other spirits after death to men on earth.

But many thoughtful minds, considering this evidence not so "positive" as the case demands, seek for the *natural* grounds of belief in immortality, and so this chapter is devoted to a consideration of this subject.

As more than once stated in this work, evolutionists, especially Mr. Spencer and his school, think that man first conceived the idea of life after death from the phenomena of dreams, swoons, etc., during which the "other-self" was supposed to leave the body and return to it after a while; and so at death it was supposed that the soul had merely gone away for a longer period, and this belief is asserted to be universal. "Travelers," says Prof. Fiske, "have now and then reported the existence of races of men quite destitute of religion, or of what the observer has learned to recognize as religion; but no one has ever discovered a race of men devoid of a belief in ghosts."* This universal belief in a life after death is one fact commonly urged in proof of immortality. It is not reasonable to suppose, it is said, that all men have been deceived; there must be some basis for this universal faith. Again, it has been urged that a future state is necessary in order to recompense man for "the ills which flesh is heir to." † The wicked so often during this life seem to triumph over the righteous that, it is claimed, Eternal Justice must recompense the latter in the future world. The validity of this argument, of course, depends upon whether there *is* a Moral Governor of the Universe, and to us who believe this to be a fact, but only to us, does the argument appeal.

Thirdly, belief in immortality is said to be a *direct intuition*, a natural dictate of the Soul; and the Soul, it is urged, is its own proper witness on this subject. Thus, the late W. R. Greg says: " The truth we believe to be that a future existence is and must be a matter of *information* or *intuition*, and not of *inference*. The intellect may imagine it, but could never have discovered it, and can never prove it; the Soul must

---

* "The Idea of God," p. 66.
† Canon Liddon's Sermon on "Immortality," University Sermons, first series, No. V.

have revealed it; must, and does, perpetually reveal it. It is a matter which comes properly within the cognizance of the Soul—of that Spiritual Sense, to which on such topics we look for information, as we look to our bodily senses for information touching the things of the earth, things which lie within their province. We never dream of doubting what they tell us of the external world, though a Berkeley should show us that their teaching is at variance with or indefensible by logic. We therefore at once cut the Gordian knot by conceding to the Soul the privilege of instructing us as to the things of itself—we apply to the Spiritual Sense for information on spiritual things. This appears to me," he adds, "the only foundation on which the belief in a future life can legitimately rest, to those who do not accept a miraculous external revelation" (as Mr. Greg himself did not). " It is a belief anterior to reasoning, independent of reasoning, unprovable by reasoning; and yet, as *no logic can demonstrate its unsoundness*, or can bring more than negative evidence to oppose it, I can hold it with a simplicity, a tenacity, an undoubting faith, which is never granted to the conclusions of the understanding." *

But, of course, the force of this argument depends upon whether there *is* a soul to bear such witness, for, as Mr. Greg frankly admits, " to the man who disbelieves the Soul's existence" this line of argument " will appear unwarrantable and illogical." Now, the existence of *something* in man distinct from physical and chemical forces is freely admitted by even Mr. Spencer, Profs. Tyndall and Huxley, and other eminent skeptics.

---

* Greg's "Creed of Christendom," pp. 373, 374.

Modern Physiology has been utterly unable to write Mind in terms of Matter, to translate Thought, Consciousness, Emotion, Will, into material phenomena or products of matter. So far from this being true, we are told by Mr. Spencer that " were we compelled to choose between the alternatives of translating mental phenomena into physical phenomena, or of translating physical phenomena into mental phenomena, the latter alternative would seem to be the more acceptable of the two." * Dr. Romanes, in his " Mental Evolution of Animals" (chapters iii and iv), maintains that there is a " Physical *Basis* of Mind," but he explains that by this he simply means that "every psychical change of which we have any experience is invariably *associated* with a definite physical change." This was also affirmed by Prof. Tyndall in his celebrated " Belfast Address," and has been frequently affirmed by Prof. Huxley and others, and this is all that Modern Physiology has been able to prove; it has not by any means been able to translate mental phenomena into physical phenomena; it is just as true as in days of yore that to talk of a *square* thought, a *round* thought, a *hexagonal* thought, a *hard* thought, a *soft* thought, etc., is literally nonsense. " Physiologists," says Dr. Le Conte, "have proved in every act of perception, first a physical change in the sense-organ, then a vibratory thrill along the nerve-fiber, and a resulting physical change in the brain ; and in every act of volition a return vibratory thrill along the nerve from the brain to the muscle, and even the velocity of transmission of this vibratory thrill has been measured and found to be only one

---

* Spencer's " Principles of Psychology," vol. i, p. 159.

hundred feet per second. They have also established the existence of chemical and molecular changes in the brain corresponding to changes of mental states, and with great probability an exact *quantitative* relation between these changes of the brain and the corresponding changes of mind. In the near future they may do more; they may localize *all* the different faculties and powers of the mind in different parts of the brain, each in its several place, and thus lay the foundations of a truly scientific Phrenology.*

"In the far-distant future we may do even much more; we may connect each kind of mental change with a different and distinctive kind of molecular brain change. We may find, for example, as has been humorously remarked (by Tyndall), a *right-handed rotation of atoms associated* with *love*, and a *left-handed* rotation of atoms associated with *hate*, or a gentle sideways oscillation associated with consciousness, and a vertical pounding associated with will. We may do all this and much more. We have thus (triumphantly exclaims the Materialist) completely identified mental changes with brain changes—spirit with matter. Thought and emotion, will and consciousness, become products of the brain in the same sense that bile is a product of the liver, or urine the product of the kidneys."

The answer to all this is plain. The materialist mistakes *association* for *causation*. There is just about as much reason in this assumption as there would be in the supposition that the cock's crow, which invariably

---

* See "Popular Science Monthly" for October, 1889, article by Dr. Starr on "The Old and the New Phrenology."

accompanies the day-dawn, is the *cause* of the dawn! "Molecular motion and chemical change, on the one hand," continues Prof. Le Conte, "sensation and consciousness on the other; the two sets of phenomena belong to different orders, different planes—planes so different that it is impossible to construe the one in terms of the other. This inability is not the result of our imperfect knowledge, but of the fundamental difference of the phenomena. It is not one which will disappear with the advance of science, as many seem to think, but is for us an eternal impossibility. Suppose an infinitely perfect human knowledge—infinite in *degree* but human in *kind;* suppose an absolutely perfect science— a science which shall have so completely subdued its whole domain, and reduced it to such perfect simplicity, that the whole cosmos (universe) is expressed in a single mathematical formula—a formula which, worked out with *plus* signs, shall give every phenomenon which shall ever occur in the future, and with *minus* signs every event which has ever occurred in the past history of the cosmos. Surely this is an infinitely perfect science, an absolutely unattainable ideal. Yet even to such a science the relation of molecular motion on the one hand, to sensation, consciousness, will, thought, and emotion on the other, would still be as great a mystery as ever. Like the essential nature of matter and the ultimate cause of force, this relation lies beyond the realm of Science." Then, after answering a materialist's attempt to refute the above argument, Prof. Le Conte concludes: "I repeat, therefore, with still more confidence, that the two series of phenomena, the physiological and the psychological, though invariably *associated* with each other, term for term, can not by any effort of the imagination be construed the one in the terms of the other, or explained the one by the other. They can not, therefore, be imagined to be correlated or mutually convertible as are the different forms of physical and chemical force. Nor can they be imagined to stand in the relation of cause and effect in the *same sense* in which we use these terms when we speak of lower forces and phenomena, where cause and effect express only change from one form of *motion* to another." *

The great importance of this demonstration of the radically distinct nature of mind and body, or of mental and physical phenomena, it seems to me, can not be overestimated. It is generally considered only "negative evidence" in favor of immortality, but I think it is quite positive; for, granting that sensation, consciousness, will, thought, emotion—i. e., mental phenomena —the essential constituents of mind—are immaterial entities, we may proceed at once to argue, with Bishop Butler,† that death can not affect these, since it affects only material things, such as flesh, skin, bones, etc. Of course, it may be urged that the body—the brain especially—though it be but the organ or instrument of the mind, is yet necessary to the mind's activity, just as the piano is necessary to the production of music by the musician. To which it may be replied: While this is true in this material world, we have no right to assume that it is true in "the unseen universe." On the contrary, the action of the spirit in that sphere might be impossible if it were united to a material form such as

---

* "Princeton Review," November, 1878, pp. 789-792.
† "Analogy," Part I, chap. i.

we know it. But, however this may be, it is a grand triumph for Theology to have a scientific demonstration of the fact that man is something else than a bundle of matter and material forces.

We come, now, to the evidence which Evolution specially contributes to this important subject, and to my mind it is quite satisfactory.

According to Evolution, there has been going on from the beginning a twofold development, viz., a development of material *forms* and a development of immaterial *forces*. The first has resulted in the human frame, which is a completion of the evolutionary movement from a physical point of view. And it may be remarked, by the way, that the popular idea that, if Evolution is true, man should develop into a higher animal is, on Evolution-principles, absurd, since, by the very supposition man is the realized ideal of the process of development. "Upon the Darwinian theory," says Prof. Fiske, " it is impossible that any creature zoölogically distinct from man, and superior to him, should ever at any future time exist upon the earth. " According to Darwinism, the creation of man is still the goal toward which Nature tends from the beginning." *

Side by side, and, indeed, as the moving cause of this physical development, there has been an evolution of Force. The first form of Force which manifested itself was what we call " gravity "—the force by which the original chaotic mass or *nebula* was gradually organized into the heavens and the earth. Almost contemporaneously, but one step above this manifestation of force, appeared what we call "chemical affinity," in

---

* " Destiny of Man," p. 31.

the production of compounds, water, etc. This was followed by a still higher development of Force, viz., Life, which appeared first in plants and then in animals. This was succeeded by a still higher manifestation of Force in the mind or *anima* of the lower animals, and this slowly developed into the self-conscious spirit of Man.

Thus, there is profound truth in a certain philosopher's assertion, " Mind sleeps in the plant, dreams in the animal, and awakes in Man." In Man it becomes conscious of *itself* and capable of independent existence. This process of spiritual evolution has been so well wrought out by Prof. Le Conte, and it is so necessary that it should be clearly understood, that I shall quote without apology his entire exposition. "In the beginning," he says, "the Divine Spirit, brooding upon primal chaos, energized dead, inert Nature, communicating an influence, an energy, a life, which became through all time the force of evolution of the comos (universe). This all-pervading divine energy, which Science calls *force*, was at first wholly and equally diffused; but through all time individuated (divided up) itself more and more under favoring conditions (I speak the language of Science), and thus assumed higher and more special forms, until finally, by *completed individuation*, it reached the condition of immortal Spirit—the image of God, whence it originally came. Such is a condensed statement of the process. Now the steps in more detail:

"1. In its original diffused, generalized, unindividuated condition we call this pervading divine energy physical and chemical forces, for these are the most universal, the lowest and evidently the earliest form of force. This is the general fund, the bank from which all other forms are drawn.

"2. A portion of this diffused force, a spark of this divine energy, drawn from the common fund, partially and imperfectly individuates itself under the favoring condition of organization, attains new powers and properties, viz., assimilation, and thus becomes the vital force of plants or non-sentient living beings.

"In this case, observe, even the material organic individuality is not yet complete, much less the kinetic or *force* individuality.

"3. A portion of this already partially individuated energy (for animals draw their vital force from planets) becomes more highly individuated under conditions of higher organization, especially the presence of a nervous system, attains in addition still higher new properties and powers, viz., sensation, consciousness, will, intelligence—and thus becomes the sentient principle—the *anima*—the soul of animals.

"4. In man the progressive individuation of forces becomes at last complete. Force in him becomes a complete, separate, independent entity; with new and far more wonderful powers and properties added; not only consciousness but self-consciousness; not only will, but also free, self-determining will; not only intelligence, but also reason and moral sense; not only a mere semblance of, but a true personality. This completed kinetic (force) individuality is what we call the spirit of man. Self-consciousness, moral sense, and reason to discern good and evil, and free-will to choose the right or wrong, in a word personality—the possession of these makes him the image of God.

"But why immortal? I answer, *because individu-*

ation is complete; because this portion of force is *separated* completely from the general fund of material forces as a distinct entity capable of independent existence. In plants force-individuation is very imperfect; therefore, when the condition of this partial individuation—viz., organization—is removed by death, the individuation also is destroyed, and the forces are again merged into the common fund of natural forces. In animals the individuation of resident forces is far greater; it may even simulate in the higher forms a true individuality (spirit); but only simulates, for, remove the conditions of individuation by death of the material organism, and the nearly completed individuation of resident forces is destroyed, and these again merge back into the common fund of natural forces. But if once the individuation be completed to actual separation, if once the resident force attains spiritual individuality or personality, it then becomes a separate entity capable of independent life. Destroy, now, the original conditions of its individuation—viz., organic life—and the already individualized and separate force entity (spirit) is not again refunded.

"In so difficult and intangible a subject I can make myself clear only by several material illustrations, each perhaps imperfect, but all combining to place the subject in a clearer light. Let the dead level of unindividuated, physical and chemical forces of Nature be separated by a water surface A B.

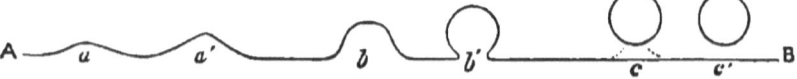

"In this watery mass tending ever to perfect level, let 'gravity' be abolished and only *cohesion* remain as the refunding force, or the tendency to return to a dead level. Now, suppose some force to pull upward against cohesion, a small portion of the watery mass above the common level, to form, as it were, a drop, as shown in the figure above. Then, if the upward-acting, drop-forming force suffice only to form a commencing drop, a mammilla *a a'*, then we have the condition of force as it exists in plants. If the upward-pulling, individuating force be greater, so that we have the semblance of a drop, though not a complete drop—a nipple-shaped protuberance *b*, or even a round button connected by a neck *b'*—then we have a representation of the condition of force as the sentient principle or *anima* of animals. If, lastly, the drop be completed and separated, we have the condition of force as the spirit of man, separated yet seemingly connected, as shown by the dotted lines in *c*. Now, it is evident that in *a a'* and in *b b'*, if we remove the lifting or individuating force, cohesion prevails and the commencing or even the nearly completed drop is refunded. But in *c* remove the original lifting or individuating force, and there is no longer any tendency to return, for the cohesive ligature is already severed. The drop is a separate entity, *totus teres atque rotundus* (completely smooth and round), and therefore capable of independent existence. Even the semblance of cohesive connection, represented by the dotted lines in *c*, is severed by death in *c'*.

"To illustrate again: The vital principle of plants and the sentient principle or *anima* of animals are *spirit in embryo*, inclosed and fast asleep in the womb of Nature—in the latter case, indeed, already *quickened* but *not yet viable*.

"In man spirit *comes to birth*, emerges into new and

higher conditions, becomes capable of independent life, though still drawing nourishment from his nursing mother, Nature. Death only weans us. Thus, as the organic embryo by birth comes to independent *temporal* life in the lower plane of matter, so the spiritual embryo, by birth in man, comes to independent *eternal* life on the higher plane of spirit. The mature embryo how like the *new-born!* The higher animals how like to man! Yet in both cases there is an immense difference; in both cases there is a sudden entrance on an entirely new and higher plane of existence—a sudden entrance into a new world; in both cases there is a sudden appearance of a new creature with entirely different capacities—a passing out of an old world and a waking up in a new and higher. Man, alone, is the child of God." *

Upon this important quotation I would make two remarks:

First, let it be remembered that Prof. Le Conte is not here sketching an *imaginary* process. All evolutionists, and indeed philosophers of all schools, believe that "gravity" or physical force was the first form of force that appeared, and that there has been a gradual development or production of higher and higher forces until the human mind—the highest of all forces—appeared. Then—

Secondly, Prof. Le Conte removes the objection to a belief in immortality which the doctrine of the "Correlation of Forces" suggests. According to this doctrine, all the so-called "natural forces" are simply different sides, different manifestations of one and the same thing. Heat, light, electricity, magnetism, chemical affinity,

---

* "Princeton Review" for November, 1878, pp. 795–798.

mechanical, vital and (some claim) mental forces are transmutable into each other back and forth; and this is what Prof. Le Conte means when he speaks of the partially individuated forces being returned at the death of the organism to the common fund from which they were originally drawn. But, according to his theory, mental force is so highly developed as to be completely separated from the lower forces, and therefore capable of independent, unending existence. It may be said that his assertion that mental force is thus perfectly individuated is a begging of the question, since this is the very point to be proved. But no, it is not a begging of the question, since he bases his conclusion upon the acknowledged and indisputable fact that there is and has been from the beginning an *elevation*, a development of forces; and he merely urges that this elevation had only to continue long enough in order to attain the height he claims it has. Moreover, *self-consciousness* confirms his allegation that kinetic or force-evolution is complete, and hence his theory has the best sort of support.

Prof. Fiske seems to share this view, or to hold one essentially like it. "The question," he says, "is reduced to this: Are man's highest spiritual qualities into the production of which all creative energy has gone, to disappear with the rest? Has all this work been done for nothing? Is it all ephemeral, all a bubble that bursts, a vision that fades? Are we to regard the Creator's work as like that of a child, who builds houses out of blocks, just for the pleasure of knocking them down? I can see no good reason for believing any such thing. On such a view the riddle of the universe becomes a riddle without a meaning. . . .

"For my own part, therefore, I believe in the immortality of the soul, not in the sense in which I accept the demonstrable truths of science, but as a supreme act of faith in the *reasonableness* of God's works. . . . The greatest philosopher of modern times," he adds (and this is the point I would emphasize), " the master and teacher of all who shall study the process of evolution for many a day to come, holds that consciousness is not the product of a collocation of material particles, but is in the deepest sense a *divine effluence.* According to Mr. Spencer, the divine energy which is manifested throughout the knowable universe is the same energy that wells up in us as consciousness.* Speaking for myself," Prof. Fiske concludes, " I can see no insuperable difficulty in the notion that at some period in the evolution of Humanity this divine spark may have acquired sufficient *concentration* and *steadiness* to survive the wreck of material forms and endure forever. Such a crowning wonder seems to me no more than the fit climax to a creative work that has been ineffably beautiful and marvelous in all its myriad stages." †

The same idea seems to have been entertained by Mr. Darwin. "Believing as I do," he says, "that in the distant future man will be a far more perfect creature than he now is, it is an intolerable thought that he and all other sentient beings are doomed to complete annihilation after such long-continued, slow progress." ‡

But apart from all authority and all other considerations, he who accepts the Idealistic view of Nature set forth in the first chapter of this book, will find little or

---

* See Spencer's " Ecclesiastical Institutions," p. 839.
† " Destiny of Man," pp. 114–119.
‡ " Life and Letters," vol. i, p. 282.

no difficulty in believing in the immortality of the human spirit, since Spirit, according to this view, is the only real, absolute, and eternal substance. The great Power which is manifested in every throb of the mighty rhythmic life of the universe is, we believe, spiritual in its nature. The human spirit and, in fact, all things, "live and move and have their being" *in* this Power; the human spirit is an "image," a *finite embodiment*, of this Power, and differs from all things else in that it is *self*-conscious and *self*-dependent now, and may continue so forever; while they (the lower animals, etc.), being not so highly developed, living a dependent life now, are at death returned to the source whence they came, as bubbles on the ocean wave.

Thus it appears that, so far from evolution disproving immortality, as many superficial minds imagine, it really affords the strongest argument in favor of this article of faith by showing that the human spirit is

"The one far-off, divine event
To which the whole creation moves."

Indeed, the popular idea that evolution destroys man's immortality by uniting him genetically with the lower animals is so superficial as not to require refutation, were not prejudice and ignorance more potent than even the strongest argument.

It would be far more rational to hold, with Bishop Butler, that the lower animals may themselves possess "some modified form of being".* in the future state, than it would to believe that, because all creatures are related, all must be destroyed together; and were we

---

* Canon Liddon's "University Sermons," first series, Sermon V, p. 378; "Butler's Analogy," chap. i.

reduced to such an alternative we should not long hesitate to accept Butler's view. Again: Mr. Darwin himself long ago urged that if the development of the individual from a little germ (and this happens in every case) does not conflict with the existence and immortality of the human soul, the development of the race does not.* Indeed, as another truly observes, "It is more remarkable that immortality should emerge in the few months of the growth of an individual in the uterus than that it should appear in the course of the dim ages of a vast series of successive species." † And when we once see that individual evolution does not necessarily destroy either the existence or the immortality of the soul, we shall readily conclude that racial evolution does not, but that, in the words of Prof. Fiske, again, "Darwinism places Humanity upon a higher pinnacle than ever before. The future is lighted for us with the radiant colors of hope. Strife and sorrow shall disappear. Peace and love shall reign supreme. The dream of poets, the lesson of priest and prophet, the inspiration of the great musician, is confirmed in the light of modern knowledge; and, as we gird ourselves for the work of life, we may look forward to the time when in the truest sense the kingdoms of this world shall become the kingdom of Christ, and he shall reign for ever and ever, king of kings and lord of lords."

NOTE.—The supreme importance of the question discussed in this chapter leads me to urge the reader to consult all the books referred to. If he does not possess them, he should buy or borrow

---

* "Descent of Man," one vol. edition, p. 613.

† "A Symposium on Christianity and Evolution," p. 115, by Dr. Matheson, etc. (Whittaker, 1887).

them, and in addition he might profitably consult the following works: Prof. Alexander Winchell's "Science and Religion," *passim;* "A Symposism on Immortality," by Canon Row, etc. (Whittaker, 1885); Dr. Martineau's "Study of Religion," Book IV; Prof. Fiske's "Unseen World," Essay I (review of "The Unseen Universe," which should also be specially consulted); Drummond's "Natural Law in the Spiritual World"; chapters on "Death" and "Eternal Life"—a not very satisfactory though a suggestive book.

CHAPTER X.

THE CHURCH OF THE FUTURE.

LET no one imagine from the title of this chapter that the author claims any special powers of the prophet: far from it! But as an evolutionist, who considers the present state of things ecclesiastical a development from a lower state, and as an observer of the tendencies of the present theological and ecclesiastical world, he may, without claiming the vision of seer or prophet, indicate the probable stage of evolution upon which we are about to enter.

The thoughtful reader, as he has noted the rise and fall of the theological idols, the history of which is briefly sketched in this volume, has doubtless asked more than once, And what shall be the *end* thereof? And perhaps he has often been tempted to conclude either that this question is unanswerable or that the end is to be—*nothing*. If so, he may be reassured by these words of Mr. Spencer: "Though Ecclesiastical Institutions hold less important places in higher societies than in lower societies, we must not infer that they will hereafter wholly disappear. If in time to come there remain functions to be fulfilled in any way analogous to their present functions, we must conclude that they will survive under some one form or other." The question, then, is, "Under what form?" Mr. Spencer thinks it will be *manifold*. State churches, in his opinion, will gradually disappear, and sects will be increased. "And along with the acquirement of complete autonomy by each religious body, there is likely to be a complete loss of the sacerdotal character by any one who plays the part of minister." But, although the priest is destined to disappear, the preacher and pastor will not.

"There will ever be a sphere," says Mr. Spencer, "for those who are able to impress their hearers with a due sense of the Mystery in which the origin and meaning of the universe are shrouded." * In these degenerate days, when the clergyman is in many quarters considered a sort of respectable beggar, it is quite comforting to him to be assured, by one of the greatest philosophers, evolutionists, and skeptics of the age, that he is not a worthless thing which is destined to be thrown overboard as the ship of progress moves over the ocean of time. "The Church of the future" probably can not be better described than by sketching the clergyman of the future.

There are two radically different ideas of the functions of the clerical office now prevailing, and these find expression in an Episcopal "charge" delivered in June, 1889, and in an editorial in "The Christian Union" (Rev. Lyman Abbott, D. D., editor) for June 20, 1889. While the (Protestant Episcopal) Bishop of Rhode Island, Dr. Clark, was expounding to his clergy, in the aforementioned "charge," one idea of preaching, the editor of "The Christian Union" was formulating ex-

---

* "Ecclesiastical Institutions," pp. 823-825.

actly the opposite idea, and I can not do better than to quote from these eminent divines.

"In a general way," said Bishop Clark, "it may be remarked that nothing is to be regarded as suitable for the pulpit that has not an ethical side. Social and political opinions, especially where there exists a divided public opinion, should be excluded from the sanctuary, unless they involve some clearly marked moral issue.

"There are other subjects which are more likely to find their way into our pulpits, that should not be made too conspicuous, and never allowed to usurp the place of those truths which pertain directly to the salvation of sinful man. Elaborate Biblical criticism, disquisition of doubtful and disputed texts, enlarging upon the cavils of unbelievers and heretics, discussions of abstract philosophical questions, dwelling at length upon the various theories of inspiration and miracle and the supernatural in general, attempts to solve the hidden mysteries of the Atonement, to philosophize upon the nature and contents of the Holy Sacraments, the new birth and the workings of the Spirit, the sovereignty of God and the freedom of men, beyond the obvious limits indicated in the Scriptures—in regard to all such matters it becomes us to exercise the greatest caution and reticence." Thus all the questions that agitate thinking minds of all classes are excluded from pulpit discussion. On the one hand, the social and political problems, which interest the laborer and employer; on the other, critical, scientific, and philosophic questions, which interest the educated—all must be ignored, or merely glanced at by the way. On the contrary, Dr. Abbott tells us that "the ancient minister was almost purely theological. In his department he was an expert, and to his department he generally confined himself. He dealt with one section of thought and life. The modern minister is not permitted—if he is a true man he does not permit himself—this limitation. Whatever concerns the moral life of his people concerns him. Temperance, sociology, the industrial problems, education; the relation of religion to the state; summer vacations, and how to get the good out of them; Darwinism; the last catastrophe, and its moral lessons; the centennial and its significance; the latest religious novel; evolution; positivism, and its prophets; the higher criticism—all come before him for treatment. He is talking to a congregation in which are men and women who have had as good an education as himself, who have better libraries, who have possibly nearly as much leisure, and who do as earnest thinking. He is no priest to tell them *ex cathedra* what they ought to believe. He is a brother student telling them what he believes and why. And he speaks to men and women who will believe nothing, in morals, politics, or religion, unless he shows them a reason for his convictions. The books and magazines accumulate on his table, and he despairs ever to overtake the rapid work of modern thought; or, in his poverty, and far from public libraries, he gets only the echoes of the books and magazines in daily newspapers, and is in despair because he must speak on living themes and thoughts, himself uninformed as to the latest utterances of the greatest thinkers. The ancient preacher pulled a leisurely stroke on a placid lake; the modern preacher pulls an oar upon a tempestuous current, and has all he can do to give his boat movement enough to secure for it steerage-way. Nor is his task lightened when a preacher of pious platitudes bids him leave these themes alone and 'preach the Gospel.' His Master has told him to 'teach *all* things whatsoever I have commanded you'; and, to apply Christ's commands to all the complicated problems of modern civilization, he must study those problems, and know the latest and best interpretations of the word duty when applied to them. But he no longer makes pastoral calls! Some do, and some do not. But those who do not are generally men of executive and administrative ability, whose time and thought are fully absorbed in directing the energies of a working church. The minister may regard his church as a hospital, a retreat for the lame, the halt, and the blind, and his duty is fulfilled in visiting and nursing his sick. Or he may regard his church as an army, and his first duty to be that of marshaling his forces and directing the campaign." It is not difficult to understand from this what Dr. Abbott thinks the Church of the Present, as well as the Church of the Future, ought to be and will be. It will be an army consisting of various divisions officered in different ways and pursuing different lines of operation, but all moving toward one point, viz., the social, intellectual, moral, and religious elevation of the human race. In the words of Canon Fremantle: "The Church has often been presented to men as if it had no object but public worship and teaching, with some few accidental adjuncts of beneficent action. It is regarded as a society, but a society of which public prayer and preaching are the supreme, if not exclusive, *ratio essendi*" (reason for its existence). "If a further object is assigned, it is to prepare men for another world. In contrast to this limited view of its functions, the Church will be here" (in his Bampton Lectures) "presented as the *social state* in which the Spirit of Christ reigns; as embracing the general life and society of men, and identifying itself with these as much as possible; as having for its object to imbue all human relations with the Spirit of Christ's self-renouncing love, and thus change the world into a kingdom of God." * This is the only sort of Church which will win the allegiance of thinking men and women everywhere. The clergyman of the future will aim to make his pulpit an *educating* power and his parish a *social and moral* power. On the one hand, he will aim to meet the intellectual wants of the educated who may form a part of his congregation, and to this end he will preach on the scientific, philosophic, literary, and other topics suggested by Dr. Abbott, discussing, of course, their moral and religious bearing chiefly, if not exclusively—that is to say, he will " preach Christ crucified," not according to mediæval views, but according to modern ideas and aim to infuse the Christ's life and spirit into *all* departments of activity. On the other hand, without " entering politics " proper, he will consider the ethical aspect of every social and political question—labor organizations and agitations, Georgeism, the tariff, etc., etc. In short, he will appear among the professional and laboring classes as their friend and brother who desires to contribute his *quota* toward the solution of the problems agitating their minds. And as the ministers of the various denominations meet on this common platform, they will gradually agree to disagree on " the distinctive features " of their " Churches." The Protestant will allow

---

* "The World as the Subject of Redemption," by Rev. W. H. Fremantle, M. A., Canon of Canterbury, England—an admirable book.

the Roman Catholic to worship the God of his fathers according to that Liturgy which he deems most rational and Scriptural; and the Romanist will not quarrel with the Protestant because he can not believe in the infallibility of the Pope or the Immaculate Conception. May we not hope that brethren that are thus separated by (apparently) insurmountable *doctrinal* hedges may yet be drawn very closely together in their efforts to promote the common weal of their fellow-men? May there not be such a union of the Churches in the near future? Only such a union seems possible. As the various Christian bodies are thus drawn together; as they begin to recognize essential unity under the manifold variety of doctrine and ritual which prevails among them, the question will arise, What shall be the attitude of the Christian Church and religion toward other religions—the so-called "Heathen Religions"? For, after all, Christianity is only one of many religions, and, when we are discussing the Church of the Future, we must not ignore the heathen religions. It is beginning to be more and more fully recognized that Christianity is the fruit of which all other religions are the flowers. One of the most striking instances of the recognition of this fact is that of the Rev. James Freeman Clarke who, in an admirable work on this subject,* aims to show that other religions—Brahmanism, Confucianism, Zoroastrianism, Buddhism, Mohammedanism, etc., are *ethnic* or national religions, while Christianity is the *catholic* or universal religion. He points out most clearly the distinctive features of these religions, and shows that

---

* "Ten Great Religions," by J. F. Clarke. Houghton, Mifflin & Co., 1882.

Christianity comprehends all these and much more. It embraces the deep *spirituality* of Brahmanism (" God is Spirit," etc.); the *prudence and humanity* of Buddhism; the reverence for the *family* and the *state* of Confucianism; the conflict of light with darkness, of right with wrong, of Zoroastrianism; and the *monotheism* of Judaism and Mohammedanism. In short, he shows that "each of the great ethnic religions is full on one side, but empty on the other, while Christianity is full all around. Christianity is adapted to take their place, not because they are false, but because they are true as far as they go. They know in part and prophesy in part; but when that which is perfect is come, then that which is in part shall be done away." *

Thus far I have spoken of the Church from a strictly external or ecclesiastical point of view. I now turn to a consideration of the *doctrinal* development which it is destined to undergo. Mr. Spencer correctly points out that the base and center of this development will be the idea of *God*. " This one supernatural power," he says, "has, by what Mr. Fiske aptly calls *deanthropomorphization*, lost the grosser attributes of humanity. If things are hereafter to follow the same general course as heretofore, we must infer that this dropping of human attributes will continue." † What will be the result? Our ideas of God being elevated, the whole plane of our theological and religious thought will be elevated.

First, our idea of Miracle will be changed. We will not think of it as a contradiction of law—as the result

---

* Compare "Symposium on Non-Biblical Religions," by Farrar, etc. (Whittaker, 1887), and Hawers's "Light of the Ages."

† "Ecclesiastical Institutions," p. 833 *et seq.*

of a special intervention of the Divine Power altering the course of things He has once established, but we will think of it as only a manifestation of a higher or a hitherto unrecognized law.

Secondly, our idea of Divine Justice will be exalted and purified. We will no longer teach that infinite punishment will result from a finite course of sin; we will no longer believe that an innocent being will be made (or allowed) to suffer in the place of the guilty. *In short, our views on all the subjects discussed in the foregoing pages will be elevated and purified—will be dematerialized and more and more spiritualized.*

The *practical* result of all this will be the realization of that ideal Church for which a Robertson and a Carpenter sighed—the ecclesiastical anathema will descend, not upon *views held*, but upon *life led*, and the Church will "admit into Christian communion every one who desires to be accounted a disciple of Christ, and humbly endeavors to follow in the footsteps of his Divine Master." *

So shall the kingdoms of this world become the kingdom of our God and of his Christ, and the Church Militant shall finally be merged into the Church Triumphant.

---

* Robertson's "Sermons," third series, Sermon I; Carpenter's "Mental Physiology," *last lines.*

INDEX.

Abbott, Dr. C. C., on the age of man, 101, 102.

Abbott, Rev. Lyman, on the modern clergyman, 396–398.

Acts of the Apostles, its authorship and date, 181–186.

Alford, Dean, on the Gospel of Mark, 162, 163.
   on corruptions of the Scriptural text, 179.

Arnold, Matthew, on the cause of bibliolatry, 232.

Arius, his doctrine of the Godhead, 266.

Athanasius, his doctrine of the Godhead, 265.

Barrett, Prof. F W., on the influence of mind upon dead matter, 228.

Barrows, Charles M., on mental healing, 203, 204, 206, 207.

Baur, F. C., on the Book of Revelation, 153.
   his law of development, 182.

Boscovich, his hypothesis on the nature of matter referred to, 26.

Brooks, Rev. Phillips, on the doctrine of the Trinity, 273–275.

Browne, Bishop Harold, on inspiration, 243.
   on the future state, 320, *note*.

Bushnell, Horace, on faith-cures, 204, 208–210.
   on the meaning of omnipotence, 346.
   on moral character, 361.

Butler, Bishop, on use of the understanding, 138.
   on immortality, 382.
   on possible future existence of lower animals, 391.

Campbell, McLeod, on "The Nature of the Atonement," 311, *note*.

Carlisle, Bishop of, on German philosophers, 198, 199.
   on virgin-birth of Jesus, 222.
   on bodily resurrection, 369.
   on evolution and the fall of man, 135–137.

Carpenter, Dr. W. B., his plea for a liberal religion, 291.

INDEX.

Carlyle, Thomas, on hero-worship, 293, 294.
Channing, Dr. W. E., an Arian, 266.
Christlieb, Dr., on the doctrine of the Trinity, 265.
Clark, Bishop, on functions of the pulpit, 396.
Clarke, James Freeman, his view of the Godhead, 273, *note*.
   on the relation of the Christian to other religions, 400.
Clement of Rome, his reference to *First Corinthians*, 147.
   his reference to *Galatians*, 148.
Coleridge, his view of inspiration referred to, 248.

Darwin, Charles, on the immortality of the soul, 390.
Davidson, Dr. Samuel, on the *Epistle to the Galatians*, 149.
   on the *Epistles to the Thessalonians, Philippians*, and *Philemon*, 150, 151.
   on the *Epistle to the Hebrews*, 152, 153.
   on the *Book of Revelation*, 153-156.
   on the *Gospel of Mark*, 163.
   on the *Gospel of Luke*, 164.
   on the internal evidence of the genuineness and authenticity of the Gospels, 167.
   on the *Fourth Gospel*, 172.
   on the *Acts of the Apostles*, 184.
Demoniacal possession, 200.
Devil, origin of the idea of a, 353-357.

Ely, Prof. R. T., his "Labor Movement" referred to, 8, *note*.

Encyclopædia Britannica, quoted on Biblical chronology, 87.
   on Gnosticism, 145.
   on Philo, 146.
   on the canon, 159.
   on leprosy, 202.
   on inspiration, 235.
   on sacrifices, 302-304.
   on a future state, 318-321.
   on the idea of a devil, 351-357.
Ewald, Prof. Heinrich, on *Genesis*, 111, *note*.
   on the miraculous feeding of the four and the five thousand, 213.

Faith-cures, 203-211.
Farrar, Archdeacon, on the *Epistle to the Hebrews*, 153.
   on corruptions of the Scriptural text, 179, *note*.
   on decadence of Biblical interpretation, 231, 232.
   on bibliolatry, 251, 253, 254.
   on sacrifice and penance, 301, 302.
   on hell, 313, 314, 323, 324.
   on the nature of heaven, 332.
   on retribution, 334, 335.
Fathers of the Church, 141, 142.
Fisher, Dr. George P., on the Gospels, 166.
   on the Fourth Gospel, 176.
Fiske, Prof. John, on development of the idea of God, 129, 130.
   on primitive man's idea of world, 195.
   on development of Jewish ideas of Deity, 196.
   on development of monotheism, 261, 262.
   on spiritual evolution, 284.

INDEX. 405

Fiske, Prof. John, on universal prevalence of belief in ghosts, 377.
   on Darwinian exaltation of man, 383, 392.
   on the immortality of the soul, 389-391.
Forces, the correlation of, 35.
Fremantle, Canon, on God's immanence in Nature, 30.
   on the functions of the Church, 398.
Froude, J. A., on miracles, 197.

Geikie, Dr. C., on the origin of man, 76.
   on archæologic periods, 93.
   on uncertainty of archæologic facts, 97.
   on the locality of Eden, 113.
   on man's primitive condition, 121, 123.
   on Adam's creed, 126, 127.
   on Chaldean sacrifices, 303.
Godet, M., on the *Fourth Gospel*, 173, 176.
Gnosticism, 143-145.
Gospels, their origin, 166.
   their date, 170.
Goulburn, Dean, on the celestial hierarchy, 318.
Greg, W. R., on the character of Jesus, 288.
   on the immortality of the soul, 377, 378.

Hagenbach, Dr., on the doctrine of the Trinity, 263.
Hamilton, Sir William, his "Philosophy of the Unconditioned" referred to, 275.

Haweis, Rev. H. R., on the *Fourth Gospel*, 176.
   on the authorship of the *Acts*, 185.
Hodge, Dr. Charles, on the origin of man, 74.
   on man's primitive condition, 116.
   on the meaning of Genesis iii, 117.
   on the atonement of Christ, 297-299.
   on the cause of physical death, 338.
   on the relation of man to the lower animals, 339.
   on ideas of bodily resurrection, 367.
Huxley, Prof. T. H., on argument from design in Nature, 24.
   on materialism, 22, 26.
   on Berkeleyism, 29.
   on the border-line between plants and animals, 74.
   on the unity of the human race, 105.
   on man's primitive condition, 119.
   on origin of the word "agnostic," 143.
   on the authorship of the Gospels, 177.
   on the historic value of the New Testament, 188.
   on the possibility of miracles, 192, 193.
   on inspiration, 247, 248.
   on the necessity of Bible-teaching, 254, 255.
   on evolution and the problem of evil, 344.
Hyatt, Prof. Alpheus, on the change of species, 61.

Idealism, definition of, 27.
Ingersoll, Colonel R. G., his tribute to Jesus, 15.
  on the truths of the Bible, 248, 249.
  on the mystery of motive, 359.
Irenæus, his reference to *First Corinthians*, 148.
  his reference to *Second Corinthians*, 148.
  his reference to *Galatians*, 149.
  his reference to *Romans*, 149.
  his attribution of the *Fourth Gospel* to St. John, 171.
  his attribution of the *Acts* to St. Luke, 182.

John, Gospel of, its author, date, etc., 170–177.
Joly, M., on the age of man, 90–101.
  on primitive man's language, 125.
  on the primitive idea of God, 130, 131.
Justin Martyr, his reference to *First Corinthians*, 147.
  his alleged quotation of the *Gospel of Luke*, 181.

Keim, Dr. Theodor, on apocryphal Gospels, 157, 158.
  on Bible miracles, 197–202, 211–214.
  on the virgin-birth of Jesus, 220.
  on the resurrection of Jesus, 228.
  on Christ's view of demoniacal possession, 250.
  on God-begotten persons, 280, 281.

Kingsley, Charles, on mind and body, 32.
  on causes of cholera, etc., 348, 349.
Krauth, Dr., his edition of Berkeley's "Principles of Human Knowledge," 27.
  on Berkeleyism, 28.
Kuenen, Dr., his work on the Hexateuch referred to, 238, *note*.

Lamarck on the causes of evolution, 44, 45.
Le Conte, Prof. Joseph, on the change of traditional beliefs, 7.
  his definition of evolution, 39.
  his laws of evolution, 39–44.
  on certainty of evolution, 48.
  on uniformitarianism, 51.
  on the evolution of the horse, 53, 54.
  on the evolution of vertebrates, 57, 58.
  on change of species, 62–66.
  on upheaval of the Alps, 91, *note*.
  on virgin-birth, 217, *note*.
  his Sabellianism, 267, *note*.
  on Divine persons of the Trinity, 269.
  on man's place in Nature, 339.
  on the problem of evil, 340–343.
  on the function of the brain in the production of thought, 379–382.
  on spiritual evolution, 384–388.
Lecky on the character of Jesus, 287, 288.
Leslie, Prof. J. P., on the character of Jesus, 289.
  on worshiping Jesus, 293.

INDEX.

Liddon, Canon, his sermons referred to, 311, *note*.
on the immortality of the soul, 377.
Lubbock, Sir John, on language, 125, *note*.
on religious evolution, 128.

Maitland, Rev. Brownlow, on revelation, 243–246.
Mansel, Dean, his Bampton Lectures referred to, 269.
Martensen, Dr., on the knowableness of God, 23.
on the nature of the future state, 324, 325.
Materialism, 25, 26.
Matter, its definition, 25.
Maurice, F. D., his "Theological Essays" referred to, 311, *note*.
on meaning of "aionios" in New Testament, 326.
on the problem of evil, 337, 338.
Medd, Canon, his "One Mediator" referred to, 311, *note*.
Meyers, Frederick, on inspiration, 242.
Milman, Dean, on the origin of Jewish ideas of bodily resurrection, 368.
Mozley, Canon, on miracles, 193.
Müller, Prof. Max, on language, 125, *note*.
on inspiration of the Vedas, 236, 237.
on *Henotheism*, 260.

Newton, Rev. R. Heber, on the origin of the Old Testament canon, 232–234.

Newton, Rev. R. Heber, on the doctrine of the Trinity, 262, 263.
on the meaning of the Trinitarian dogma, 271, 272.

Papias, his reference to Matthew and Luke, 161, 162.
Patton, John M., his "Death of Death" referred to, 361, *note*.
Pharisees, their origin and their belief in bodily resurrection, 368.
Philo, 143, 145, 146.
Polycarp, his reference to *First Corinthians*, 147.

Rawlinson, Canon George, on the date of Noah's flood, 103.
on the Chaldean religion, 259.
on early prevalence of monotheistic beliefs, 262.
on the Zoroastrian doctrine of the resurrection, 367.
Reimensnyder, Rev. J. B., his "Doom Eternal" quoted, 314, 315.
Renan, Ernest, on the Epistles to the Thessalonians, the Philippians, Philemon, and Colossians, 150, 151.
on the Epistle to the Ephesians, 151, 152.
on the legendary character of the Gospels, 167.
on the authorship of the *Acts*, 186.
on the historic value of the New Testament, 188, 189.
on the possibility of miracles, 192.

Renan, Ernest, on the time necessary for the growth of myths, 216.
   on the character of Jesus, 286.
Resurrection of Jesus, 223–229.
Robertson, F. W., on doubt, 9, 10.
   on persecution, 72.
   on popular Tritheism, 270.
   on the doctrine of the Trinity, 272, 273.
   on suffering, as a law of being, 343, 344.
   on relationships in the spirit-world, 358.
Robertson, Canon, on Arianism, 266.
Row, Canon C. A., on freedom of the will, 34, *note*.
   on Genesis iii, 118, 132, 133.
   on the time necessary for the growth of myths, 216.
   on inspiration, 242.
   on superhuman action of Jesus in history, 287, 288.
   on future punishment, 325.
   on the use of reason in religious studies, 329.
   on the meaning of the serpent in the story of Eden, 355, *note*.
Romanes, Prof. G. J., on physiological selection, 46.
   on development of language, 125, *note*.
   on physical basis of mind, 379.

Sabellius, his view of the Godhead, 207.
Sadducees, their origin and their rejection of the doctrine of bodily resurrection, 368.
Samaritans, their origin, 87.
Semper, his "Animal Life" referred to, 48.
Schlegel, Frederick, his definition of idealism, 27.
Shakespeare on the dissolution of the body, 363.
Smith, Miss Jennie, her remarkable cure, 203.
Smith, Dr. William, on the data of Biblical chronology, 84, 86.
Spencer, Herbert, on the existence of God, 21.
   on mind and matter, 32, 33.
   on causes of evolution, 44, 48.
   on embryological argument for evolution, 66, 67.
   on man's primitive condition, 122, 123, 129.
   on religious evolution, 129.
   on the origin of the ideas of the supernatural, 194–196.
   on inspiration, 241.
   on the Abrahamic covenant, 261.
   on God-begotten persons, 278, 279.
   on the incarnation of Christ, 282.
   on propitiations of deities, 301.
   on the future life and world, 316–318, 321, 322.
   on physical immortality, 342, *note*.
   on evolution and the problem of evil, 347, *note*.
   on ideas of resurrection, 366, 367.
   on materialism and idealism, 379.

INDEX. 409

Spencer, Herbert, on the future of ecclesiastical institutions, 394, 395.
Stewart and Tait, their "Unseen Universe" quoted, 369-371.
Stewart, Prof. Balfour, on miracles, 229.
Stanley, Dean, quoted, 13, 14.
— on moral defects in the Bible, 240.
Strauss, David, on the credulity of the Church Fathers, 160.
— on Justin Martyr's "Memoirs," 165.
— on God-begotten persons, 279, 280.
"Symposium on the Atonement," by Archdeacon Farrar, etc., 311, *note*.
"Symposium on Future Probation" by Dr. Leathes, etc., 325, *note*.
"Symposium on Immortality," by Canon Row, etc., p. 393, *note*.
"Symposium on Christianity and Evolution," by Dr. Matheson, etc., p. 392.
"Symposium on Non-Biblical Systems of Religion," by Archdeacon Farrar, etc., 401, *note*.
Swedenborg a Sabellian, 267, *note*.

Talmage, Rev. T. De Witt, on bodily resurrection, 365, 366.
Taylor, Bishop Jeremy, on hell, 312.
Thompson, Dr. W. H., on the meaning of Genesis iii, 355, *note*.
Tuke, Dr. D. H., on mental cure of the blind, 179.

Tuke, Dr. D. H., on mental healing, 208.
Tylor, Dr. E. B., on the age of man, 97, 104.
— on the unity of the human race, 105.
— on development of civilization, 120, 121.
— on primitive language, 124.

Ullmann, Dr., his "Sinlessness of Jesus" referred to, 287.
Usher, Archbishop, his Biblical chronology, 84.
"Unseen Universe," its argument against bodily resurrection, 369-371.

Van Oosterzee, Dr., on the origin of man, 73, 78.
— on hell-fire, 315.
Virgin-birth of Jesus, 217-223.

Wallace, Alfred Russel, on "materialization" of spirits, 226.
Winchell, Prof. Alexander, on the paleontological evidence of evolution, 52, 53.
— on connecting links, 54, 55.
— on the morphological evidence of evolution, 56, 57.
— on change of species, 60.
— on the embryological evidence of evolution, 62.
— his summary of the evidences of evolution, 67, 68.
— on Biblical chronology, 88.
— on Preadamitism, 106-111.
— on primitive man's home, 114, 115.
— on primitive man's condition, 122-124.

Whitney, Prof. W. D., on language, 124.

White, Dr. A. D., on demoniacal possession, 200, *note*.

Young, Dr., his "Christ of History" referred to, 287.

Zeller, Dr., on the authorship of the Acts of the Apostles, 185.

THE END.

CHARLES DARWIN'S WORKS.

ORIGIN OF SPECIES BY MEANS OF NATURAL SELECTION, OR THE PRESERVATION OF FAVORED RACES IN THE STRUGGLE FOR LIFE. From sixth and last London edition. 2 vols., 12mo. Cloth, $4.00.

DESCENT OF MAN, AND SELECTION IN RELATION TO SEX. With many Illustrations. A new edition. 12mo. Cloth, $3.00.

JOURNAL OF RESEARCHES INTO THE NATURAL HISTORY AND GEOLOGY OF COUNTRIES VISITED DURING THE VOYAGE OF H. M. S. BEAGLE ROUND THE WORLD. New edition. 12mo. Cloth, $2.00.

EMOTIONAL EXPRESSIONS OF MAN AND THE LOWER ANIMALS. 12mo. Cloth, $3.50.

THE VARIATIONS OF ANIMALS AND PLANTS UNDER DOMESTICATION. With a Preface, by Professor Asa Gray. 2 vols. Illustrated. Cloth, $5.00.

INSECTIVOROUS PLANTS. 12mo. Cloth, $2.00.

MOVEMENTS AND HABITS OF CLIMBING PLANTS. With Illustrations. 12mo. Cloth, $1.25.

THE VARIOUS CONTRIVANCES BY WHICH ORCHIDS ARE FERTILIZED BY INSECTS. Revised edition, with Illustrations. 12mo. Cloth, $1.75.

THE EFFECTS OF CROSS AND SELF FERTILIZATION IN THE VEGETABLE KINGDOM. 12mo. Cloth, $2.00.

DIFFERENT FORMS OF FLOWERS ON PLANTS OF THE SAME SPECIES. With Illustrations. 12mo. Cloth, $1.50.

THE POWER OF MOVEMENT IN PLANTS. By Charles Darwin, LL. D., F. R. S., assisted by Francis Darwin. With Illustrations. 12mo. Cloth, $2.00.

THE FORMATION OF VEGETABLE MOULD THROUGH THE ACTION OF WORMS. With Observations on their Habits. With Illustrations. 12mo. Cloth, $1.50.

New York: D. APPLETON & CO., 1, 3, & 5 Bond Street.

D. APPLETON & CO.'S PUBLICATIONS.

JOHN TYNDALL'S WORKS.

ESSAYS ON THE FLOATING MATTER OF THE AIR, in Relation to Putrefaction and Infection. 12mo. Cloth, $1.50.

ON FORMS OF WATER, in Clouds, Rivers, Ice, and Glaciers. With 35 Illustrations. 12mo. Cloth, $1.50.

HEAT AS A MODE OF MOTION. New edition. 12mo. Cloth, $2.50.

ON SOUND: A Course of Eight Lectures delivered at the Royal Institution of Great Britain. Illustrated. 12mo. New edition Cloth, $2.00.

FRAGMENTS OF SCIENCE FOR UNSCIENTIFIC PEOPLE. 12mo. New revised and enlarged edition. Cloth, $2.50.

LIGHT AND ELECTRICITY. 12mo. Cloth, $1.25.

LESSONS IN ELECTRICITY, 1875–'76. 12mo. Cloth, $1.00.

HOURS OF EXERCISE IN THE ALPS. With Illustrations. 12mo. Cloth, $2.00.

FARADAY AS A DISCOVERER. A Memoir. 12mo. Cloth, $1.00.

CONTRIBUTIONS TO MOLECULAR PHYSICS in the Domain of Radiant Heat. $5.00.

SIX LECTURES ON LIGHT. Delivered in America in 1872–'73. With an Appendix and numerous Illustrations. Cloth, $1.50.

ADDRESS delivered before the British Association, assembled at Belfast. Revised with Additions. 12mo. Paper, 50 cents.

RESEARCHES ON DIAMAGNETISM AND MAGNE-CRYSTALLIC ACTION, including the Question of Diamagnetic Polarity. With Ten Plates. 12mo, cloth. Price, $1.50.

New York: D. APPLETON & CO., 1, 3, & 5 Bond Street.

D. APPLETON & CO.'S PUBLICATIONS.

THOMAS H. HUXLEY'S WORKS.

SCIENCE AND CULTURE, AND OTHER ESSAYS. 12mo. Cloth, $1.50.

THE CRAYFISH: AN INTRODUCTION TO THE STUDY OF ZOÖLOGY. With 82 Illustrations. 12mo. Cloth, $1.75.

SCIENCE PRIMERS: INTRODUCTORY. 18mo. Flexible cloth, 45 cents.

MAN'S PLACE IN NATURE. 12mo. Cloth, $1.25.

ON THE ORIGIN OF SPECIES. 12mo. Cloth, $1.00.

MORE CRITICISMS ON DARWIN, AND ADMINISTRATIVE NIHILISM. 12mo. Limp cloth, 50 cents.

MANUAL OF THE ANATOMY OF VERTEBRATED ANIMALS. Illustrated. 12mo. Cloth, $2.50.

MANUAL OF THE ANATOMY OF INVERTEBRATED ANIMALS. 12mo. Cloth, $2.50.

LAY SERMONS, ADDRESSES, AND REVIEWS. 12mo. Cloth, $1.75.

CRITIQUES AND ADDRESSES. 12mo. Cloth, $1.50.

AMERICAN ADDRESSES; WITH A LECTURE ON THE STUDY OF BIOLOGY. 12mo. Cloth, $1.25.

PHYSIOGRAPHY: AN INTRODUCTION TO THE STUDY OF NATURE. With Illustrations and Colored Plates. 12mo. Cloth, $2.50.

HUXLEY AND YOUMANS'S ELEMENTS OF PHYSIOLOGY AND HYGIENE. By T. H. HUXLEY and W. J. YOUMANS. 12mo. Cloth, $1.50.

New York: D. APPLETON & CO., 1, 3, & 5 Bond Street.

D. APPLETON & CO.'S PUBLICATIONS.

SIR JOHN LUBBOCK'S (Bart.) WORKS.

THE ORIGIN OF CIVILIZATION AND THE PRIMITIVE CONDITION OF MAN, MENTAL AND SOCIAL CONDITION OF SAVAGES. Fourth edition, with numerous Additions. With Illustrations. 8vo. Cloth, $5.00.

"This interesting work—for it is intensely so in its aim, scope, and the ability of its author—treats of what the scientists denominate *anthropology*, or the natural history of the human species; the complete science of man, body, and soul, including sex, temperament, race, civilization, etc."—*Providence Press.*

PREHISTORIC TIMES, AS ILLUSTRATED BY ANCIENT REMAINS AND THE MANNERS AND CUSTOMS OF MODERN SAVAGES. Illustrated. 8vo. Cloth, $5.00.

"This is, perhaps, the best summary of evidence now in our possession concerning the general character of prehistoric times. The Bronze Age, The Stone Age, The Tumuli, The Lake Inhabitants of Switzerland, The Shell Mounds, The Cave Man, and The Antiquity of Man, are the titles of the most important chapters."—*Dr. C. K. Adams's Manual of Historical Literature.*

ANTS, BEES, AND WASPS. A Record of Observations on the Habits of the Social Hymenoptera. With Colored Plates. 12mo. Cloth, $2.00.

"This volume contains the record of various experiments made with ants, bees, and wasps during the last ten years, with a view to test their mental condition and powers of sense. The author has carefully watched and marked particular insects, and has had their nests under observation for long periods—one of his ants' nests having been under constant inspection ever since 1874. His observations are made principally upon ants, because they show more power and flexibility of mind; and the value of his studies is that they belong to the department of original research."

ON THE SENSES, INSTINCTS, AND INTELLIGENCE OF ANIMALS, WITH SPECIAL REFERENCE TO INSECTS. "International Scientific Series." With over One Hundred Illustrations. 12mo. Cloth, $1.75.

The author has here collected some of his recent observations on the senses and intelligence of animals, and especially of insects, and has attempted to give, very briefly, some idea of the organs of sense, commencing in each case with those of man himself.

THE PLEASURES OF LIFE. 12mo. Cloth, 50 cents; paper, 25 cents.

CONTENTS.—THE DUTY OF HAPPINESS. THE HAPPINESS OF DUTY. A SONG OF BOOKS. THE CHOICE OF BOOKS. THE BLESSING OF FRIENDS. THE VALUE OF TIME. THE PLEASURES OF TRAVEL. THE PLEASURES OF HOME. SCIENCE. EDUCATION.

New York: D. APPLETON & CO., 1, 3, & 5 Bond Street.

D. APPLETON & CO.'S PUBLICATIONS.

Professor JOSEPH LE CONTE'S WORKS.

EVOLUTION AND ITS RELATION TO RELIGIOUS THOUGHT. By JOSEPH LE CONTE, LL. D., Professor of Geology and Natural History in the University of California. With numerous Illustrations. 12mo. Cloth, $1.50.

"Much, very much has been written, especially on the nature and the evidences of evolution, but the literature is so voluminous, much of it so fragmentary, and most of it so technical, that even very intelligent persons have still very vague ideas on the subject. I have attempted to give (1) a very concise account of what we mean by evolution, (2) an outline of the evidences of its truth drawn from many different sources, and (3) its relation to fundamental religious beliefs."—*Extract from Preface.*

ELEMENTS OF GEOLOGY. A Text-book for Colleges and for the General Reader. By JOSEPH LE CONTE, LL. D. With upward of 900 Illustrations. New and enlarged edition. 8vo. Cloth, $4.00.

"Besides preparing a comprehensive text-book, suited to present demands, Professor Le Conte has given us a volume of great value as an exposition of the subject, thoroughly up to date. The examples and applications of the work are almost entirely derived from this country, so that it may be properly considered an American geology. We can commend this work without qualification to all who desire an intelligent acquaintance with geological science, as fresh, lucid, full, authentic, the result of devoted study and of long experience in teaching."—*Popular Science Monthly.*

RELIGION AND SCIENCE. A Series of Sunday Lectures on the Relation of Natural and Revealed Religion, or the Truths revealed in Nature and Scripture. By JOSEPH LE CONTE, LL. D. 12mo. Cloth, $1.50.

"We commend the book cordially to the regard of all who are interested in whatever pertains to the discussion of these grave questions, and especially to those who desire to examine closely the strong foundations on which the Christian faith is reared."—*Boston Journal.*

SIGHT: An Exposition of the Principles of Monocular and Binocular Vision. By JOSEPH LE CONTE, LL. D. With Illustrations. 12mo. Cloth, $1.50.

"Professor Le Conte has long been known as an original investigator in this department; all that he gives us is treated with a master-hand. It is pleasant to find an American book that can rank with the very best of foreign books on this subject."—*The Nation.*

COMPEND OF GEOLOGY. By JOSEPH LE CONTE, LL. D. 12mo. Cloth, $1.40.

New York: D. APPLETON & CO., 1, 3, & 5 Bond Street.

D. APPLETON & CO.'S PUBLICATIONS.

DR. HENRY MAUDSLEY'S WORKS.

BODY AND WILL: Being an Essay concerning Will in its Metaphysical, Physiological, and Pathological Aspects. 12mo. Cloth, $2.50.

BODY AND MIND: An Inquiry into their Connection and Mutual Influence, specially in reference to Mental Disorders. 1 vol., 12mo. Cloth, $1.50.

PHYSIOLOGY AND PATHOLOGY OF MIND:

PHYSIOLOGY OF THE MIND. New edition. 1 vol., 12mo. Cloth, $2.00. CONTENTS: Chapter I. On the Method of the Study of the Mind.—II. The Mind and the Nervous System.—III. The Spinal Cord, or Tertiary Nervous Centres; or, Nervous Centres of Reflex Action.—IV. Secondary Nervous Centres; or, Sensory Ganglia; Sensorium Commune.—V. Hemispherical Ganglia; Cortical Cells of the Cerebral Hemispheres; Ideational Nervous Centres, Primary Nervous Centres; Intellectorium Commune.—VI. The Emotions.—VII. Volition.—VIII.—Motor Nervous Centres, or Motorium Commune and Actuation or Effection.—IX. Memory and Imagination.

PATHOLOGY OF THE MIND. Being the Third Edition of the Second Part of the "Physiology and Pathology of Mind," recast, enlarged, and rewritten. 1 vol., 12mo. Cloth, $2.00. CONTENTS: Chapter I. Sleep and Dreaming.—II. Hypnotism, Somnambulism, and Allied States.—III. The Causation and Prevention of Insanity: (A) Etiological.—IV. The same continued.—V. The Causation and Prevention of Insanity: (B) Pathological.—VI. The Insanity of Early Life.—VII. The Symptomatology of Insanity.—VIII. The same continued.—IX. Clinical Groups of Mental Disease.—X. The Morbid Anatomy of Mental Derangement.—XI. The Treatment of Mental Disorders.

RESPONSIBILITY IN MENTAL DISEASE. (International Scientific Series.) 1 vol., 12mo. Cloth, $1.50.

"The author is at home in his subject, and presents his views in an almost singularly clear and satisfactory manner. . . . The volume is a valuable contribution to one of the most difficult and at the same time one of the most important subjects of investigation at the present day."—*New York Observer.*

"Handles the important topic with masterly power, and its suggestions are practical and of great value."—*Providence Press.*

New York: D. APPLETON & CO., 1, 3, & 5 Bond Street.

D. APPLETON & CO.'S PUBLICATIONS.

GEORGE J. ROMANES'S WORKS.

MENTAL EVOLUTION IN MAN: Origin of Human Faculty. One vol., 8vo. Cloth, $3.00.

This work, which follows "Mental Evolution in Animals," by the same author, considers the probable mode of genesis of the human mind from the mind of lower animals, and attempts to show that there is no distinction of kind between man and brute, but, on the contrary, that such distinctions as do exist all admit of being explained, with respect to their evolution, by adequate psychological analysis.

"The vast array of facts, and the sober and solid method of argument employed by Mr. Romanes, will prove, we think, a great gift to knowledge."—*Saturday Review.*

JELLY-FISH, STAR-FISH, AND SEA-URCHINS. Being a Research on Primitive Nervous Systems. 12mo. Cloth, $1.75.

"Although I have throughout kept in view the requirements of a general reader, I have also sought to render the book of service to the working physiologist, by bringing together in one consecutive account all the more important observations and results which have been yielded by this research."—*Extract from Preface.*

"A profound research into the laws of primitive nervous systems conducted by one of the ablest English investigators. Mr. Romanes set up a tent on the beach and examined his beautiful pets for six summers in succession. Such patient and loving work has borne its fruits in a monograph which leaves nothing to be said about jelly-fish, star-fish, and sea-urchins. Every one who has studied the lowest forms of life on the sea-shore admires these objects. But few have any idea of the exquisite delicacy of their structure and their nice adaptation to their place in nature. Mr. Romanes brings out the subtile beauties of the rudimentary organisms, and shows the resemblances they bear to the higher types of creation. His explanations are made more clear by a large number of illustrations."—*New York Journal of Commerce.*

ANIMAL INTELLIGENCE. 12mo. Cloth, $1.75.

"A collection of facts which, though it may merely amuse the unscientific reader, will be a real boon to the student of comparative psychology, for this is the first attempt to present systematically the well-assured results of observation on the mental life of animals."—*Saturday Review.*

MENTAL EVOLUTION IN ANIMALS. With a Posthumous Essay on Instinct, by CHARLES DARWIN. 12mo. Cloth, $2.00.

"Mr. Romanes has followed up his careful enumeration of the facts of 'Animal Intelligence,' contributed to the 'International Scientific Series,' with a work dealing with the successive stages at which the various mental phenomena appear in the scale of life. The present installment displays the same evidence of industry in collecting facts and caution in co-ordinating them by theory as the former."—*The Athenæum.*

New York: D. APPLETON & CO., 1, 3, & 5 Bond Street.

D. APPLETON & CO.'S PUBLICATIONS.

ERNST HAECKEL'S WORKS.

THE HISTORY OF CREATION; OR, THE DEVELOPMENT OF THE EARTH AND ITS INHABITANTS BY THE ACTION OF NATURAL CAUSES. A Popular Exposition of the Doctrine of Evolution in general, and of that of Darwin, Goethe, and Lamarck in particular. From the German of ERNST HAECKEL, Professor in the University of Jena. The translation revised by Professor E. Ray Lankester, M. A., F. R. S., Fellow of Exeter College, Oxford. Illustrated with Lithographic Plates. In two vols., 12mo. Cloth, $5.00.

THE EVOLUTION OF MAN. A Popular Exposition of the Principal Points of Human Ontogeny and Phylogeny. From the German of ERNST HAECKEL, Professor in the University of Jena, author of "The History of Creation," etc. With numerous Illustrations. In two vols., 12mo. Cloth. Price, $5.00.

"In this excellent translation of Professor Haeckel's work, the English reader has access to the latest doctrines of the Continental school of evolution, in its application to the history of man. It is in Germany, beyond any other European country, that the impulse given by Darwin twenty years ago to the theory of evolution has influenced the whole tenor of philosophical opinion. There may be, and are, differences in the degree to which the doctrine may be held capable of extension into the domain of mind and morals; but there is no denying, in scientific circles at least, that as regards the physical history of organic nature much has been done toward making good a continuous scheme of being."
—*London Saturday Review.*

FREEDOM IN SCIENCE AND TEACHING. From the German of ERNST HAECKEL. With a Prefatory Note by T. H. HUXLEY, F. R. S. 12mo. $1.00.

New York: D. APPLETON & CO., 1, 3, & 5 Bond Street.

D. APPLETON & CO.'S PUBLICATIONS.

DR. W. B. CARPENTER'S WORKS.

PRINCIPLES OF MENTAL PHYSIOLOGY. WITH THEIR APPLICATION TO THE TRAINING AND DISCIPLINE OF THE MIND, AND THE STUDY OF ITS MORBID CONDITIONS. By WILLIAM B. CARPENTER, M. D., LL. D., etc. 12mo. Cloth, $3.00.

"It is the object of this treatise to take up and extend the inquiry into the action of body upon mind, as well as of mind upon body, on the basis of our existing knowledge, so as to elucidate, as far as may be at present possible, the working of that physiological mechanism which takes a most important share in our psychical operations, and thus to distinguish what may be called the *automatic* activity of the mind from that which is under *volitional* direction and control."

MESMERISM, SPIRITUALISM, ETC., HISTORICALLY AND SCIENTIFICALLY CONSIDERED. By WILLIAM B. CARPENTER, M. D., LL. D., etc. 12mo. Cloth, $1.25.

"The reader of these lectures will see that my whole aim is to discover, on the generally accepted principles of testimony, what *are* facts; and to discriminate between facts and the inferences drawn from them. I have no other 'theory' to support than that of the constancy of the well-ascertained laws of Nature."—*From the Preface.*

NATURE AND MAN: ESSAYS, SCIENTIFIC AND PHILOSOPHICAL. By the late WILLIAM BENJAMIN CARPENTER, M. D., F. R. S. With an Introductory Memoir by J. ESTLIN CARPENTER, M. A., and a Portrait. 12mo. Cloth, $2.25.

"Mr. Estlin Carpenter's memoir of his father is just what such a memoir should be—a simple record of a life uneventful in itself, whose interest for us lies mainly in the nature of the intellectual task, so early undertaken, so strenuously carried on, so amply and nobly accomplished, to which it was devoted."—*Spectator.*

H. CHARLTON BASTIAN'S WORKS.

THE BRAIN AS AN ORGAN OF MIND. By H. CHARLTON BASTIAN. With numerous Illustrations. 12mo. Cloth, $2.50.

"The fullest scientific exposition yet published of the views held on the subject of psychology by the advanced physiological school. It teems with new and suggestive ideas."—*London Athenæum.*

ON PARALYSIS FROM BRAIN-DISEASE IN ITS COMMON FORMS. By H. CHARLTON BASTIAN. 12mo. Cloth, $1.75.

D. APPLETON & CO., Publishers, 1, 3, & 5 Bond Street, New York.

D. APPLETON & CO.'S PUBLICATIONS.

Dr. H. ALLEYNE NICHOLSON'S WORKS.

TEXT-BOOK OF ZOÖLOGY, for Schools and Colleges. 12mo. Half roan, $1.60.

MANUAL OF ZOÖLOGY, for the Use of Students, with a General Introduction to the Principles of Zoölogy. Second edition. Revised and enlarged, with 243 Woodcuts. 12mo. Cloth, $2.50.

TEXT-BOOK OF GEOLOGY, for Schools and Colleges. 12mo. Half roan, $1.25.

INTRODUCTION TO THE STUDY OF BIOLOGY. Illustrated. 12mo. Cloth, 60 cents.

THE ANCIENT LIFE-HISTORY OF THE EARTH. A Comprehensive Outline of the Principles and Leading Facts of Palæontological Science. 12mo. Cloth, $2.00.

"A work by a master in the science who understands the significance of every phenomenon which he records, and knows how to make it reveal its lessons. As regards its value there can scarcely exist two opinions. As a text-book of the historical phase of palæontology it will be indispensable to students, whether specially pursuing geology or biology; and without it no man who aspires even to an outline knowledge of natural science can deem his library complete."—*The Quarterly Journal of Science.*

"The Professor of Natural History in the University of St. Andrews has, by his previous works on zoölogy and palæontology, so fully established his claim to be an exact thinker and a close reasoner, that scarcely any recommendation of ours can add to the interest with which all students in natural history will receive the present volume. It is, as its second title expresses it, a comprehensive outline of the principles and leading facts of palæontological science. Numerous woodcut illustrations very delicately executed, a copious glossary, and an admirable index, add much to the value of this volume."—*Athenæum.*

New York: D. APPLETON & CO., 1, 3, & 5 Bond Street.

www.ingramcontent.com/pod-product-compliance
Lightning Source LLC
Chambersburg PA
CBHW030557300426
44111CB00009B/1012